THE
JAMES SPRUNT STUDIES
IN HISTORY
AND POLITICAL SCIENCE

*Published under the Direction of
the Departments of History and Political Science
of the University of North Carolina*

VOLUME 25
NUMBER I

———————— * ————————

Editors

ALBERT RAY NEWSOME
WILLIAM WHATLEY PIERSON
MITCHELL B. GARRETT
FLETCHER M. GREEN
KEENER C. FRAZER

NORTH CAROLINA BOUNDARY DISPUTES INVOLVING HER SOUTHERN LINE

By

MARVIN LUCIAN SKAGGS, Ph. D.
*Head of the Department of Social Sciences,
Campbell College, Buie's Creek, N. C.*

CHAPEL HILL
———————— * ————————
THE UNIVERSITY OF NORTH CAROLINA PRESS
1941

PREFACE

My interest in boundary controversies in general was first aroused by study in connection with the Oregon boundary dispute. I later took up the question of North Carolina's southern line for exhaustive study, and the present work has been the result.

An earnest attempt has been made to present the facts relative to the rights and claims of the States concerned in an unbiased way, for the most part relating rather than interpreting.

I desire to express deep appreciation of the valuable aid rendered by many individuals and institutions in the course of the preparation of this study. The library staffs of the University of North Carolina, the University of South Carolina, Duke University, the State Library of Georgia, and the Carnegie Library of Atlanta have given effective aid. Generous privileges in the use of materials have been granted by Dr. A. R. Newsome and his assistants formerly in the North Carolina Historical Commission, by Mr. A. S. Salley, Secretary of the South Carolina Historical Commission, and by Miss Ruth Blair, State Historian of Georgia. Mr. George F. Syme, Senior Engineer of the North Carolina State Highway Commission, kindly permitted the use of his private correspondence with the governors and other officials of North Carolina and South Carolina in connection with the survey of 1928, in which he was commissioner for North Carolina. He also made valuable mathematical calculations in connection with the earlier surveys. Dr. R. L. Meriwether, Head of the Department of History of the University of South Carolina, and Dr. J. F. Jamison of the Library of Congress have supplied valuable information for use in this study. My wife has rendered indispensable aid in the task of preparing the manuscript. Dr. J. G. deR. Hamilton and Dr. C. C. Crittenden have read the manuscript and made valuable suggestions. Special gratitude is expressed to Dr. H. M. Wagstaff of the University of North Carolina for patient assistance and constant advice throughout the period of research.

Chapel Hill, N. C.   M. L. SKAGGS
April 10, 1941

CONTENTS

PART I
THE DISPUTE WITH SOUTH CAROLINA

PREFACE v

CHAPTER I. BACKGROUND OF THE BOUNDARY
    CONTROVERSY 1
    The importance of boundary disputes.............. 1
    Growing consciousness of division between northern
        and southern Carolina........................ 3

CHAPTER II. PROGRESS OF THE SURVEY DURING THE
    COLONIAL PERIOD..................................... 23
    Section I. The boundary question during the
        Proprietary period............................. 23
    Section II. Progress of the survey during
        the reign of George II......................... 30
    Section III. Extension of the line to the mountains...... 59

CHAPTER III. THE CONTROVERSY RESUMED BY THE
    INDEPENDENT STATES............................... 92
    Section I. Fruitless negotiations...................... 92
    Section II. A basis for settlement reached............. 125
    Section III. Agreements modified and the
        line surveyed.................................. 140
    Section IV. Confusion and a new survey............... 145

PART II
THE DISPUTE WITH GEORGIA

CHAPTER I. ORIGIN OF THE DISPUTE AND EARLY EFFORTS
    TOWARD SETTLEMENT.............................. 161
    The changing ownership of the disputed territory..... 162

CONTENTS

Early efforts to locate the line..................... 164
Georgia organizes the territory.................... 164
Local violence.................................. 166
Georgia appeals to Congress to intervene............ 176
A coöperative survey............................ 183

CHAPTER II. THE CONTROVERSY RENEWED AND
FINALLY CLOSED................................ 191

Georgia repudiates the work of her own commissioners
and astronomers............................. 192
Georgia's second appeal to the Federal
government 197
Georgia's independent survey..................... 198
North Carolina's contentions sustained—collapse
of the opposition............................ 202
The dividing line surveyed....................... 203

Conclusion 206

Bibliography 212

Index 229

PART I
THE DISPUTE WITH SOUTH CAROLINA

CHAPTER I

BACKGROUND OF THE BOUNDARY CONTROVERSY

It is the plan in the first chapter to show the importance of boundary controversies by quoting scholars of American history regarding them, and by brief references to some of the disputes to indicate the significant issues involved.

It will also be shown that North Carolina's boundary problems involved more than the mere use of surveyor's instruments and the erection of line markers—that the topographical features in the region of the boundary, divergent racial settlements, different institutions, lack of frequent contacts as a result of poor methods of transportation and communication, ungenerous attitudes, and other factors collectively contributed to the development of a spiritual division which preceded and accompanied a physical division of the territory.

Controversies with regard to boundary limits have characterized the relations of the political units within the territory of the United States from their beginnings. These controversies have not only been the subject of negotiations between the units concerned, but have often become so acrimonious as vitally to affect their peaceful relations and permanently to color their history and shape their destinies.

Scholars of American history recognize the importance of these disputes in the relations of colonies and States, and cause them to stand out in bold review in their published works. Dr. R. D. W. Connor, National Archivist, says regarding such controversies that before 1700 few of the colonies had such well-defined boundaries as to be free from boundary disputes. In those between crown colonies and proprietary colonies, both king and proprietors had interests to be considered. The colonies themselves were deeply concerned as the controversies frequently involved the enforcement of criminal laws, the collection of taxes, Indian affairs, and other governmental problems. Conflicting land titles often led to riots and bloodshed. Dr. Connor adds that no better illustration of conditions growing out of a disputed boundary can be found than these which arose along the North Carolina-South Carolina border.[1] Professor William K. Boyd of Duke University refers to North Carolina boundary issues as questions productive of controversies.[2] Professor Allan Nevins states that boundary lines constituted a theme of bickering between almost every pair of adjacent provinces; and he ranks her boundary controversies among North Carolina's four most important problems before the Revolution when he enumerates her "marked" disputes as involving finances, boundaries,[3] representation, and the courts.[4] Other writers even claim that only six States had definite boundaries at the close of the Revolution.[5]

A principle enunciated by Vattel in the eighteenth century, relative to the relations of nations, readily applies to the relations of American colonies and States in regard to their boundaries. He wrote as follows:

The tranquility of the people, the safety of the State, the happiness of the human race, do not allow that the possessions, empire and other rights of nations should remain uncertain, subject to dispute and ever ready to occasion bloody wars.[6]

Local boundary disputes often became dangerous, involving as they did the question of ownership of homes and farms, and challenging the patriotism and pride of colonies and States. Such a dispute between Virginia and Pennsylvania just before the outbreak of the Revolution almost caused the two colonies to resort to warfare. Such controversies were so numerous[7] and so important after the American States had declared their independence

[1] R. D. W. Connor, *The Colonial and Revolutionary Periods*, 1584-1783, volume I in Connor, Boyd and Hamilton, *History of North Carolina*, 2 vols. (Chicago and New York, 1919), pp. 241-242. (Cited hereafter as Connor, *History*).

[2] W. K. Boyd, *The Federal Period*, volume II in Connor, Boyd and Hamilton, *History of North Carolina*, 2 vols. (Chicago and New York: Lewis Publishing Co., 1919), pp. 70, 72.

[3] It should be noted that boundaries are mentioned second in the order.

[4] Allan Nevins, *The American States During and After the Revolution, 1775-1789* (New York: The Macmillan Co., 1927), pp. 17, 547.

[5] Cf. W. R. Garrett, "History of the South Carolina Cession," *Tennessee Historical Papers* (Nashville, 1884).

[6] M. de Vattel, *The Law of Nations* (New York: Campbell, 1796), Bk. II, Chap. 11, sec. 149.

[7] See Georgia Governor's Letter Book, 1809-1814 (MSS), p. 11. Various State boundary disputes are there mentioned.

that national leaders took notice of them with evident concern.[8] Connecticut and Vermont, for example, quarrelled with every one of their neighbors over State boundaries.[9] In the dispute between the former and Pennsylvania, actual civil war resulted, known as the first and second "Pennamite Wars."[10] Silas Deane, writing on October 15, 1775, said that the Connecticut settlers "have conducted [sic] in a most shocking manner." And he added that the excitement in Philadelphia was so great that "the very union of the colonies" was thrown into a "critical situation."[11] Nevins adds that the Pennsylvania and Vermont disputes "genuinely alarmed the lovers of State concord for a time."

Even minor disputes demanded the most careful attention and the most delicate handling, because their dangers were cumulative. The psychological effect of continuous minor altercations all over the nation, national leaders knew, would be destructive to the spirit of union, which had been developing ever since 1754. Hence, in 1782 John Jay wrote Livingston that "The boundaries between the States should be immediately settled and all cause of dispute between them removed." Less than one year later he counselled Gouverneur Morris: "Settle your boundaries without delay. It is better that some improper boundaries be fixed, than any left in dispute. In a word, everything conducive to union and constitutional energy of government should be cultivated. . . ."[12]

Such caution was timely. Some States had already threatened radical action unless their territorial demands were acceded to. A mere glance at the controversies reveals the important issues involved and their great significance in the history of the States and the Union.

Early in the history of Carolina there appeared a consciousness of separateness between the northern and southern sections of the

[8] The Continental Congress regarded the question of State boundaries of so much importance that as early as 1777 frequent agitation for ascertaining them was carried on. See *Journals of the Continental Congress,* October 15, 1777, IX, 806-807.

[9] Henry Gannett, *Boundaries of the United States and of the Several States and Territories with an Outline of the History of all Important Changes of Territory* (U. S. Geological Survey, Bulletin No. 171. Washington: Government Printing Office, 1900), *passim.*

[10] Nevins, *op. cit.,* pp. 283-285. The term "Pennamite" seems to be an adjective derived from the abbreviation for the State in which the violence occurred.

[11] Quoted by Nevins, *op. cit.,* p. 583.

[12] Quoted by Nevins, *op. cit.,* p. 590.

province which developed into a positive movement toward physical delimitation. Administrative division influenced the growth of this consciousness to some extent. A governor was appointed by the Governor of Virginia to administer the Albemarle section in 1664. After the granting of the second charter in 1665, the Proprietors administered the whole of Carolina, including Albemarle, as they saw fit. The terms North and South Carolina were applied to the two sections within a few years after the settlement was made near Charleston in 1670. In the following year a governor was appointed for the southern portion of Carolina, and in 1689 the Proprietors appointed a governor of the section north and east of Cape Fear. Two years later he was made governor of all Carolina and he appointed a Deputy-Governor of the northern section. After 1711 the deputies were entirely independent of other colonial governors, and were governors in their own right. But this point is anticipatory; the subject of administrative division will be treated in full later in this study as the first step toward definite physical division. It should be borne in mind, however, regarding spiritual division of the province, that Albemarle began as a part of Virginia and the minds of the inhabitants were long inclined to look northward.

Topographical features, however, had much to do with the origin of the feeling of logical division. The Cape Fear River was of great length, extending from the seacoast northwestward into the interior for a distance of over 300 miles, and forming a sort of marker which tended to force upon all occupants of the province a recognition of a natural division.[13] The Pee Dee River also tended to divide the territory into geographical units. Rising in northwestern Carolina and flowing southeastward through the province as Yadkin River, it flows into Winyaw Bay on the coast, forming a natural and most logical boundary line between the two sections. A third great river course extending from the seacoast of southern Carolina far into the northwest was composed of the Santee, Wateree, and Catawba rivers. The southern portion of this

[13] Hugh Meredith, writing in 1731, speaks of a number of smaller rivers and streams in the Cape Fear region as though they, as a group, marked a sort of natural territorial limit. See *An Account of the Cape Fear Country*, p. 15. Four years later, surveyors were greatly hindered by "the many large and Rapid Rivers as well as Creeks" which they had to cross. *State Records of North Carolina*, Walter Clark, ed., 16 vols. (1895-1905), XI, 29. (Cited hereafter as *S.R.*)

NORTH CAROLINA BOUNDARY DISPUTES 5

natural line, the Santee River, was early recognized as the boundary between the provinces.[14] In addition to the presence of river courses tending to divide the territory, there were forests, barren lands, and occasional swamps which constituted barriers to the joining of northern and southern settlements. In August, 1720, Governor Boone and Colonel Barnwell of South Carolina informed the Board of Trade that there was a "vast uninhabited wood between North and South Carolina."[15] Conditions had not changed fifteen years later, for the commissioners and surveyors who made the first survey in 1735, which will be later described, complained to the Crown of having been forced to run the line "thro' Desert and uninhabited Woods in many Places absolutely impassible . . ."[16] without first cutting a passage way.

The accuracy of this description as applied to the region of the boundary itself, even at the opening of the Revolution, is borne out by testimony of a minister, Nicholas Christian, who wrote from Brunswick in July, 1774, as follows:

I perform divine service . . . at the Boundary between the North and South Province and at a place called Waccamaw . . . from Brunswick upwards of forty miles, the roads exceeding bad especially to Waccamaw there being upwards of twelve swamps to cross some of which are so deep that horses are frequently up to the Saddle in crossing them. . . . This place is out of the way of all Society.[17]

[14] *Colonial Records of North Carolina*, W. L. Saunders, ed., 10 vols. (1886-1890), II, vii. (Cited hereafter as *C.R.*). As the terms North and South Carolina were used as early as 1688 to refer in a general way to the two sections, they will be so used here for the sake of convenience. Definite location of dividing lines will be given in the discussion of the surveys.

[15] Public Records of South Carolina, 36 vols., VIII, 257. (Cited hereafter as Pub. Rec. of S. C.).

[16] Skene and Abercromby to the King in Council, April 19, 1737. *C.R.*, IX, 28-29. As late as 1755, the Governor and Council of North Carolina were urging natural boundaries instead of surveys on account of "almost impenetrable Thickets or Swamps." *Ibid.*, V, 384. Allusions here to the surveys are anticipatory, and are used simply to show physical conditions tending to divide Carolina, and the general ignorance of those conditions in the colonies and in England.

[17] Christian to the Society for the Propagation of the Gospel, London. *C.R.*, IX, 1022. These swamps and wilderness barriers were keeping the Carolinas separated in population and, consequently, in spirit even after the middle of the nineteenth century. Edmund Ruffin, writing of eastern North Carolina in general about 1861, stated that "there is no equal space of territory in all the States of the American Union that has been so little

The greatest misfortune for the colonies regarding these topographical features and conditions was the fact that the authorities in England were ignorant of them when they prepared the instructions for locating the boundary line. Members of the Board of Trade were "entire strangers to the Geography of Carolina" when they issued instructions in 1730 for a survey; and the Proprietors' governors knew "very little of ye maritime part of the Province" south of New River, "& nothing at all of the Courses of the Rivers, or of the Country to the westward at any distance from the Sea coast."[18] Hence, the authorities were forced to depend upon whatever information they could secure from the two provinces, which was always colored to favor the province concerned. They came to believe that the Waccamaw River extended northwestward, parallel to the Cape Fear, instead of northeastward and almost parallel to the coast line practically all of its length. Under such an impression, they favored the Waccamaw as the dividing line between the two sections.[19] The governor at Charleston was forced to protest that the acceptance of such a line would extend North Carolina into the "bowels" of his province.[20]

Similar ignorance abounded among officials both in England and America regarding the Catawba River. Even the governor of South Carolina was in error regarding the South Branch of the Catawba. In proposing a line in 1768, he reported to the Board of Trade that the course of that branch was east and west, and that it extended to the mountains,[21] both of which statements were inaccurate, as standard maps indicate. Official maps of the early period, supposedly prepared by experts, speak eloquently of the

---

visited or seen by other than its residents. . . . It is rare that any stranger enters this *terra incognita.*" *Sketches of Lower North Carolina,* p. 52. He added that not even residents of other parts of North Carolina had ever been there.

[18] North Carolina Governor and Council to Board of Trade, 1755. *C.R.,* V, 380. It will be shown later in this work how ignorance of the true source of the Tugaloo River prolonged the dispute over the twelve-mile strip of territory in the west, involving North Carolina, South Carolina, and Georgia in serious boundary controversies.

[19] Pub. Rec. of S. C., XVIII, 257. British officials were persistent if not stubborn in this opinion. In 1735 they "were of the opinion that Waccamaw River . . . is the intended Boundary," according to instructions, and ordered that both governors act accordingly. *Ibid.,* XVII, 257.

[20] *S.R.,* XI, 21.

[21] *C.R.,* VIII, 563; XI, 220. North Carolina constantly protested against these erroneous claims. Cf. *C.R.,* VII, 897. Tryon to Hillsborough, December 12, 1768; *ibid.,* VIII, 457.

general ignorance of the geographical and topographical features of the territory composing the Carolinas.[22]

The young colony north of the Cape Fear was born of its Mother Britain a deformed child in the beginning. Its heart was in the wrong part of its body. The Albemarle section logically belonged to Virginia. There was no logical proceeding connected with the establishment of North Carolina. Practical considerations called for division at least as far southward as the Pee Dee River, which would have made of the province a true natural unit.[23] The great Cape Fear River section would thus have been the nucleus from which the State would have grown, and a natural boundary would very probably have been early accepted.

A condition which was productive of a desire for separation was the immense distance intervening between the northern section of the province and the seat of government at Charleston. Members of the colonial assembly would have found it very burdensome to travel the great distance from northern and northwestern areas to Charleston.[24] Attendance from the remote sections would have necessitated travel of 300 to 400 miles by very poor methods of transportation. The inhabitants themselves resented having to go to Charleston to obtain government services and to perform civil duties. County courts were not allowed in the southern province,

[22] Cf. inaccurate early maps in North Carolina Historical Commission. For example, "A New Description of Carolina," Francis Lamb (1676); "Carte General de la Carolina," Le Siena (about 1700).

[23] The idea of a geographical unit north of the Pee Dee is attributable to Governor Burrington in his testimony before the Board of Trade, June 13, 1735, when he said the only natural boundary was the "pedee River." Pub. Rec. of S. C., XVII, 260-261. John Spenser Bassett repeated the idea in his enlightening monograph "The Influence of Coast Line and Rivers on North Carolina," *American Historical Association Reports* (1908), I, 58-61.

[24] In the additional instructions to Governor Phillip Ludwell in 1691, the following order appears: "If you should find it impracticable for to have the Inhabitants of Albemarle County to send Delegates to the Genl. Assembly held at South Carolina, you are then to issue writs to the Sheriffs to hold elections in Berkeley, Colleton, and the portion of Craven County lying south and west of Cape Fear." He was further empowered to appoint a deputy-governor of North Carolina, if deemed necessary. *Journal of the Commons House of Assembly of South Carolina*, October 12, 1692. (Cited hereafter as *Commons House Journal*). Cf. Edward McCrady, *The History of South Carolina under the Proprietary Government, 1670-1719* (New York: The Macmillan Company, 1897), p. 236. The same orders were given by the Proprietors to Governor Thomas Smith, in 1693. *Records in the Public Record Office Relating to South Carolina, 1691-1697* (A. S. Salley, ed.), November 30, 1693.

and all inhabitants having lawsuits over small debts were forced to endure the hardships of a very long journey in order to reach the Charleston Courts.[25]

The attitude and policy of the government played a part in drawing the sections apart. The Lords Proprietors forbade the sale of any land within twenty miles of Cape Fear,[26] and, regardless of the fact that Governor Burrington ordered this instruction to be disregarded, it played an important part in preserving a wilderness barrier, and thereby prevented the two sections from joining their grants and settlers in neighborly proximity. The growth of a spirit of unity was thus forestalled. New Hanover precinct, embracing the infant settlement on the Cape Fear River, was not established until November, 1729,[27] a period long after the boundary question had become an important problem.[28]

The Proprietors from the earliest times had been conscious of a natural division between the northern and southern sections of the proprietary lands, and this consciousness took definite form in their communications. In the commissions and instructions to colonial officials in South Carolina there appears with impressive frequency the phrase, "that part of the Province of South Carolina that lies South and West of Cape Fear."[29] Moreover, the Proprietors "regarded with particular favor"[30] the settlement on the Ashley and Cooper rivers, and "directed all their energies toward building up" that section.[31] They had little interest in

---

[25] *C.R.*, VI, 1038.

[26] *C.R.*, II, 236; Connor, *op. cit.*, p. 132.

[27] *C.R.*, VI, 227; Connor, *op. cit.*, pp. 133-134.

[28] It will be shown later that the movement to secure a definite dividing line began as early as 1713.

[29] *Commissions and Instructions from the Lords Proprietors of Carolina to Public Officials of South Carolina, 1685-1715* (A. S. Salley, Jr., ed.). The phrase, which clearly demonstrates that official thinking throughout the period was in terms of a division at Cape Fear, appears from one to three times on each of the following pages: 16, 17, 18, 22, 23, 27, 36, 39, 40, 42, 45, 46, 62, 68, 69, 70, 77, 78, 80, 84, 86, 88, 91, 95, 96, 106, 107, 108, 109, 110, 111, 113, 114, 120, 132, 142, 155, 158, 159, 160, 162, 165, 166, 171, 172, 173, 185, 188, 190, 191, 194, 195, 196, 201, 210, 213, 215, 216, 219, 221, 222, 228, 229, 233, 235, 236, 237, 239, 242, 246, 248, 249, 250, 251, 254, 260, 263, 264, 268, 272. Cf. Pub. Rec. of S. C., *passim*. These numerous references are here cited for later use in support of a position taken by the writer relative to the Cape Fear River as the boundary line. Cf. *infra*, p. 27.

[30] S. A. Ashe, *History of North Carolina*, 2 vols. (Vol. 1, Greensboro: Van Noppen, 1908; Vol. II, Raleigh: Edwards & Broughton, 1925), I, 75.

[31] Connor, *op. cit.*, p. 145.

building up the northern section. The progress it made was in spite of them, and not because of their aid.

The result of such special interest was the development of a superiority complex among the inhabitants of the southern section, with its accompanying condescending spirit, which became a source of irritation and resentment for the northern province. Charleston was the source and center of this ungenerous attitude. It was for a time the greatest exporting point on the American Continent,[32] in theory the capital of both provinces from 1691 to 1711, the center of their political life, and the object of British favors. In that center an air of superiority was cultivated on every convenient occasion. It is clearly demonstrated in correspondence between the governors. Governor Dobbs, in replying to a letter from Governor Glen of South Carolina regarding the boundary line, accused him of writing "in a very extraordinary style, I may say dictatorial, not as one Governor to another having equal powers from his Majesty, and independent of each other, but as if I was dependent upon you, and obliged to give you an account of my behavior in transmitting affairs of this Government."[33]

The Charlestonians missed no opportunity of lauding their city, the namesake of a King;[34] and British officials came to look upon the section surrounding it as the dominant one. The more democratic northern section naturally resented the whole system, and developed a desire to leave the south to itself. Hence the demand for a division.

The divergence of racial elements in the settlement of the Carolinas encouraged the growing apart of the two sections. Southern Carolina was settled by a much greater proportion of English than was the northern portion of the province. The failure of the

[32] U. B. Phillips, *History of Transportation in the Eastern Cotton Belt* (New York: Columbia University Press, 1908), p. 45.

[33] *C.R.*, V, 387. Professor Connor says regarding this incident that "Glen's air of superiority and condescension ruffled his adversary's sense of dignity." *Op. cit.*, p. 243. The North Carolina Governor refused to have any further dealings with his contemptuous neighbor.

[34] Professor U. B. Phillips testifies to the truth of this irritating egotism around Charleston when he says: "Throughout the whole period, from the establishment of the colony until well into the nineteenth century the public policy of South Carolina was entirely controlled by the city of Charleston.... Outlying localities might make feeble demands for various things; but to be effective, every important demand must either be the demand of Charleston originally or secure the full support of that city." *Op. cit.*, p. 35.

attempted English settlement on the Cape Fear in 1667 gave opportunity a half century later for the settlement by other racial elements.[35] However, these transatlantic elements were preceded by settlers from the rival southern section some time prior to 1725.[36] These settlers only encouraged the desire for separation from the southern section, however, for they had "always been troublesome" to the southern government.[37] The settlement on the Cape Fear prospered, and by 1740 had 3,000 inhabitants, some of whom were of direct European origin.[38] A small settlement of Scotch Highlanders existed at the head of navigation on the Cape Fear in the early part of the royal period, and by the middle of the century they were coming into the province in impressive numbers. A few had arrived as early as 1729. Within a short period they had settled widely in the present Anson, Bladen, Cumberland, Harnett, Moore, Richmond, Robeson, Sampson, Hoke and Scotland counties,[39] reinforcing the sparse numbers of the English stock already in this area. Thus a large racial element appeared with no knowledge of or friendship for southern Carolina. As they were Dissenters in religion, they could not harmonize their religious convictions with the Anglican Establishment in South Carolina. Finally, having to give up their own customs, they adopted those of the region in which they had settled and developed a distinct provincial consciousness and patriotism, a result which was aided by the fact that Gabriel Johnston, a fellow

[35] Connor, *op. cit.*, p. 147.

[36] The discussion here given is only intended to treat briefly the immigration into northern Carolina of new racial elements, principally during the second quarter of the eighteenth century, and assumes a general knowledge on the part of the reader that the coastal region had long been settled by a population largely English in origin. Regions toward the interior were sparsely settled.

[37] Connor, *History*, p. 148. These southern Carolinians "chose rather to be inhabitants of North Carolina." South Carolina Assembly to Board of Trade, 1757. *S.R.*, XI, 128.

[38] Professor John Spencer Bassett states that the Cape Fear region drew its population from "extraneous sources"; Highlanders, Scotch-Irish, colony-born, West Indian-born, and English-born Britons were there mingled. He further states that it was about 1730 that this region was opened to civilization. *Op. cit.*, I, 58-61.

[39] Connor, *op. cit.*, p. 157. For a full discussion of the Scotch-Highlanders, see R. D. W. Connor, *Race Elements in the White Population of North Carolina* (North Carolina State Normal & Industrial College Historical Publications, 1920), no. 1, pp. 44-68.

Scot, became governor in 1734 and was greatly interested in promoting the settlement of the whole Cape Fear region.[40]

Meanwhile, the Scotch-Irish were coming into the Piedmont region. They were also Calvinistic Protestants, with a keen dislike for the Anglican church, dominant among their southern neighbors. Many of them had been driven from Ireland by the Test Act of 1714 and by England's persistent application of it in North Ireland, while relaxing it in England itself. The Woolens Act of 1699 hastened the movement. A few of this group were in northern Carolina as early as 1676, though the great exodus from Ireland came in the eighteenth century. The first organized group came in 1737 at the instance of a land company sponsored by Henry McCulloh, a London merchant, Arthur Dobbs and other Scotch-Irish. They settled in modern Duplin and Sampson counties, in the southern portion of the province but with nothing in common with the inhabitants of South Carolina. They became attached to their new home, and one of their leaders, Arthur Dobbs, became governor of the province in 1753.[41] Mathew Rowan, who was acting-governor in 1753, was also of Scotch-Irish blood. Large numbers of Scotch-Irish also came from Pennsylvania and settled in the province. Some Irish immigrants arrived at New Bern in the fall of 1753 harboring a deep hate for anything Anglican. Others had settled on the Northeast River.[42] A small body of Swiss also settled there, as they had on the Cape Fear.[43]

In 1736 McCulloh, Crymble, Huey, Dobbs, and others were granted 1,200,000 acres of land in interior North Carolina, chiefly along the Catawba, Eno, and Yadkin rivers, McCulloh agreeing to bring into the region a large number of settlers. Though the plan failed, a nucleus of population was brought to the province which had nothing in common with South Carolinians. Those in Anson and Mecklenburg counties particularly developed bitter enmity toward them over the location of the boundary line.[44] About the middle of the century another divergent race entered

[40] R. D. W. Connor, *Cornelius Harnett* (Raleigh: Edwards & Broughton, 1909), chapter I, *passim*. [41] *C.R.*, V, 17.

[42] *C.R.*, IV, 685 *et seq.;* Ashe, *op. cit.*, I, 254. See also J. J. McConnell, *Catholicity in the Carolinas and Georgia* (New York: D. & J. Saddler, 1879), *passim*. [43] Ashe, *op. cit.*, I, 254.

[44] See, for example, *C.R.*, VI, 795.

when settlers from Germany began to arrive.[45] Also, as early as 1730 Welsh emigrants from Pennsylvania and Delaware were settling in the Cape Fear region.[46] Six years later they secured valuable lands in the Pee Dee valley, eight miles on either side of the river to the confluence of its two main branches.[47]

The Scotch-Irish settled on the headwaters of the Catawba, Yadkin, Cape Fear, and Neuse rivers. After 1750 many of this group moved to the region west of the Yadkin River, and the following year they were moving rapidly toward the mountains. By 1775 they were in the region of Rocky River, a tributary of the Yadkin.

By the time Dobbs became governor, there were almost 15,000 Irish Protestants and Germans in Anson, Orange, and Rowan counties alone.[48] Within sixteen years after 1746 six counties—Granville, Johnston, Anson, Orange, Rowan, and Mecklenburg—were erected to care for the stream of Scotch-Irish and Germans.[49] Two of these were southern boundary counties and a third was near the line. The German settlers began occupying North Carolina about 1745, settling along the foothills of the Alleghenies and on the mountain sides; along the banks of the Catawba and Yadkin rivers, on small farms. In religion they were Moravians, Lutherans, and German Reformed—all Protestant groups. Forsyth County became a center of the first group. However, German settlements were made in the present counties of Guilford, Alamance, Orange, Randolph, Davidson, Iredell, Cabarrus, Stanly, Union, Mecklenburg, Lincoln, Catawba, Rowan, and Burke before the Revolution. In 1750 the frontier counties—Anson, Orange, and Rowan—were settled for the most part by Irish Protestants and Germans.[50]

Thus it is seen that from the early appearance of the boundary question there were racial groups in the northern section of Caro-

---

[45] Connor, *History*, pp. 167-168.

[46] Hugh Meredith, *An Account of the Cape Fear Region*, 1731, p. 11. A tract in New Hanover County is called the Welsh Tract to this day. Meredith, *op. cit.;* Ashe, *op. cit.*, I, 254.

[47] The facts relating to the Welsh Tract were also secured from a summary of a study by Professor R. L. Meriwether, Head of the Department of History and Government in the University of South Carolina, kindly sent to the writer by Professor Meriwether, August 29, 1932.

[48] Connor, *History*, p. 169.   [49] *Ibid.*, pp. 169-170.

[50] The presence of the Catawba Indians in a strategic location in the west also constituted a sort of mark of division between the sections, as will later appear.

lina who were distinctly different from the people of southern Carolina in customs, in religion, in ideals; who were provincial in their nature and fundamentally opposed to remaining under the dominance of South Carolina. The inflow of these new elements increased in volume so rapidly that by the close of the French and Indian War they constituted considerably over half of the population.[51]

Divergent tendencies in the economic life of the two colonies also were pronounced. This was particularly true of agriculture. In the northern colony landholdings were small and numerous. In southern Carolina, chiefly in the low country, there was a considerable number of great estates. A marked difference also appeared in the kind of products grown on those farms and estates. In North Carolina they varied, consisting of naval stores, corn, wheat, peas, tobacco, lumber, furs, leather, flax, and many miscellaneous products. The colony produced no great staples comparable to those produced by her southern neighbor. South Carolina produced two of these—rice and indigo.

Large plantations were characteristic of the southern colony, and the type of labor employed on them served to accentuate the divergent tendencies in the two colonies. A comparison of the growth of servile population is instructive in considering the causes and development of a spiritual division in the two sections. The increase in the number of negro slaves in northern Carolina during the first half of the eighteenth century was as follows:[52]

```
1712  . . . . . .     800
1717  . . . . . .   1,100
1730  . . . . . .   6,000
1754  . . . . . .  15,000
```

In 1754 only nineteen negroes entered her territory through the port of Bath; and in the preceding seven years, the average number entering Beaufort was only seventeen. The negro population was concentrated in the East, and even in that area it was not until 1767 that the negroes surpassed the white population in numbers. North Carolina was developing along more democratic lines.

[51] Cf. Connor, *History*, p. 178.
[52] The statistics relating to North Carolina are taken from Professor Connor's *History*, p. 184.

As early as 1708, however, South Carolina had 4,000 slaves,[53] surpassing the number of white population; and "Early in the eighteenth century the blacks began to outnumber the whites about three or four to one."[54] In the five years preceding 1708, the increase by importation reached 500;[55] and the increase by birth during the same period was 600.[56] It was estimated that in 1724 the number of slaves was about 32,000,[57] the great majority of whom were negroes.[58] Their numbers had trebled within a period of nine years. By 1739 they numbered approximately 40,000, and in 1760, 60,000.

With the great increase of a servile class and its medieval socio-economic system, "sharp and clear" class distinctions developed[59] which produced the theory and attitude that honest toil was a disgrace. This was resented by the masses of more democratic North Carolinians.

Industrial development was much more important in South Carolina than in the northern colony. That of the latter consisted mainly of lumbering and the production of naval stores; whereas, in South Carolina there was the raw silk industry, tanning, lumbering, brick making, manufacture of naval stores, printing, the fishing industry, ship building, manufacture of leather goods, iron works, and other forms of industry. It was a natural step to the growth of important commercial interests.

North Carolina, with her dangerous coast and lack of safe harbors, could never hope to develop a great overseas commerce. Travel by water was hazardous, communication with the outside

[53] Edward McCrady, *The History of South Carolina under the Proprietary Government* 1670-1719 (New York: The Macmillan Co., 1897), p. 477.

[54] W. Roy Smith, *South Carolina as a Royal Province* (New York: The Macmillan Co., 1903), p. 179. In 1734 Governor Johnson stated the negroes outnumbered the whites three to one. McCrady, *South Carolina under Royal Government*, p. 183. This is an exaggeration. Professor Connor says that by 1760 the proportion was two to one. Unpublished lectures, University of North Carolina.

[55] During the four years following 1733, 10,447 negroes were imported into South Carolina. *The South Carolina Gazette*, April 2, 1737. Cited by McCrady, *South Carolina under Royal Government*, pp. 182-183.

[56] McCrady, *South Carolina under Proprietary Government*, p. 477.

[57] McCrady, *Royal Government*, pp. 182 et seq.

[58] A portion of these slaves were Indians. Governor Johnson states that in 1708 there were 1,400 Indian slaves in South Carolina. McCrady, *Proprietary Government*, p. 722.

[59] Connor, Unpublished Lectures, University of North Carolina.

world was difficult, and prices for native products were low. Obviously she could never develop an overseas commerce comparable to that of South Carolina. In Charleston the latter colony had a safe and convenient harbor which invited trade with the outside world, and she took advantage of the opportunity. She far surpassed her northern neighbor in both imports and exports. The tonnage entering North Carolina ports was negligible compared with that entering Charleston harbor. As early as 1724 commerce to the amount of about £60,000 entered the port of Charleston.[60] On the other hand, it was frequently quite impossible for a vessel going to North Carolina to find a cargo.[61] With such divergence of interests developing in the Carolinas, there appeared a feeling of separation which resembled the unsympathetic spirit which developed between the industrial North and the agricultural South in the country at large during the first half of the nineteenth century. Is it any wonder that a demand arose for permanent separation of Carolina, or that once the process was begun, it should be carried to a final conclusion?

Trade relationships between the colonies themselves constituted a primary cause of distrust and ill feeling.[62] The principle of geographical determinism played a large part in this. The southeastward course of North Carolina rivers tended to encourage trade with South Carolina.[63] In the early period it was much more convenient for the settlers on the Pee Dee and Catawba to use the valleys of those streams as trade routes than to transport their commodities by land to New Bern and Wilmington. However, South Carolina took unfair advantage of this situation. Her government laid heavy duties on products imported from the north.[64] North Carolina began to retaliate. As late as 1762 her Council petitioned the Crown to direct that the boundary line should be located on the Pee Dee River and Winyaw Bay,

[60] McCrady, *Proprietary Government*, p. 124.
[61] The above facts regarding industry and commerce in North Carolina were taken largely from a doctoral dissertation, "Transportation and Commerce in North Carolina, 1763-1789" (Yale University, 1930), kindly loaned to the writer by the author, Dr. C. C. Crittenden, Secretary of the N. C. Historical Commission.
[62] On commercial relations, see, for example, *C.R.*, VII, 155.
[63] C. C. Crittenden, "Inland Navigation in North Carolina, 1763-1789," *North Carolina Historical Review*, VIII (April, 1931), 145-154; Crittenden, "Ships and Shipping in North Carolina, 1763-1789," *op. cit.*, VIII (January, 1931), 1-13.
[64] *C.R.*, VI, 778; Connor, *History*, p. 247.

as by our having one side of Winyaw we should have a free navigation to the Sea and enjoy the Benefit of the inland navigation of the Yadkin, Rocky, Great and Little Pee Dee River, which though they all run through the heart of this province we [they] are from that reason totally useless to both provinces as the Boundary now stands.[65]

The Board of Trade replied that South Carolina's policy of levying heavy tariff duties "must in its consequence destruct the Commerce of his Majesty's subjects in North Carolina," and they promised to take action which would give the colony the desired relief. But the Board failed to give relief, and North Carolina adopted measures of her own. In 1751 the Assembly levied heavy duties on spirituous liquors imported into Anson County from South Carolina,[66] and later forbade the grazing of South Carolina cattle within the limits of North Carolina.[67] In 1762 an act was passed to incorporate a market town[68] called Campbellton[69] at the head of navigation of the Cape Fear River. The Assembly hoped that "the trade of the counties of Anson and Rowan, which at present centers in Charleston, South Carolina to the great injustice of this Province, will be drawn down to the said town."[70] This policy was furthered by the passage of two acts providing for the building of roads from Dan River on the Virginia line and from Shallow Ford on the Yadkin River to the new market town.[71] By 1775 it was the distributing point for trade as far west as Guilford, Yadkin, and Iredell counties.[72] South Carolina countered in 1790 by chartering the Santee Canal, joining the Santee River with Charleston in order to make that market more attractive and convenient to the northwest.[73] However, commercial trends were away from Charleston because of the very low prices offered there for products. In 1731 North Carolina commodities brought at least fifty per cent less on the Charleston

---

[65] *C.R.*, VI, 778.

[66] *C.R.*, IV, 1260, 1262, 1265, 1266, 1273, 1280, 1285.

[67] Connor, *History*, p. 247.   [68] *S.R.*, XXIII, 592.

[69] Modern Fayetteville.

[70] *C.R.*, XXV, 470; Crittenden, "Inland Navigation"; Connor, *History*, p. 248.

[71] Professor Connor states that "these wise measures" turned much of the trade of the back country to Wilmington by way of Campbellton and the Cape Fear, and helped unify North Carolina, in opposition to South Carolina influence. *History*, p. 247.

[72] Bassett, *op. cit.*, I, 60.   [73] Phillips, *op. cit.*, p. 15.

market than did those imported from the northern colonies.[74] North Carolinians resented this unfair discrimination.

The opposition to those conditions was effective. North Carolina resorted to other markets and sought largely to ignore her neighbor. A considerable amount of trade in lumber, naval stores, and farm products was built up with other colonies, the West Indies, and with England. In 1734, for example, in the midst of negotiations for a definite boundary survey, forty-two vessels cleared for Wilmington.[75] The northern province was rapidly working toward economic independence of Charleston and unity for herself. She demanded a definite and permanent dividing line.

The lack of adequate means of transportation and communication tended to isolate the two colonies and became a chief cause of the development of a provincial consciousness, with its accompanying desire for definite and permanent separation. Lack of frequent and intimate contacts tended to weaken the ties that bound the sections to each other. This effect was evident in credit transactions. It was often difficult to secure credit in Charleston when residing at a great distance from that center, and having secured credit, it was often difficult to collect and pay accounts.[76]

The condition of the roads in Carolina during the first half of the eighteenth century greatly limited intercommunication of the inhabitants, even in the most highly developed portion of the northern section. Reverend John Blair, a minister of North Carolina writing in England in 1704, described the roads in the province as "the worst roads that ever I saw"; and he added that anyone who had tried it would rather make the journey from England to Holland than from Albemarle County to Pamlico River.[77]

From the settlement of the colony down to the Revolution, road making consisted mostly of chopping "blazes" on trees.[78]

[74] Meredith, *op. cit.*, p. 29. [75] Connor, *History*, p. 150.
[76] C. C. Crittenden, "Means of Communication in North Carolina, 1763-1789," *North Carolina Historical Review*, VIII (October, 1931), 373-383. I am indebted to Dr. Crittenden for many facts here used relative to transportation and communication.
[77] *C.R.*, I, 602-603; F. W. Clonts, "Travel and Transportation in Colonial North Carolina," *North Carolina Historical Review*, III (January, 1925), 21.
[78] J. F. D. Smith, *A Tour of the United States of America: Containing an Account of the Present Situation of that Country*. 2 vols. (London,

Many of the roads themselves were hardly more than winding paths. Blair states that if a stranger ever loses his way "it is a great hazard if he ever finds his road again," for the roads were very "difficult to be found."[79] Governor Spotswood of Virginia, writing to the Board of Trade in 1711, described the "almost insuperable difficulties" of travel in the Albemarle—the most highly developed section of the province—stating it was "without any conveniency of carriage."[80]

The colonial governments took very little interest in road building in their early history. There was a general reliance on individual enterprise for transportation, whether by boat, pack train, or wagon. The South Carolina Assembly made its first provision for road building as early as 1682, but the roads were usually in "wretched order."[81] It made no effort to extend the road system beyond the limits of the tidewater area until 1737 and 1762 when two acts were passed for building roads to the northeast and northwest. Before that period no effort was made by the Assembly to draw the sections into commercial unity. The movement for separation, with a permanent boundary, had been in progress a quarter century when the first of these acts was passed. By the date of the second act, North Carolina was unifying herself by building east-west roads. Only four years later she passed "An Act for laying out a Public Road from the Frontiers of this Province, through the counties of Mecklenburg, Rowan, Anson, and Bladen, to Wilmington and Brunswick."[82] Five years later a similar act was passed for building a road from the frontier to Campbellton.[83]

Lack of adequate means of travel was as great an obstacle to contacts between the sections as the condition of the roads. Land

---

Robson and Sewell, 1784), I, 178; W. C. Watson, ed., *Men and Times of the Revolution* (New York: Dana & Co., 1856), p. 59; Crittenden, "Overland Travel and Transportation in North Carolina, 1763-1789," p. 247.

[79] *C.R.*, I, 600. Obstructions, such as fallen trees, were very reluctantly removed if they could be gone around. See "Journal of a French Traveler in the Colonies, 1765," March 17. *American Historical Review*, XXVI (1920-21), 734.

[80] *C.R.*, I, 782; F. W. Clonts, *op. cit.*, p. 17.

[81] Phillips, *op. cit.*, p. 27. Professor Phillips states that, even when a system of turnpikes was constructed, "it was permitted by the planters to fall into absolute neglect and decay." *Ibid.*, p. 12.

[82] *S.R.*, XXIII, 753.   [83] *Ibid.*, XXIII, 870.

travel was by foot, ox-cart,[84] and horse-back or crude carriage.[85] The use of horses was by no means common in the early period. Some horses were imported into South Carolina at an early date and used with both saddle and harness by the planters "when quick locomotion was needed."[86] But horses were "so monstrous extravagant"[87] that the great majority of the inhabitants could not afford them at that time. Travel was very slow even on horseback. Under favorable conditions thirty-five miles was considered ample for one day.[88] Wagon travel was much slower, often less than twenty miles a day.[89]

In time of peace there was little travel in North Carolina. Economic strain and bad facilities for travel kept the people at home.[90] Comparatively few inhabitants of North Carolina ever visited South Carolina.[91]

[84] Phillips, *op. cit.*, p. 25.

[85] The stagecoach did not come into use until about the close of the 18th century. Crittenden, "Overland Travel," p. 255. A footnote in Watson, *op. cit.*, p. 43, is enlightening, both for the revolutionary period and the middle nineteenth century. The author, describing his twelve-hundred mile trip from Providence to Charleston in 1777, says, "I performed the whole route either on horse-back or in a sulky." The editor then states in a footnote, "At that day, and under the circumstances of the country, this was the most commodius and practicable way of traveling. A fact almost surpassing belief, in those days of stage-coach and railroad facilities."

[86] Phillips, *loc. cit.*   [87] *C.R.*, IX, 1022.

[88] Crittenden, "Overland Travel," p. 252. In 1779 Whitmell Hill, delegate to the Continental Congress, writing to Thomas Burke in Philadelphia, says, "the Friday after leaving you I was at my home, so that I performed the journey in about seven and a half days, a ride scarcely performed before in so short a time." *S.R.*, XIV, 1.

[89] Four wagons going from Wachovia to Brunswick in 1767 required thirteen days to reach the town on account of "bad roads," a distance of approximately two hundred and twenty-five miles, or about eighteen miles a day. Adelaide L. Fries, ed., *Records of the Moravians in North Carolina*, 4 vols. (Raleigh: Edwards and Broughton, 1922-1930), 1, 356. Wagons from Wachovia to Charleston required about four weeks.

[90] Cf. Crittenden, "Overland Travel."

[91] In the spring of 1778 a traveler from South Carolina to Wilmington lost his way near Wilmington. The following day he overtook his former companions, "covered with mud, . . . giving . . . a most piteous account of his trials the night previous, . . . he had pressed forward through the pine wilderness in the region of Lockwood's Folly, and when night overtook him, he fell into a by-path, became bewildered, among swamps, and at length totally lost. His horse failed, exhausted by hard traveling without food. Fortunately . . . he carried flint and steel, and thus lighted a fire. He spent the night in fighting wolves, attracted by the light from the wilds, with pitch-pine flaming brands. At daylight he ascended a tall sapling, . . . 'to look out for land,' and saw the ferry-house not far off."

Travel by water was also slow, and very hazardous. As a result, communication with other sections by this mode was difficult. De Graffenreid, in his account of the founding of New Bern about 1712, says, "we had thought to accomplish our voyage [from Neuse River to Chowan Precinct] in twice 24 hours, and it took us 10 days."[92] Even in the greatest emergencies during this early period the most rapid means of communication between northern and southern Carolina was by large canoe.[93]

Communication between provinces was further retarded in the early period by lack of a postal system. Letters were often sent by any means that chanced to offer. In official business, expresses were usually employed. As late as 1780 Governor Jefferson of Virginia was writing the governor of North Carolina that he was employing "a sufficient number of expresses to station one at every 40 miles"[94] for bearing messages relative to the war. A Charleston bi-monthly express was established in 1765 by a group on the Cape Fear, but this was a private enterprise. In 1715 a primitive system was established by the passage of an act ordering that public letters concerning "divers Business" be carried promptly from plantation to plantation "under penalty of Five pounds for each default."[95] Nothing approaching regular postal service was established until 1757 when three private citizens were appointed for one year to carry the post twice a month from Wilmington to Suffolk. A regular time schedule was fixed and salaries allowed.[96] The contract was renewed the following year.[97] However, even these poor facilities were allowed to lapse within a few years.[98] In 1760 Governor Tryon complained that, "it is a disagreeable reflection . . . that the chain of communication . . . should be broken within this province."[99] Though regular postal service was established in North Carolina by the

---

Watson, *op. cit.*, p. 57. This would indicate that there was a veritable barrier between the Carolinas even as late as the Revolution.

[93] *C.R.*, I, 951.

[93] Orders to Foster, North Carolina agent, during the Tuscarora War, 1711-1713, read as follows: "After having Canoe hands, provisions & other necessaries you are with the first conveniency & all expedition you can make the best of yr way to Charles Town in South Carolina." *C.R.*, I, 898; Clonts, *op. cit.*, p. 18.

[94] Thomas Jefferson to Abner Nash, June 16, 1780. *S.R.*, XIV, 852.

[95] Laws of North Carolina—1715, chapter LVI, in *S.R.*, XXIII, 81.

[96] *C.R.*, V, 886, 920.   [97] *Ibid.*, V, 1038, 1101.

[98] Crittenden, "Means of Communication in North Carolina," p. 376.

[99] *C.R.*, VIII, 66.

opening of the Revolution[100] and continued in operation during most of the war, it was slow and unreliable. There were strong complaints of poor service from South Carolina even as late as 1777,[101] which is indicative of earlier conditions.

This lack of facilities for communication had a marked effect on the region north of the Cape Fear. Northern Carolina became self-reliant and self-conscious, feeling that she did not need union with the southern section of the province. Constant demands for a division, and for extension westward of a boundary line, once it was begun, were only a natural consequence.

Thus it is seen that North Carolina's southern boundary disputes were characteristic of the relations of the American colonies and States throughout much of their history. The issues involved in all these disputes were often of great importance to the future of the colonies and states and of the Federal Union. Security of territory, state rights, peace and war, economic welfare, right of settlement, national politics, international relations, and even the existence of the States and the Union were among those issues. Statesmen and scholars have not failed to point out their great significance.

The dispute between North and South Carolina was one of the oldest and the most lengthy of all of those boundary controversies, and involved elements which were unique in their

[100] North Carolina and South Carolina had postal service only once a fortnight at that time. Crittenden, "Means of Communication in North Carolina," p. 378.

[101] One such complaint, for example, read as follows: We beg leave "to acquaint your Excellency that, unless the post is established on a better footing in future, than it is at present, it will be impossible for us to maintain that regular intercourse with your State that is necessary, as the post which set off from North Carolina, previous to Mr. Le Poole's departure from thence is not yet arrived—there being three mails now due." Jas. Jamieson & Co. to Governor Caswell, Charles Town, January 6, 1777, quoted in *S.R.*, XI, 359-366. In 1774 it took twenty-seven days for post riders to carry a letter 435 miles from Charlestown to Suffolk— an average of only sixteen miles a day. Newspaper circulation was also very poor in the Carolinas, even as late as the opening of the Revolution. A letter written from North Carolina in December, 1775, contained the complaint: "We have but little communication with neighboring provinces." Quoted in Crittenden, "Means of Communication . . ." p. 381. William Hooper, at Hillsboro, complained that, "I have not seen a paper or magazine since I came hither. We hold no more intercourse with the public and political world than if we were no part of it." William Hooper to James Iredell, February 7, 1784. C. J. McRae, *Life and Correspondence of James Iredell*, 2 vols. (New York: D. Appleton & Co., 1858), II, 90.

nature and character. The northern section of the province was settled by an immigration to a great degree alien in origin and race to that of the southern section and remained so throughout the period of their boundary bickerings. Physical, commercial, and social conditions played a great part in maintaining the ever-widening differences between the two sections, while an ungenerous attitude of superiority on the part of South Carolina tended to alienate the good will of North Carolina. All of these elements combined to cause the development of a spiritual division between the two sections which preceded and accompanied the agitation for and progress of the permanent division of Carolina.

With a brief description of these contributing conditions and elements as a background, we now turn to a description of the actual drawing of North Carolina's southern boundary line.

CHAPTER II

PROGRESS OF THE SURVEY DURING THE COLONIAL PERIOD

Section I

THE BOUNDARY QUESTION DURING THE PROPRIETARY PERIOD

The possibility of a division of the province of Carolina was recognized at its inception. The Charter of 1663 to the Lords Proprietors, though it referred to the territory as one province, granted to them the authority to lease any amount of the territory within their charter limits. That of 1665 gave the specific power "to erect, constitute, and make several counties, baronnies, and colonies, of and within the said province, territories, lands and hereditaments . . ." and to enact laws appertaining to a "county, baronny, or colony. . . ."[1]

The germ of physical division of Carolina appeared in the establishment of such separate and distinct governmental units in the northern and southern sections. As we have seen, the system was begun in the year of the granting of the first charter. In the fall of 1663 Sir William Berkeley, Governor of Virginia, was instructed to organize a government at Albemarle, and was authorized to appoint two governors for that region should he deem it wise and practical.[2] The following summer he appointed William Drummond governor. By 1665 the first Assembly was held, and the settlement became self-governing.[3] The charter of the latter date included Albemarle in the Carolina grant, and the Proprietors thereafter set up administrative divisions as they desired.

Pursuant to the commission of the Lords Proprietors, dated

[1] Francis N. Thorpe, ed., *The Federal and State Constitution, colonial Charters, and other Organic Laws of the States, Territories, and Colonies now or heretofore Forming the United States of America* (Washington: Government Printing Office, 1909), V, 2763.
[2] *C.R.*, I, 49.
[3] On January 11 of the same year the Lords Proprietors appointed Sir John Yeamans governor of "a Collony or plantation to the southward of Cape Romania," that is, of all Carolina south of the cape. *C.R.*, I, 93-94

December 26, 1671, Sir John Yeamans was proclaimed governor "of all this Territory or part of the Province of Carolina that lyes to the Southward and Westward of Cape Carterett," by the Grand Council of South Carolina.[4] In the previous year the region around Charleston was settled, and the settlements at Albemarle and Charleston were soon spoken of as North Carolina and South Carolina. Albemarle was called North Carolina by the Virginia Council as early as 1688.[5] On December 5, 1689, the Lords Proprietors commissioned Colonel Philip Ludwell "Governour of that part of our Province of Carolina that lyes north and east of Cape feare"[6] thus separating Carolina into two political divisions with specified limits.[7] Ludwell became governor of all Carolina in November, 1691,[8] and appointed Thomas Harvey[9] as Deputy-Governor of North Carolina, as authorized in his commission. In December, 1708, the Proprietors appointed Edward Tynte "Governor of our whole province of South and North Carolina,"[10] and

[4] Journal of the Grand Council of South Carolina (MSS.), March 16, 1671/2.

[5] Other similar divisional terms were often used in referring to the northern section. For example, "This day a letter was given . . . to ye Govr & Council at ye North pt. of Carolina." *Records in the British Public Record Office Relating to South Carolina, 1663-1684* (A. S. Salley, Jr., ed., 1929), August 5, 1681. (Cited hereafter as *Rec. in B. P. R. O. Rel. to S. C.*). In 1697 the Lords Proprietors wrote to Governor Blake of Carolina that they had taken the exemplification of their charter and sent it to the Deputy-Governor and Council of "North Carolina" to adjust their boundary with the Governor of Virginia. *Ibid.*, December 22, 1697. Cf. The Act "for the determination of the General Assemblies," June 20, 1694. Nicholas Trott, *Laws of South Carolina* (1719), p. 36. Legislative division was there specified. See further, S. A. Ashe, *History of North Carolina*, I, 141. (Cited hereafter as Ashe, *History*).

[6] *C.R.*, I, 360.

[7] The original plan was to have only one Assembly for all Carolina. On November 28, 1691, Ludwell was instructed to have the counties of Albemarle, Colleton, Berkeley, and Craven elect five delegates each, to meet at a place to be designated by himself. *C.R.*, 1377. The great distance between the north and south portions, however, made this impracticable, and the Albemarle government continued unaltered. Ashe, *History*, I, 142.

[8] *C.R.*, I, 373.

[9] *Ibid.*, I, 405. Cf. Public Records of South Carolina, VII, 40. (Cited hereafter as Pub. Rec. of S. C.). The Proprietors had appointed the governor of the northern section theretofore.

[10] *C.R.*, I, 695. In the work of Chief Justice Nicholas Trott of South Carolina entitled, *The Laws of the Province of South Carolina* (1719), one of the title pages reads: "Acts passed by the General Assembly of South Carolina, during the Governments of the Honble Col. Edward Tynte, esq.; Governour of North and South Carolina." Ashe says the Proprietors ex-

NORTH CAROLINA BOUNDARY DISPUTES 25

on his death in 1711, they appointed Edward Hyde "Govern^r of North Carolina" in his own right.[11] The appointment was approved by the Crown, and on May 9, 1712, he received his commission as "Govr Capt Gen^{ll} Adm^{ll} Comand^r in Chiefe of that part of ye province of Carolina that lyes N° & E^t of Cape ffeare Called N° Carolina."[12]

Thus began the complete separation of the government of North Carolina from that of South Carolina.[13]

This development was given impetus by the glaring inefficiency of the proprietary government. Its defects were tragically evident in 1716. During the dangers to the people of South Carolina accompanying the War with the Yemassee Indians, their officials applied to England for troops for protection.[14] The Proprietors admitted their inability to afford protection to the province, and the question of its purchase by the Crown was considered,

---

pected Tynte to appoint Edward Hyde Deputy-Governor of North Carolina. *History*, I, 168. [11] *C.R.*, I, 799.

[12] *C.R.*, I, 841. It has been shown that official thinking throughout the period from 1685 to 1715 was in terms of geographical and political separation of the original proprietary province. *Supra*, p. 8. Similar expressions were frequently used before that period. Cf. *Rec. in B. P. R. O. Rel. to S C., passim*. As late as August, 1720, the Lords Proprietors were urging the King to resume their practice of appointing a deputy governor of North Carolina, subject to the orders of the governor of South Carolina, Pub. Rec. of S. C., VIII, 40, 95. But when Francis Nicholson received his instructions at that time as provisional royal governor of "South Carolina in America," they contained no provision empowering him to appoint a deputy governor of the northern province. The distinct governments were preserved. *Ibid.*, VIII, 42-57.

[13] Permanent division was recommended in 1695 in order to improve the system of collecting the king's customs duties. When Edward Randolph, Collector of Customs, made his report to the Commissioners of Customs in that year, he included the following recommendation:

"Wherefore for prevention of so great a mischiefe to England tis humbly proposed

1st That the south part of Carolina and all the Bahama Islands be put under His Majesties immediate authority

2nd That North Carolina be annexed and put under the care and inspection of His Majesties Governor of Virginia. . . ."

C.R., I, 441. The proposal, however, was not carried out. On August 16, 1720, Colonel Barnwell of South Carolina and Boone, her agent, stated to the Board of Trade that North and South Carolina were two distinct governments and "are independent of each other in all respects." Pub. Rec. of S. C., VIII, 252.

[14] The South Carolina General Assembly ignored the Proprietors and applied for aid directly "To the Kings most Excellent Majesty" in May, 1715. Pub. Rec. of S. C., VI, 85, 116.

but with no definite action taken. By 1719, conditions in the colony had become intolerable and the people determined to revolt. Their Assembly resolved itself into a convention and threw off the authority of the Proprietors. They elected James Moore as Governor, and application was then made to the king to receive South Carolina as a royal province.[15] This raised the question of a North Carolina-South Carolina boundary line.[16]

The South Carolina authorities claimed the Cape Fear River as their boundary, asserting that their government had been granting lands on its banks for years. They were accurate regarding land grants.[17] As there were no settlements in the Cape Fear region in the earlier period, the boundary question was not so important and North Carolina also granted lands on the southern bank of the Cape Fear before the line was run.[18] The Lords Proprietors—the real owners of the whole region—called the Cape Fear the line of division. In August, 1713, they were complaining of injuries from illegal grants being issued for lands south of that stream.[19] Governor Boone and Colonel Barnwell of South Carolina reported to the Board of Trade in November, 1720, that many of the prevailing controversies regarding the boundary were caused by the carelessness of the Proprietors in referring to Cape Fear as the boundary without mentioning the Cape

---

[15] Francis Yonge, *A Narrative of the Proceedings of the People of South Carolina, in the year* 1719; *and of the True Causes and motives that induced them to Renounce their Obedience to the Lords Proprietors, as their Governors, and to put themselves under the Immediate Government of the Crown* (London, 1726), *passim*. B. R. Carroll, ed., *Historical Collection of South Carolina*, 2 vols., II, 141-196.

[16] There was consideration of Carolina boundaries as early as 1681 but it is not clear what portion is referred to. In the records of a meeting of the Proprietors in July of that year the following entry appears:

Agreed y^t—

"The [That] ye bounds be adjusted." *Rec. in B. P. R. O. Rel. to S. C.*, 1663-1684.

[17] For example, on August 17, 1714, one Thomas Hughes received a grant for 409 acres of land in Craven County, "butting and bounding to the . . . East on Cape Fear River. . . ." Proprietors Grants (MSS., S. C.), vol. 39, no. 2. On September 6 of the same year, Price Hughes received a grant of 3184 acres on Cape Fear River in the same county, "butting and bounding to the Northeast on said River. . . ." *Ibid.*, vol. 39, no. 2. A grant to Thomas James in the same year is recorded as follows:

"James, Thomas Crav. | 409 | 39 | 164 | 17 | Aug. 1714." Index to Grants, A to K, 1695 to 1776 (S. C.); Commons House Journals, 1734-1736 (MSS.), no. 9, p. 197.

[18] Ashe, *History*, I, 215. [19] Pub. Rec. of S. C., VI, 56.

Fear River.[20] The Board of Trade was also specifying Cape Fear as the northern limit. In its report to the King on September 8, 1721, the following item appears:

"South Carolina—
extends from Cape Fear to the River St. Mathias. . . ."[21]

The writer has some doubt as to the accuracy of a statement by W. L. Saunders, editor of the *Colonial Records of North Carolina*, to the effect that Cape Fear River never was the dividing line between the Carolinas.[22] The Proprietors were definitely designating Cape Fear as the boundary between the two provinces, South Carolina officials clearly indicated that it was only through carelessness of statement that the Proprietors were referring to Cape Fear as the line instead of Cape Fear River; those officials themselves understood and insisted that the river was the boundary; the Board of Trade reported to the King that the northern limits of South Carolina were at Cape Fear; South Carolina was granting lands on the southern bank of the Cape Fear with the full knowledge of the Proprietors; and the Proprietors were complaining that North Carolina was granting lands in the same region. Hence, that stream may have been for a time the dividing line. It will be shown later that in 1757 South Carolina still insisted that the Cape Fear River was the "Ancient Boundary."[23]

The first occasion of agitation for determining a permanent boundary line between the Carolinas was a constant failure of the southern province to secure the return of fugitives from justice. In the fall of 1713, the Governor and Council of South Carolina had made a formal request of the Proprietors to have the dividing line permanently established, but after considering the request the latter "thought it a matter of such consequence" as to require more mature consideration.[24] Their secretary stated to Thomas Pollock that action had been postponed, but that he would present the request again at their next meeting and "endeavor all I can to have a determination of the Matter in your favor."[25] Nothing was done toward establishing the line at that time, however, though disputes were frequently arising and fugitives constantly escaping to the Cape Fear region. The South Carolina Assembly represented to the Board of Trade in September, 1721,

[20] *C.R.*, II, 395.
[22] *C.R.*, II, vii.
[24] *C.R.*, II, 63.
[21] Pub. Rec. of S. C., IX, 66.
[23] *Infra*, p. 65.
[25] *C.R.*, II, 63.

"how much this province suffers by the Inhabitants and slaves running away there where they are succoured"; hence, they declared, it is imperative that the boundary be permanently established.[26] Businessmen were taking notice of the situation and the abuses which it made possible. For years they had observed the practice of evasion of debts by taking advantage of the lack of a permanent boundary. They had frequently called the attention of the London merchants to "a desertion" to the Cape Fear "where they think theire Credit[rs] can't reach them." In 1727, they renewed the demand of 1719 for immediate establishment of a royal government, and they urged the appointment of a royal governor with specific instructions "to have Cape Fear ascertained in this Government."[27] Two months later, another London merchant, acting as agent for the President and Council of South Carolina, presented a memorial to the Board of Trade requesting that an order be secured from the Royal Council placing Cape Fear with "all its Settlem[ts]" in South Carolina.[28] In December, Governor Robert Johnson used his influence in support of this request, and for the same reasons. He wrote to the Secretary of the Board of Trade that the boundary line must be determined in order to prevent South Carolinians from running to "Cape Fair" and permanently settling there "to defraud their Creditors. . . ."[29] Cape Fear, he urged, should be declared within the limits of South Carolina to check this evil.

As early as 1721, the situation had acquired sufficient importance to cause South Carolina to take positive steps toward securing an adjustment. As a result of her revolutionary change in government, that province expected a radical change in the relations of North Carolina with the Proprietors and the Crown. Consequently, South Carolina instructed her newly appointed agents in London, Francis Yonge and John Lloyd, to endeavor to

[26] Pub. Rec. of S. C., IX, 123. The Board of Trade was sufficiently concerned over the general confusion that they reported it to the King immediately. *C.R.*, II, 419.

[27] Extract of a letter from "Considerable Merchant" in South Carolina to another in London, May 24, 1727. He declared that all friends of South Carolina should strongly discourage settlement of Cape Fear, which "Mr. Moor" and his friends in South Carolina are working to establish as an independent government. Pub. Rec. of S. C., XII, 215-216. See also, *supra*, p. 10.

[28] Memorial from Mr. Godin in behalf of the President and Council of South Carolina, July 23, 1727. Pub. Rec. of S. C., XIII, 338, 341.

[29] Governor Johnson to the Secretary, December 19, 1729. *C.R.*, III, 51.

bring about a definite settlement. If North Carolina should remain a distinct government, they were to apply for the King's orders to the governors of North and South Carolina to meet and make an agreement regarding the line, and to urge that "the head of the North Branch of the Cape Fear River and from thence by a due west line parallel to Virginia be the settled bounds for ever. . . ."[30] If the northern province should be made a royal colony, they were to urge that it be put under the jurisdiction of South Carolina. The expected change in the form of government was not made at that time, however, and no action was taken to determine a permanent line.

The possibility of a "fatal" contraction of her territory on the south and west intensified South Carolina's demand for her northernmost claims. Following the Yemassee War and the accompanying threat of a Spanish advance from the south, the Proprietors determined to established a government south of South Carolina with the Savannah River as its northern boundary, in the region of modern Georgia.[31] This plan ultimately led to the first definite action toward an adjustment of the line.

In April, 1725, South Carolina again petitioned the king to issue instructions that "Effectual means may be taken to Ascertain the Boundaries of this Your Province towards the Government of North Carolina,"[32] but without results.

In the meantime, there had been a permanent change in the form of government in North and South Carolina.[33] In January,

[30] *C.R.*, II, 448.

[31] *Ibid.*, II, vii. Saunders says this was the origin of the demand for a definite northern boundary, but the writer disagrees with this view. As shown above, the demand for a dividing line preceded the Georgia question. *Supra*, p. 27. That question was, to a great extent, the result of the colony's demand for a royal government with permanent boundaries, affording the colony the King's protection. The two questions came in the order of cause and effect. The establishment of a buffer colony was calculated both to afford protection and silence the colony's demand for a definitely limited royal government. However, the chartering of Georgia in 1732 gave impetus to the movement for a permanent line and hastened the survey of 1735; but it must be remembered that boundary agitation was then two decades old.

[32] Petition of the South Carolina Assembly, sent to Francis Yonge, her Agent in London. Pub. Rec. of S. C., XII, 35.

[33] South Carolina had been under royal government since 1719, but, as we have seen, the change was only provisional. Francis Nicholson was installed as "Provisional" Royal Governor. Edward McCrady, *The History of South Carolina under the Proprietary Government, 1670-1719* (New York: The Macmillan Co., 1897), pp. 673, 750. The movement which

1728, seven of the Lords Proprietors signed a memorial offering to surrender their interests in the Carolinas,[34] and an act was passed by the British Parliament during its session of 1728 authorizing the purchase of the original province from the Proprietors.[35] Their rights to the territory were surrendered to the Crown by deed dated July 25, 1729.[36] Official division of the area into two provinces followed the purchase immediately.[37]

Thus, during the Proprietary period the controversy went through a gradual development. Topographical features of Carolina had produced a natural tendency on the part of the inhabitants toward a division of the territory into two sections separately administered; the possibility of such division into other colonies was contained in the early charters; such division was often urged, particularly at the Cape Fear and Santee rivers. Each colony claimed one of these river courses as the boundary. The Santee was the more equitable point of division. The Proprietors had admitted their inability to govern the province efficiently and had sold their shares, save one, to the Crown. With the royal purchase came specific political and administrative division of the territory into Crown colonies and direct negotiations for locating a permanent dividing line. This was the status of the boundary question at the close of the Proprietary period. To the events leading up to the original surveys we now turn.

Section II

Progress of the Survey During the Reign of George II

The administrative division by the Crown, referred to above, was direct and definite. On January 15, 1729/30, George II commissioned Captain George Burrington "Captain General and Governor in Chief in and over our Province of North Carolina in America."[38] Colonel Robert Johnson was likewise commissioned Governor of South Carolina, December 11, 1729.

Both of the royal governors resumed the efforts they had put forth while proprietary governors of their respective provinces

---

had been in progress toward purchase by the Crown for some time was probably interrupted by the death of George I in 1727.

[34] Ashe, *History*, I, 217.

[35] 2nd George 2nd, chap. 34. Quoted in S. C. *Statutes at Large*, I, 60-70.   [36] S. C. *Statutes at Large*, I, 405.

[37] *Ibid.*, I, 41.

[38] *C.R.*, III, 66. (The old style calendar was not changed until 1750; hence, the system of dual dating used in some of the sources.)

toward ascertaining and marking a dividing line. They held personal conferences looking toward a mutual agreement regarding the location of the boundary, and while in London in January, 1729/30, they attended a meeting of the Board of Trade and announced that they had reached an agreement.[39] Two weeks later the Board of Trade and the two governors agreed on a dividing line to begin thirty miles southwest of Cape Fear River and "to be run at that parallel distance the whole course of the said river."[40] The Board ordered that an article to that effect be inserted in the draughts of the governors' instructions. This was clearly a compromise between Cape Fear as designated by the Proprietors and the Santee River which favored North Carolina.

Governor Johnson drew up a memorial on his instructions regarding the line, which was read before the Board of Trade on June 9, 1730; and the following day his suggested line was incorporated in a set of one hundred twenty-four instructions as the one hundred tenth.[41] He modified the agreement on January 22, however, in "the following way of expresing it to answer the same intent vid: That a line shall be run (by Commissioners appointed by each province) beginning at the Sea 30 miles distant from the mouth of Cape Fear River on the South West side thereof keeping the same distance from the said River as the Course thereof runs to the main sourse or head thereof and from thence the said boundary line shall be continued due west as far as the South Seas. But if Waccama River lyes within 30 miles of Cape Fear River then that River to be the boundary from the sea to the head thereof, and from thence to keep the distance of 30 miles Paralel from Cape Fear River to the head thereof and from thence a due West Course to the South Sea."[42]

South Carolina set out immediately to have the line ascer-

[39] Journals of the Board of Trade, quoted in *C.R.*, III, 124, and in Pub. Rec. of S. C., XIV, 1. The Journal records:
"Whitehall, Thursday, Jan., 1729/30
"Col. Johnson Govr of South Carolina and Capt Burrington Govr of North Carolina attending with some other gentlemen belonging to those Provinces acquainted the Board that they had agreed upon a division line between those Provences and their Lordships desired they would mark the line upon a Map and lay the same before the Board which they promised accordingly."
[40] *C.R.*, III, 125; Pub. Rec. of S. C., XIV, 1-2. Cf. map, p. 32. The lines here indicated are approximated. It is regretted that technical difficulties make it impossible to include copies of the original surveys. They may be found in the North Carolina Historical Commission offices, Raleigh.
[41] Pub. Rec. of S. C., XIV, 206.   [42] *C.R.*, III, 84.

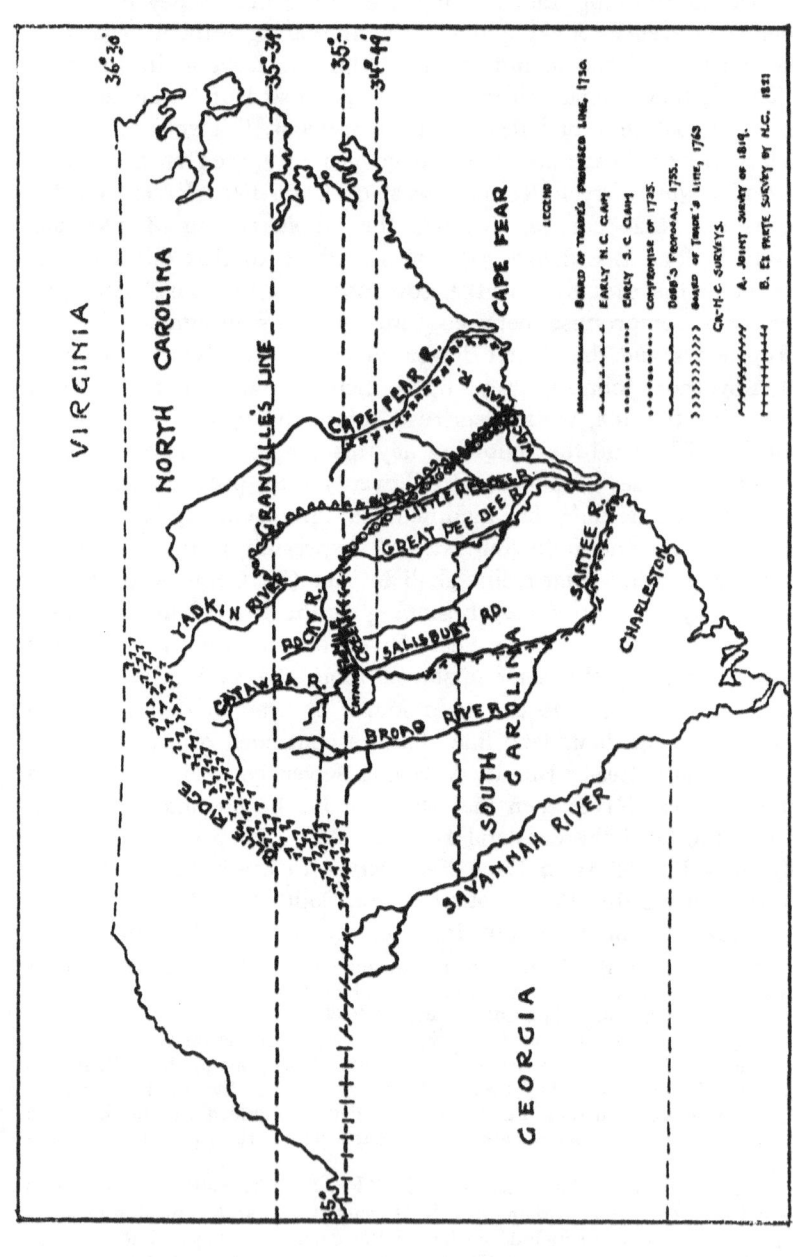

NORTH CAROLINA'S DISPUTED SOUTHERN BOUNDARY

tained and marked. On October 27, 1730/31, Governor Johnson wrote to Governor Burrington asking that commissioners be appointed "for speedy running" the line, according to royal instructions.[43] The question of a proper interpretation of these instructions then arose and the North Carolina Council, favoring Burrington's interpretation, advised him to defer appointing commissioners until the King's further pleasure was known.[44] The governor accepted their advice and let the matter rest for the time being.[45]

The difference of interpretation came over the wording of the royal instructions which described the line. Those instructions conclude as follows: "But if Waccamaw River lyes within 30 miles of Cape Fear River then that River to be the boundary. . . ."[46] Governor Johnson claimed that the Board of Trade concluded that the first clause of the instructions should stand,[47] "unless the MOUTH[48] of the Wackamaw was within thirty miles of Cape Fear River . . ."; that the word "mouth" was omitted only through mistake.[49] Governor Burrington claimed, on the other hand, that the first clause of the instructions was to stand unless the Waccamaw River, in any part of its course, was within thirty miles of the Cape Fear.

From a strictly legal standpoint, Governor Burrington's position was sound. It appears quite improbable that a whole phrase —"the mouth of"—was omitted from this document by an expert clerical force. But granting that the improbable occurred, and that the point was directly discussed between the Board and the two governors, and that Burrington and the Board agreed with Johnson on the term "mouth of the Wackamaw," as the latter contended;[50] still, the instructions to the two governors were at hand, identical, and bore out Burrington's contentions.[51] If South Carolina had been allowed to read into the instructions one addi-

[43] N. C. *Council Journal*, January 17, 1731/2. Quoted in *C.R.*, III, 398.
[44] Burrington to Board of Trade, February 20, 1731/2. He repeated the above facts, explaining his failure to act by stating that he was advised to wait until he "was honored with an answer from England on that Subject." *C.R.*, III, 336.
[45] As late as September, 1732, Governor Johnson filed a written complaint with the Board of Trade that he had urged Governor Burrington to appoint commissioners, "but he has not answered that Letter. . . ." Johnson to Board of Trade, September 28, 1732. *S.R.*, XI, 20.
[46] *Supra*, p. 31.
[47] That is, the Cape Fear parallel clause.
[48] The capitals are the writer's.
[49] *S.R.*, XI, 19.   [50] *Ibid.*, XI, 19.
[51] Pub. Rec. of S. C., XIV, 206; *C.R.*, III, 115.

tional provision, she might have been able to have added other radical changes; hence, Burrington evidently felt it safer strictly to observe the letter of the instructions. He declared that "The Head of Wackamaw is within 10 miles of Cape Fear River . . .,"[52] and the South Carolina General Assembly admitted that it was not over 14 miles distant at certain portions of its course.[53] However, there was reason in Governor Johnson's protest that such a line would extend the North Carolina boundary into the heart of his province.[54]

Governor Burrington was persistent in his efforts to prevent the running of the line parallel to the Cape Fear River. He attacked the proposal from the standpoint of the great expense it would incur—argument which he knew would be carefully weighed by the British authorities. He informed the Secretary of State that it would cost at least £2,000 to survey and mark the proposed line; whereas, the Pee Dee River could be made the boundary and save the expense and trouble of a survey.[55] He reminded the Secretary that the Santee River formerly divided the two provinces. The North Carolina Governor followed up these efforts to prevent the survey with another appeal to the Board of Trade at the beginning of the following year. He stated that nothing had been done regarding the boundary and repeated his statement that the Pee Dee River would be a "natural and proper division." South Carolina would then contain twice the amount of territory left to North Carolina, he stated, adding that if the King should order the line to be run, finances would have to be provided; and he then raised his estimate of the cost of a survey to £3,000 sterling.[56] This Pee Dee River proposal was an infinitely more equitable compromise line than that contended for by South Carolina. But regardless of cost and the great inconvenience and injustice inherent in the Cape Fear parallel line, Governor Johnson had significantly stated, "I fear no boundary can be settled" unless the line is run thirty miles south of the Cape Fear.[57] Burrington further endeavored to block Johnson's plans by publishing a warning to "unadvised people" of South Carolina against taking out

---

[52] *S.R.*, XI, 20.
[53] S. C. Council Journals, 1734-1736, no. 6, pp. 27-29.
[54] *S.R.*, XI, 21.
[55] Burrington to Newcastle, July 2, 1731. *C.R.*, III, 154.
[56] Burrington to Board of Trade, January 1, 1731/2. *C.R.*, III, 435.
[57] *S.R.*, XI, 21.

grants for lands north of the Waccamaw River and thereby "parting with their money to no purpose."[58] Johnson replied in kind, adding that he was only awaiting further instructions from the Board of Trade.[59] In the meantime, he had been pleading with the Board of Trade to continue in their original "intentions" as to the location of the line, and "to let him and me know your pleasure."[60] He declared that adoption of the Waccamaw River line would make it impossible to prevent illegal trade, for ships would simply go a short way up that stream and be out of his jurisdiction.

When their "pleasure" was revealed, it was seen that the Board of Trade had ignored the letter of the instructions and directed that the boundary line be run thirty miles south of the Cape Fear River and parallel to that stream.[61] The Board had favored South Carolina.

The matter was dropped for sometime after this order was transmitted, possibly because of the change of governors of North Carolina.[62] The new governor, Gabriel Johnston, had to adjust himself to his new government and to inform himself regarding the whole boundary question. However, Governor Burrington had succeded in preventing the survey. His greatest service in the boundary controversy was in deferring this unreasonable survey until a better line could be agreed upon.

The actions and provocations of the Tuscarora Indians, however, soon caused a renewal of efforts on the part of South Carolina to secure a definite and permanent dividing line. The governor of that province wrote to Governor Johnston regarding the Indians and the necessity of determining the boundary. The reply was read in the Upper House of the South Carolina Assembly January 24, 1734/5,[63] and after a committee was appointed, the letter and the royal instructions relative to the location were sent to the Lower House for immediate consideration.[64] Action was

[58] *South Carolina Gazette,* October 21, 1732. Quoted in S. C. *Statutes at Large,* I, 406; *S.R.,* XI, 19.
[59] S. C. *Statutes at Large,* I, 407; *S.R.,* XI, 19.
[60] Pub. Rec. of S. C., XVI, 6-7; *S.R.,* XI, 20. It must be remembered that it was Johnson himself who had the Waccamaw River provision added to the Board's original instructions.
[61] Secretary Popple to Burrington, August 16, 1732. *C.R.,* III, 355.
[62] Burrington was succeeded by Johnston in April, 1733.
[63] S. C. Council Journals, 1734-1736. no. 6, p. 22.
[64] *Ibid.,* p. 23.

prompt and the following day the Commons House returned a report of a joint committee which contended for the Cape Fear parallel line and recommended that the governor notify Governor Johnston of the sense of the Assembly. It was also recommended that commissioners be appointed to run the line as soon as the governors came to an agreement on the interpretation of their instructions. Meantime, South Carolina should require all inhabitants along the Waccamaw residing within thirty miles of Cape Fear to pay taxes, and Governor Johnston should be requested to severely reprimand the Tuscarora Indians.[65]

Definite progress was made toward an actual survey when, in 1735, the respective governors appointed commissioners to determine the line.[66] The appointments in South Carolina caused a disturbance of relations between the legislative and executive branches of the government. The Lower House displayed poor judgment in selecting their nominees, having included no one with technical knowledge. The governor urged that a surveyor be included but the House replied that their nominees were "very capable" of performing their duties and refused to alter the nominations.[67] The South Carolina Assembly had been notified a month before that North Carolina had appointed commissioners. Nevertheless, they wrangled over personnel and compensation at intervals for over a month until the governor took the matter of appointments into his own hands and with the advice of the Council, appointed commissioners on March 19. He did later appoint one nominee of the Assembly's selection, however. He had previously written Governor Johnston appointing March 25 for a meeting of the commissioners on the Cape Fear;[68] this appointment probably helps to account for his taking the appointments out of the hands of the Assembly. The disagreement between Governor and Assembly effectively delayed action on the line.

The commissioners assembled on the Cape Fear April 23[69] for the purpose of reaching an agreement as to procedure. Prospects

[65] *Ibid.*, pp. 27-29. The report was adopted.
[66] The following commissioners were appointed. For North Carolina: Robert Halton, Eleazer Allen, Matthew Rowan, Edward Moseley, and Roger Moore; for South Carolina: Alexander Skene, James Abercrombie, and William Walters. *C.R.*, V, 375; S. C. Council Journals, March 19, 1734/5; Commons House Journals, March 26, 1734/5.
[67] S. C. Commons House Journal, 1734-1736, pp. 192-193.
[68] S. C. Council Journals, February 14 to March 19, 1735, *passim.*
[69] Pub. Rec. of S. C., XVII, 311; *C.R.*, V, 374.

of reaching a mutual understanding were still dark. Governor Johnson was persisting in every effort to secure a boundary line favorable to South Carolina. He wrote to Perege Fury, Agent in London, that if the "mouth" of the Waccamaw is within thirty miles of the Cape Fear River it should be the boundary line, "and not otherwise." He also reported the approaching meeting of the commissioners to determine a line, "tho' we apprehend with little probability of success."[70] This communication was sent to the Board of Trade and, after its reading and consideration, the Board "were of opinion that Wagyamaw River is . . . [according to royal instructions] the intended Boundary";[71] and they gave orders that the secretary prepare a letter to each of the governors accordingly. When drafting the letters a week later, the Board called in former Governor Burrington and Fury, the South Carolina Agent, for consultation. Burrington expressed the opinion that the running of the Cape Fear parallel line was "hardly practicable," or if practicable it would be very expensive and difficult, the expense alone of running a line through that uninhabited wilderness would amount to "upwards of £4,000."[72] He added that the only natural boundary was the Pee Dee River, which would cost nothing to either province.[73] The Board deferred a final decision in order to consult former Governor Craven of South Carolina at a later meeting.[74] At the later meeting, however, final decision was again postponed.[75]

In the meantime, progress was being made in the colonies. After long and futile efforts had been made among the commissioners on the Cape Fear to reach an agreement, Governor Gabriel Johnston interposed as mediator and brought about an agreement "to the general satisfaction" of all concerned.[76] "In order to pre-

[70] Johnson to Fury, March 14, 1735. *C.R.*, XI, 25.
[71] Journals of the Board of Trade, June 6, 1735. Quoted in Pub. Rec. of S. C. XVII, 257; *C.R.*, IV, 27.
[72] *Ibid.*, June 13, 1735. Pub. Rec. of S. C., XVII, 260-1; *C.R.*, IV, 28.
[73] Burrington's opinion was valuable because of its impartiality. As governor of North Carolina he had been removed from office after many conflicts with the people, and it was only natural and human that he should have enjoyed any stroke against their interests. He was big enough to ignore his grievances and offer an honest opinion.
[74] *C.R.*, IV, 28.
[75] Journals of the Board of Trade, June 26, 1735. Pub. Rec. of S. C. XVII, 262-4.
[76] *Ibid.*, July 29, 1735. Pub. Rec. of S. C., XVII, 267. See also, *C.R.*, IV, 9.

serve and maintain a good correspondence between the inhabitants of both the said provinces and to prevent any future contests relating to the boundarys between the same," the commissioners agreed to the following articles, which were as agreeable "as may be" to the sense of the royal instructions:

1. The line shall begin at the sea, thirty miles "from the West side of the mouth of the Cape Fear River."
2. From thence it shall run on a northwest course to the thirty-fifth parallel of north latitude, and from thence due west "to the South Seas."[77]
3. If the said northwest course comes within five miles of Pee Dee River before reaching the thirty-fifth parallel, then a line shall be run parallel to said river at five miles distant from it to the said thirty-fifth parallel, and from thence a due west course as before; provided that such parallel line does not approach nearer to Cape Fear River than thirty miles; and in such case a northwest course shall be continued from the point where it so approaches.
4. If said westward line shall include any part of the Cherokee or Catawba Indians, it shall be "set off" so as to leave them in South Carolina, incircling them until the line shall again strike the thirty-fifth parallel and continue due westwardly.
5. The above articles shall be interchanged between the commissioners under their hands and seals.[78]

Thus after six weeks of fruitless conferences at Cape Fear,[79] during which Governor Johnston saw there was no chance of agreement on a natural boundary—either the Santee, the Pee Dee, or the Cape Fear—he brought about an agreement which was a second compromise between the original South Carolina claim to the Cape Fear, and the North Carolina claim to the Santee River. He wrote a courteous letter to Governor Johnson of South Carolina with regard to the agreement, including the text of the articles.[80] His most valuable contribution, after bringing about harmony among the commissioners, was in influencing them to agree on a straight line through the uninhabited country instead

---

[77] See map, p. 32.
[78] *C.R.*, V, 374-5; S. C. Council Journals, 1734-1737, no. 6, pp. 123-4; Commons House Journals, 1734-1736, p. 267.
[79] Abercrombie and Skene, commissioners, to the Royal Council, April 19, 1737. *S.R.*, XI, 28.
[80] S. C. Council Journals, 1734-1737, no. 6. pp. 123-4; Commons House Journals, 1734-1736, p. 267. A joint committee was appointed to consider the provisions of the articles.

of attempting the tortuous task of paralleling the winding Cape Fear.

On May 30,[81] Lieutenant-Governor Thomas Broughton of South Carolina sent to the Lower House all papers relating to the proceedings of the commissioners, with the letter from the Governor of North Carolina, stating that he and the Council "approved of their conduct," and commending them for their prudent management of the controversial question.[82] This apparently insignificant incident becomes of great importance in the later history of the dispute. The South Carolina Assembly, as will be shown, later challenged the legality of the survey carried out under this agreement. Hence, it is well to review the facts relating to the agreement in connection with this challenge.

In a report to the Board of Trade, the Assembly of South Carolina denied the legality of the survey on the following grounds: first, that it was not in accord with the royal instructions; and second, that it was not "countenanced by any Act of the Legislature of this Province."[83] The Assembly's position was untenable on both counts. First, after receiving copies of the articles of agreement, the British authorities not only raised no objection to them, but, in a spirit of generous approval, wrote Governor Johnston in September, 1735, that they find the line "has at last been adjusted by Commiss[rs] on both sides and we shall always have a proper regard to so solemn a determination agreed to by persons properly empowered by each of the provinces."[84] Second, the Council not only "approved" the articles of agreement,[85] but was very commendatory in its attitude; and the Lower House demonstrated its approval by joining the Council

[81] This delay of a month in Legislative and Executive action was caused by the death of the South Carolina Governor. Governor Johnson died May 3, and was succeeded by Thomas Broughton who prorogued the Assembly to May 27.

[82] S. C. Commons House Journal, May 30, 1734/5. Only three days before, one of the South Carolina commissioners had written the Agent in London as follows:
"On my return from Cape Fear in North Carolina, where I have been as one of three Com[rs] to settle the Boundary between this and that province which we have been so lucky as to accomplish to general satisfaction, and at last remove that bone of Contention," I received your letter. Pub. Rec. of S. C., XVII, 356. The general attitude revealed in this statement is important in view of later contentions of South Carolina regarding the agreement here referred to.

[83] *S.R.*, XI, 129. [84] *C.R.*, IV, 17.
[85] S. C. Commons House Journals, 1734-1736, p. 280.

in providing funds to extend the survey in the fall of the same year. The South Carolina commissioners, during the negotiations, had themselves asked the North Carolinians to regard the instructions lightly and agree to more "reasonable" terms, and then to aid in getting them ratified at home. An agreement was reached, and Johnston later stated to the Board of Trade that it was "ratified by their constituents."[86] The Board itself, as will be shown, later declared the line as then run to be the "final boundary" between the two colonies.[87] Thus it is evident that the British authorities approved the agreement and that South Carolina took sufficient legislative action in carrying it into effect to amount to definite approval. Hence, her later challenge of its legality was unsupported by the facts.

A mutual agreement having been reached, the commissioners proceeded to carry it out.[88] They began the survey May 1, 1735, and spent weeks running the line, working under extremely difficult conditions in a veritable wilderness.[89] They proceeded thirty miles west and southwest from Cape Fear, coming within ten poles of the mouth of Little River; thence northwestward "to the place where it crossed the country road,"[90] where they set up line markers. The commissioners then separated, agreeing to resume the survey September 18 following. If either party should fail to appear the other was to continue the line, which was "to be binding upon both."[91] This timely clause proved to be the salvation of the North Carolinians so far as they desired to expedite the survey, as will later appear.

Following this interval came a period of irritating delay and confusion arising from the refusal of one of the governments to cooperate in furthering the survey. North Carolina authorities were anxious to continue the survey as soon as possible.[92] South Carolina, however, desirous of securing a boundary line more favorable to her interests, planned to take advantage of the opportunity afforded by the death of Governor Johnson, under whose

---

[86] *C.R.*, IV, 295. [87] *S.R.*, XI, 234.

[88] The South Carolina commissioners were not originally instructed to run the line, but after they had reached an agreement and returned to Charleston, they were reappointed to run and mark the line. *S.R.*, XI, 28.

[89] *S.R.*, XI, 29; Connor, *History*, p. 246.

[90] The writer has not been able to identify this "Country road."

[91] *C.R.*, V, 381.

[92] See letter from Governor Johnston to Board of Trade, May 25, 1735. *C.R.*, IV, 9; also S. C. Council Journals, March 24, 1725/6.

administration the line had been agreed upon, to send to the authorities in England a request for new instructions for locating the boundary. Governor Johnston of North Carolina wrote a letter to protest to the Board of Trade, urging that the Board ignore requests to alter an agreement which was made in good faith by South Carolina's own representatives, to whom she had given full authority to act.[93]

If such "sollicitations" from the southern government ever reached the Board of Trade, they did not receive favorable action. The commissioners of both colonies, having completed the first part of the survey in conformity to the articles of agreement, saw South Carolina accept their work; and Perege Fury, her Agent in London, expressed the hope that that service "is now performed in such a manner as to free your Lordships from the trouble of any further enquiry into this affair."[94] The Board definitely accepted the work also, and in September ordered Lieutenant-Governor Broughton to send a draught of the survey signed by the commissioners who participated.[95] These actions by the colony and the Board of Trade should also be borne in mind when the later question of legality is raised.

The survey was resumed September 18 as agreed upon, and the North Carolina commissioners' suspicions with regard to attendance were borne out. The North Carolinians proceeded alone with the line, which they extended in the same northwestwardly direction for about seventy miles. The commissioners from South Carolina did not arrive until October, when they proceeded to retrace the survey made by the North Carolinians for about forty miles, "and finding the work right so far," they dropped the task and sent a draught of what they had done to the Board of Trade.[96] This confusion was the result of dissension between the

---

[93] "I hope," wrote the governor, "as it is now finished your Lordships wont hearken to any sollicitations from our neighbors who I hear design since Mr. Johnson's death to procure a new Instruction more in their favour than the last, in order to have a pretence for receding from an agreement made by their own Commissioners fully empowered by themselves." *C.R.*, IV, 9. South Carolina had had the advantage in the negotiations with the Board of Trade, for North Carolina had no Agent in London before 1731 (*C.R.*, III, 287); whereas, South Carolina had maintained agents there for years previously.

[94] Fury to Board of Trade, July 29, 1735. *S.R.*, XI, 26.

[95] *C.R.*, IV, 29.   [96] *Ibid.*, V, 382.

South Carolina authorities and their commissioners. The latter halted and refused to continue the survey because of their failure to receive remuneration for their services.

Governor Johnston continued to push the survey toward completion regardless of the dissension in South Carolina. He continued by correspondence to urge her authorities to act. On March 24, 1735/6, the South Carolina Council sent a message to the Lower House reading:

We hereby send you a Letter from His Excellency the Govr. of North Carolina, whereby you will see how desirous that Gentleman is to Comply with His Majesty's Royal Instructions in having the Boundary Line between the Two Provinces Finished.

We have the same very much at heart, but are at a Loss how to proceed on that Service,

as the former commissioners "Intirely decline" to serve again.[97] Abercrombie and Skene, the commissioners, felt "So very Ill rewarded" for their previous services that they refused another commission.[98] The Council urged that a resolution be sent to Governor Johnston in reply to his request, lest they be held responsible for delay in finishing the survey.

The Commons House immediately replied that they had expressed themselves on the boundary question in a message to the Council on January 30, to which they were referred.[99] That message forcefully reiterated their stand for £5 per day instead of £7. It was also recommended that a "proper person" be appointed to run the rest of the line at £3 per mile and equip himself.[100] The Council became angry and impatient, and in their reply sarcastically enquired of the Lower House "if any of the Members of your House will undertake the Service at £5 Diem in full of all Trouble and Charges." Constant wrangling among the South Carolina officials and commissioners, and between the two Houses of the Assembly, with the accompanying confusion, prevented any definite action being taken toward extending the line at that time.

Early in 1737 the colonies resumed negotiations on plans of procedure. Three of the North Carolina commissioners who had

---

[97] S. C. Council Journal, 1734-1737, p. 209; Commons House Journal, 1734-1736, pp. 557-559.

[98] S. C. House and Council Journals, *loc. cit.*

[99] House and Council Journals, March 24, 1735/6. Major Pawley was then recommended for commissioner.

[100] S. C. Council Journal, January 30, 1735/6.

signed the original compromise agreement, Moseley, Rowan and Halton, continued the survey; and James Abercrombie, Alexander Skene, and William Walters again served for the southern government. Evidently Skene and Abercrombie had been given satisfaction as to compensation for their previous services. By the end of April plans were complete, the "manner of running it . . . agreed upon by both Colonies."[101] However, the work was delayed by disagreement over the question of who should bear the expense. The commissioners were taking no chances in the second survey, and they were justified. Governor Johnston informed the Board of Trade that the survey was "farr from being compleated," that the North Carolina Assembly was refusing to pay the commissioners anything and was "very positive" it should be paid by the Crown.[102] In view of the fact that North Carolina was at that time the King's personal property, this position would seem logical and justified. At any rate, the question of who should be responsible for the cost of running the line had been a great obstacle to the progress of the survey from the beginning. It has been shown that the South Carolina commissioners dropped their work in October, 1735, on account of receiving nothing for their labors. A year later, Governor Johnston sent the unpaid account of the North Carolina commissioners to the Board of Trade, commending their "great diligence and exactness," and significantly adding, "Before they finish this Affair they want to be directed by your Lordships where to apply for payment whether to His Majesty or to Assembly here."[103] In 1737, he frankly informed the Board that the agreement on the line could not be executed until the question of remuneration was determined.

North Carolina agreed to meet the expenses and salary of her commissioners, however,[104] and the work proceeded. The survey was resumed at the termination of the line run in 1735, at "a point two miles northwest of one of the branches of Little Pedee."[105] The line was extended in the same northwestward direction for a distance of twenty-two miles to a stake in a

[101] Johnston to Board of Trade, April 30, 1737. *C.R.,* IV, 249.
[102] *C.R.,* IV, 249.   [103] *Ibid.,* IV, 178.
[104] This fact is assumed because the commissioners proceeded with the survey, and in September, 1737, the Council paid the account of the North Carolina commissioners at the rate of £1 per diem, pronouncing it "upon the whole a most just, modest and reasonable claim." Minutes of the Council, September 18, 1737. Quoted in *C.R.,* IV, 281-283.
[105] *C.R.,* IV, viii.

meadow, "erroneously supposed to be the point of intersection with the 35th parallel of north latitude."[106]

Authorities have made erroneous statements regarding these early surveys. A few examples will serve to illustrate. In the report of the Geological Survey of North Carolina of 1875, W. C. Kerr states that the North Carolina-South Carolina line was first established by commissioners from 1735 to 1746, having been run from Goat Island to the thirty-fifth parallel (supposedly); thence westward to a point near the Catawba River; thence along the Salisbury Road to the southeast corner of the Catawba Lands. But there was no survey in 1746, the line was not extended to the Salisbury Road until 1764, and was not extended directly to the southeastern corner of the Catawba Lands until 1813, as will be shown later in this study. The United States Geological Survey makes the same errors by quoting Kerr.[107] A century after the survey, Governor Swain made an error in date when he stated that the twenty-two-mile extension was made in 1735, thus ignoring completely the survey of 1737.[108]

Though official work of extending the line was discontinued when it was thought by the commissioners that they had reached the thirty-fifth degree of north latitude, it was soon extended several miles in a "due west Course" by private persons acting without authority from either government. Their work was accepted by settlers on both sides for many years.[109]

The two colonies again began wrangling immediately after the survey was made. Resentment arose when South Carolina initiated a second attempt to obtain an alteration of the line as soon as the work of 1737 was completed. Governor Johnston took a decided stand against the proposed change. He reported to the Board of Trade that he was informed that "the Gentlemen of South Carolina" were urging the Board to "set aside" the boundary line "as . . . settled at their own request about three years ago."[110] He argued against the proposed change on the following grounds:

[106] *Ibid.*, IV, viii.
[107] See Gannett, *Boundaries of the United States*, p. 101; Douglas, *Boundaries*, p. 131.
[108] Swain to Joseph T. Cogswell, March 27, 1835. Executive Letter Book, 1833-1835, XXX, 339.   [109] *C.R.*, VI, 777.
[110] Johnston to Board of Trade, June 13, 1738.

1. The question of the location of the line had been the occasion of many "warm disputes" for years before the survey was made.
2. The agreement was a result of South Carolina's initiative for ascertaining and running the line and was "consented to with great joy."
3. The South Carolina Assembly approved it.
4. South Carolina cooperated in running the most difficult portion of said line.
5. The Board of Trade approved it.
6. The Crown has granted 1,200,000 acres of land near the line to some London merchants,[111] thus confirming the agreement.
7. The Surveyor-General of the province, with sixty men and horses, have spent months surveying it.
8. All finances spent in running the line to its present extent would be a complete loss should the agreement now be set aside.
9. If this agreement is voided, South Carolina will likely want the next also set aside.
10. North Carolina's side should be fully heard and carefully considered.[112]

This array of argument was effective with the British authorities in England, and the line was allowed to stand as run and marked, causing resentment in South Carolina toward the Board.

Governor Johnston again took the lead in the work of extending the line. In a letter of June 13, 1738, to the Board of Trade he "did . . . press the Settling and adjusting of that Boundary Line." The letter was read before the Board in January following and received some consideration but nothing was done. A reply was finally written in the fall of 1739, in which the Board declared that no application had been made on behalf of South Carolina for settlement, but when such an application should be made, they would further consider it and inform him of their action.[113]

The cause of the next phase of the boundary dispute is to be attributed directly to the Board of Trade. It appears that that body either deliberately or carelessly ignored their responsibility to both of the provinces in regard to the controversy when drawing

---

[111] This large grant was in the region of Anson County. It was granted to a land company, among whose members were Henry Eustace McCulloh and Arthur Dobbs, the latter of whom later became governor of North Carolina.

[112] *C.R.*, IV, 295-296.   [113] *C.R.*, IV, 339.

up instructions to their governors. In the draught of instructions to Governor Glen of South Carolina in 1739 the Board of Trade simply inserted a paragraph identical with the old instructions given to Governors Burrington and Johnson in 1730,[114] ignoring the changes mutually made by North Carolina and South Carolina and approved by the Board itself, the survey of almost one hundred miles, and its acceptance by the settlers near the line.

With the outbreak of the War of Jenkins' Ear, the boundary question was subordinated for some years to the more important question of self-defense. In the summer of 1740 Governor Johnston received instructions to raise troops for the war, and he called a special session of the General Assembly for the purpose. Over 400 men were raised and equipped, 5 vessels were hired, and £1200 sterling appropriated to meet the military and naval expenses. The colony experienced a wave of patriotism which largely crowded out other questions.[115]

Toward the close of the war, confusion began to arise over land grants along the line. Arthur Dobbs' interest in McCulloh's lands, after receiving a grant for his portion of them in 1745, led to plans for having them surveyed. They were occupied by "lawless persons" who opposed all surveys and claimed to be in either province, as suited their policy of evasion, holding these lands by force. Many such intruders were in Anson County, on Sugar and Reedy creeks. They later formed a company of militia, pretending to have authority for such action from South Carolina. This situation caused great resentment between the colonies. Some members of the North Carolina Assembly vehemently charged that South Carolina was openly encouraging them.[116] The settlers also insulted and abused Dobbs on his own lands "to the great reproach of all Government," and defied all law. When the sheriff of Anson, with his deputies, attempted to calm their violence and in the King's name commanded the peace, they "damned the King and his peace," and wounded many of the sheriff's deputies, taking the sheriff himself prisoner. Indictments against them were returned "not executed" on account of threats against the officers of justice, "and the protection they mett with from the South Carolina Government."[117] A report was widely broadcast from South Carolina that the Receiver-General of that province would

---

[114] *Ibid.*, V, 358, 376.
[115] Governor Johnston to Newcastle, November 5, 1740. C.R., IV, 421.
[116] C.R., VI, 795. [117] C.R., VI, 795.

not demand quit rents for lands north of Crane Creek in the disputed area. In 1753, the North Carolina Council complained that many settlers, under pretense of having authority from the Surveyor-General of South Carolina, had surveyed lands in the Waxhaw region and adjacent sections in the province to the "great Disturbance" of their peace, and to the great loss of North Carolina land owners. The Council urged the governor to have the guilty apprehended and prosecuted.[118]

Abuses in the granting of lands became constantly more frequent, and disputes grew more bitter. By 1765 Governor Dobbs was complaining to the Board of Trade that South Carolina was "daily" granting warrants of survey within the different tracts belonging to the associates of Murray and Crymble, which had been held by patents from the North Carolina government since 1746.[119] In January and August of the following year he filed with the Board a similar complaint, and he closed the year by sending two accounts of "Distractions" arising from illegal grants near the boundary.

Governor Dobbs resumed his pressure on the Board of Trade at the opening of 1759. In January he again informed them that grants were issued "daily" for lands in Anson County, but he added that they were then coming from both governments, stating that if two persons apply and one secures a warrant, the other goes to South Carolina and applies for a grant, which is never refused. For this reason, he states, "the bordering Counties can't be settled."[120]

In 1762 Dobbs turned from the Board of Trade to the Governor of South Carolina to urge action. He declared that settlers on his own tracts were refusing to recognize his ownership, and pretending they were in South Carolina, because the boundary line had not been run and marked. They threaten to "violently" seize his surveyors, he said, and carry them to Charleston for trial.[121] Six weeks later he wrote Boone that South Carolina officials "went off in Triumph" with a Magistrate of Anson County, taking him "forcibly" without a warrant, for helping survey his

---

[118] *Ibid.*, V, 33.
[119] Dobbs to Board of Trade, October 31, 1756. *C.R.*, V, 641; *ibid.*, V, 739, 784.
[120] *C.R.*, VI, 7. Cf. *ibid.*, VI, 718-719.
[121] Dobbs to Governor Boone of South Carolina, May 17, 1762. *C.R.*, VI, 779-780.

lands, under pretense that they were in South Carolina territory. He charged that Simpson, the Clerk of the South Carolina Council, was the "Chief Supporter" of the applicants for "our lands."[122]

As the summer and fall of 1762 wore on, the correspondence between the two governors became more heated. Upon the eviction of two South Carolina grantees by North Carolina, the governor and Council of the southern province threw off all restraint and expressed their feelings in a bitter message to the northern governor.[123]

Governor Dobbs corresponded in kind, concluding by declaring that such threats and proceedings "shall no way intimidate me. . . ."[124]

In December following, the North Carolina Council stated in a message to the King in Council that Boone had written Gover-

---

[122] C.R., VI, 783.

[123] As this letter marks the climax of irascible correspondence between the two colonies prior to the revolution, it is here copied in full. It must be read in view of the two positions held regarding the boundary line, for which the Board of Trade was to blame. It reads as follows:

Sir—

I was extremely surprised today with an application from two men who have held Lands for several years by virtue of Grants from this Government to know how they should conduct themselves with regard to Ejectments that have been served upon them from North Carolina and in which you yourself are a party, a step of this sort which can tend to nothing but to throw both provinces into confusion taken precipitately and unseasonably by you sir to whom the tranquility of one is entrusted both affects and astonishes me, but you have indeed relieved me of the pain of doubting or even of deliberating, one resolution only was left me to take, one General Order to issue, and that is already done, A principle of candour and sincere desire to prevent the mischiefs that must insue induce me to communicate to you by express, that I have strictly enjoined a Magistrate to employ every Lawful means to protect and secure everybody in their properties and persons that are settled under the sanction of this Government I have ordered the persons concerned to treat the Ejectment with the contempt it deserves and in no respect to acknowledge the Jurisdiction of North Carolina. I was in great hopes Sir that you would have been Contented to have waited the decision of our Superiors upon a Subject which you and I are neither competent or impartial Judges of, But if you have too much impetuosity to wait this determination, I have too little Tameness to submit to yours, and really flatter myself that when I communicate to the Lords of Trade this Transaction which I shall do immediately that my proposals and requests which so plainly bespoke an Inclination to preserve a Harmony between the Colonies will be full as acceptable to their Lordships as your manifest indifference to a matter of so much moment, because a few paultry Acres of your own are in Question. Governor Boone to Governor Dobbs, October 5, 1762. C.R., VI, 792-793.

[124] C.R., VI, 789.

nor Dobbs a letter which was approved by the South Carolina Council, charging him with "Creating disturbances between this province and that of South Carolina," declaring he will "immediately" lay the case before the Board of Trade. The Council exonerated Dobbs by stating that he was only endeavoring to quiet the associates of Huey and Crymble in their possessions in North Carolina, as directed in his instructions. The North Carolina Council accused the South Carolina officials of encouraging settlers to "persist to insult and abuse your Majesty's Governor and maltreat the Officers of the Crown" in a "contemptuous and open manner."[125]

Both colonies continued to issue land grants, however, and by the close of 1763 North Carolina had granted lands far southward of the thirty-fifth parallel of north Latitude, both east and west of the Catawba Lands.[126]

Confusion over the payment of taxes on lands along the boundary was as great as that arising from the question of land grants. Evasion and disorder had become so prevalent by 1749 that Governor Glen of South Carolina reported the situation to the Board of Trade, stating that land holders refuse to pay taxes when approached by officials of either government and pretend they are within the territory of the other.[127] Governor Dobbs made a similar report, stating that settlers who had been paying taxes in North Carolina for eight years were refusing to pay them, imprisoning the tax collectors, and expecting to be supported in their refusal by the government of South Carolina. Dobbs states that if the practice continues "I shall be obliged to use force also, & consequently throw both provinces into a flame. . . ."[128] He adds that even the settlers on lands north of the thirty-fifth parallel are "all in a flame," claiming they are encouraged by South Carolina; and that this is the condition along the line for one hundred and fifty miles. By 1757, the settlers living near the thirty-fifth parallel would "not take out Grants from this Province being all in Rebellion, and will pay of late no quit rents" under pretense that the lands belong to South Carolina. Dobbs stated to the Board of Trade that their refusal was caused by South Carolina's claiming all territory west of the northwest branch of Cape

[125] N. C. Council Journal, December 10, 1762.
[126] C.R., V, 387; S.R., XI, 153.
[127] Glen to Board of Trade, July 19, 1749. C.R., XI, 113.
[128] C.R., V, 364, 641, 642.

Fear River if thirty miles distant.[129] At the close of the same year the tax collector for Anson County stated in a deposition that there were great "divisions and distractions" among the people regarding payment of taxes; that they seemed unanimously resolved not to pay their rents until the boundary line was determined and marked. He stated that he had been warned against prosecuting for recovery of rents, lest he "run the risk of loosing [sic] his life."[130] He was firmly convinced that if the line was run all disputes would subside.

The confusion resulting from the Cherokee War added to the difficulties of collecting taxes on the disputed lands. Writing from Brunswick in May, 1762, Governor Dobbs stated that the settlers who were driven off of their lands by the Indians were returning, to find only "great confusion" over the question of a boundary line, and were therefore refusing to pay any taxes. They had not paid a farthing of taxes in North Carolina, though they were charged with taxes in both provinces. South Carolina was claiming all lands south of Lord Granville's line by the original instructions.[131]

Great confusion and some violence arose over the question of jurisdiction over the Catawba Nation and their lands. They numbered about three hundred fighting men and occupied a section of territory through the center of which ran the thirty-fifth degree of north latitude, which was called for in the original instructions to Burrington and Johnson.

Governor Dobbs appears to have taken an impartial attitude on the question of jurisdiction in the beginning.[132] He stated to the Board of Trade that the Catawba Lands were on the "Verge" of the thirty-fifth parallel and should be declared wholly within the limits of one of the provinces. However, on August 29, 1754, his representative, at the treaty with the Catawbas, argued his right to divide a part of their lands for public sale; and a year

[129] *C.R.*, V, 739-740. He repeated this statement to the Board three months later. *Ibid.*, V, 762.

[130] Deposition of John Hamer, Receiver for Anson County, December 12, 1757. *C.R.*, V, 938.

[131] Dobbs to Board of Trade, May 17, 1762. *C.R.*, VI, 718-719. On the same day he sent a similar protest to the governor of South Carolina, and in December his Council sent a representation to the King in Council. *Ibid.*, VI, 779, 777. Relations with both South Carolina and the British authorities were becoming more strained.

[132] At least that was the attitude shown in his communications to the Board of Trade. See *C.R.*, V, 358.

later he requested of the Board of Trade permission to hold a meeting with them for purchasing the lands adjoining their town in order to prevent their violence, which was encouraged by South Carolina.[133] Dobbs even attempted to interfere in their local politics by commissioning a popular half-breed, called "Prince of Wales," as a captain to make him more eligible for election as King in King Haglar's stead. This Indian was friendly to the claims of North Carolina; whereas, Haglar favored the pretentions of the southern government.

The authorities of South Carolina were even more aggressive. Governor Glen cultivated the Catawbas' friendship on every convenient occasion. In April, 1754, he wrote a letter to King Haglar stating that the Indians' lands were reserved to them, by himself and the Council, including their hunting grounds within a radius of thirty miles from their towns; and as he had ordered all white men to remove, he urged Haglar to drive off all white people within that territory. The Indians were told that Glen had written to the English King regarding the grant and were assured that King George would approve it.[134]

North Carolina strongly resented these actions. The settlers complained of the Catawbas killing their stock and destroying their crops. The governor protested against the excessive amount of land allotted to them. He stated that they had been promised 1,808,640 acres, or 2,500 acres each; whereas, the Tuscaroras had been granted an area of only ten miles radius, containing 200,960 acres, or only 287 acres to each person. Governor Dobbs protested to the Board of Trade that Glen had "buoyed up" the Catawbas, attempted to give them nine times as much territory as the Tuscaroras had received, and set them against North Carolina, "alledging they are his Indians."[135]

The aggressive policy of Glen was followed by his successor,

---

[133] Dobbs to Board of Trade, August 24, 1755. *C.R.*, V, 360.

[134] Letter from Glen to King Haglar, April 8, 1754. Reported by Acting-President Rowan. *C.R.*, V, 124, 144, 358. Glen was still acting on the basis of his interpretation of the old instructions, which had been re-issued in 1739.

[135] Dobbs to Board of Trade, August 24 and October 28, 1755, and January 20, 1757. *C.R.*, V, 364, 440, 742. In August, 1757, Dobbs again reported that the Indians had been "spirited up" by Glen's tactics and had even "had the impudence" to insult the Chief Justice of the Supreme Court sitting at Salisbury. *Ibid.*, V, 784. See *ibid.*, VI, 58, and Ashe, *History*, I, 304.

Governor Bull, who claimed to have made an agreement with King Haglar and his headmen in 1761 whereby a tract of fifteen miles square was allotted to them. When commissioners from South Carolina and representatives of the Catawba Nation arrived in Anson County in July, 1762, to run the lines pursuant to this agreement, protest was made on the part of North Carolina on the grounds that neither her government nor the British authorities were consulted, and that there was the "highest probability" that the whole area would fall within North Carolina when the boundary was determined.[136] Governor Dobbs proposed that the survey of the tract be suspended for a time, offering to suspend the issuing of land grants in that area until the dividing line was run. He also warned the Indians that their agreement with South Carolina could not be carried out until the war then in progress had closed and peace was signed.

After the proclamation of peace in March, 1763, a conference with the Indians was called at Augusta, Georgia.[137] During its sessions the boundaries agreed upon between the Catawbas and the South Carolina government were confirmed and a treaty signed November 10, 1763, providing that the survey formerly begun by South Carolina should be completed immediately. Governors Dobbs and Boone cooperated in furthering this survey in order to expedite the extension of the North Carolina-South Carolina line.[138] The survey was completed,[139] giving the colonies a free hand to extend their dividing line.

At this point it will be well to review the status of the controversy at the close of the reign of George II and to attempt an estimate of its general effects on the life of the two colonies up to that time.

The governors of the two colonies, in an effort to compromise the opposing claims of North Carolina to the Santee and South Carolina to the Cape Fear rivers, had reached an agreement in

[136] Their line to extend northward from Twelve Mile Creek and from east to west fifteen miles—7½ miles on either side of Catawba River. *C.R.*, VI, 786. Dobbs suggested a tract twelve miles square, since the Indians had been reduced in number by disease to fifty warriors.

[137] *C.R.*, VI, 1020; *S.R.*, XI, 201-202.

[138] Dobbs, writing in behalf of himself and Boone, informed the Board of Trade that, "we have now fixed the Catawba's Claim and a Surveyor is employed to survey and mark their Boundary Line. Please inform me whether we shall continue our line along the thirty-fifth parallel west of the Catawba Lands." Dobbs to Board of Trade, January 14, 1764. *C.R.*, VI, 1024.   [139] *C.R.*, VII, 147, 290.

1730 that the line should run parallel to the Cape Fear River at a distance of thirty miles southwest of that stream. It was accepted by the Board of Trade but Governor Johnson of South Carolina influenced the Board to add a provision which included the Waccamaw River as a part of the line, but on account of gross ignorance regarding the course of the Waccamaw, the line was hopelessly confused. Governor Burrington was strongly opposed to the Cape Fear parallel line, while Johnson and the Board of Trade joined against him in favor of that location.

Such was the status of the dispute when Gabriel Johnston succeeded Burrington as Governor of North Carolina. The South Carolina Assembly then supported their governor and the Board of Trade in opposition to North Carolina, in demanding that the Cape Fear parallel line be accepted. Governor Johnston, however, in spite of the decision of the Board of Trade and the insistence of South Carolina, brought about a very sensible compromise when he led the commissioners of the two colonies to agree on a straight line from the seacoast to the thirty-fifth parallel of north latitude. The colonies were therefore expected to run a line accordingly.

The line was surveyed to the thirty-fifth parallel (supposedly) and discontinued. Proceedings regarding the boundary during the remainder of the reign of George II consisted of agitation, proposals, and counter proposals.

By the time of the Seven Years War the boundary question had vitally affected every phase of the life of the two colonies, as well as the relations between the British authorities and the colonies. Those relations became tense soon after the purchase of the province by the Crown over the question of payment of the cost of running the line in 1735. North Carolina insisted that, since the colony was royal property, the Crown was obligated to pay the costs of the division—a very logical position. And, although the Council later paid their commissioners, the popular branch of the Legislature consistently refused to meet the expense. The Governor of South Carolina even defied the Board of Trade in 1755 by ignoring their instructions to submit a new proposal for the location of the dividing line. He urged the Governor of North Carolina to ignore those instructions also and join him in having the line run according to the old instructions. The South Carolina governor was later removed from office for his insubordination. During the previous year the Board of Trade received numerous complaints from the colonies against the location of the old line, and the King was informed of these serious complaints. The colonies, as will later appear, were further displeased when, at the close of the Seven Years War, the Crown forbade settlement of the territory near the Catawba Lands until the Indian boundaries could be determined. Exercise of jurisdiction over the Indians by either province was also forbidden pending such settlement.

The land policy of the two colonies was also affected by the controversy. Soon after the original agreement on the location of a line, North Carolina adopted the policy of granting no lands south of the thirty-fifth parallel, as then located, proving her faith in the agreement and the work of the commissioners. South Carolina, however, after her repudiation of the old line, freely granted lands in the disputed territory, duplicating the North Carolina grants in many cases. A report was widely spread in South Carolina that the Surveyor General would not demand quit rents for lands taken up by South Carolinians in the disputed area; and many settlers took advantage of the offer, especially in the Waxhaw region and adjacent sections. This policy resulted in considerable loss to North Carolina land owners. Governor Dobbs' attempts to survey his own lands in Anson County after 1745 were vigorously opposed. The settlers all claimed to be in South Carolina. North Carolina then adopted the policy of ejecting South Carolina grantees in that region from their lands. By 1756 the latter colony was "daily" granting Dobbs' lands and hopeless confusion was resulting from the duplications. Dobbs reported that the settlers finally refused to take out any grants from North Carolina, claiming the whole region was in the southern province. In 1762 he proposed that the survey of the Catawba Indian line be suspended for a time, offering in return to suspend the issuing of North Carolina land grants. South Carolina was claiming all lands south of Granville's line, basing her claim on the old instructions.

Such confusion over land grants served to interfere with the settlement of the territory in the region of the boundary. It has been shown, for example, that settlement near the Catawba Lands was forbidden until their location was definitely established. The duplication of grants and the consequent uncertainty of receiving legal titles created a state of extreme caution on the part of prospective settlers which greatly retarded the settlement of the border counties.

These uncertainties seriously affected the system of tax collection in the two colonies, producing as much confusion in this regard as in that of land grants. In 1735, South Carolina demanded that all inhabitants along the Waccamaw River within thirty miles of the Cape Fear River pay taxes to her government until the governors agreed on the interpretation of their instructions. This requirement was made, of course, before the line was run, and therefore before the inhabitants could have known to which government they were obligated to pay taxes. The payment of taxes in the boundary region farther west was evaded by claiming to be in the other province when approached by the tax collectors of one government. When evasion appeared unsuccessful, the grantees would often imprison the collectors. Governor Dobbs charged that many grantees in North Carolina expected to be supported by South Carolina in their refusal to pay taxes, and he threatened to use force in collecting the revenues unless a remedy could be found for the evasions. He declared that similar confusion existed along the boundary for a distance of one hundred and fifty miles. Occasionally, in a very businesslike way, settlers would simply but positively refuse to pay taxes to either government until the boundary line was definitely determined, insuring them against dual payments. The collector of Anson County was even threatened with the penalty of death by the more radical settlers should he persist in his efforts to collect the revenues.

The possibility of making the Cape Fear River the permanent line created at once the most favorable interest in South Carolina and the greatest concern in North Carolina on account of its effect upon the revenues of the respective colonies. Such a permanent line would have greatly increased the income of the southern government while, at the same time, it would have ruined the income of the northern government and of the Crown; for Granville's line extended southward to 35° 41', and his agents were therefore collecting the revenues of two thirds of modern North Carolina. The prospect was disturbing. Prospective loss of revenue from the area between the Pee Dee and Cape Fear rivers, as will be further shown, prompted South Carolina's strong opposition to the proposed Pee Dee River boundary which was greatly desired by North Carolina. Dobbs' attempted compensation for such loss in taxes, by securing the extension of South Carolina west of the Savannah River and allowing her to continue collecting revenues in the former region until the latter should yield an equal amount of income, was an effective reply to a selfish demand. The tax systems and policies of the two colonies were seriously disturbed at the close of the Cherokee War, when the governors felt compelled to agree to mutual suspension of all process relative to delinquent taxpayers. This policy probably resulted from the fact that many settlers who had been driven off their lands during hostilities, on returning to them had refused to pay their taxes until the boundary was determined.

Interference with and confusion in court procedure was common in the border counties. Court action regarding the validity of a land title or the sale of property for taxes was almost always opposed with vigor. South Carolina officers even arrested magistrates in Anson County and carried them to Charleston for trial and imprisonment. The lack of local courts in the southern province often led citizens of the border counties to desire to be included in North Carolina in order to escape the necessity of traveling long distances to attend the Charleston courts.

Agriculture and commerce were affected either directly or indirectly by the proposed location of the line, and in turn affected the proposals and claims. As will later appear, South Carolina contended that the number of negroes to be purchased from British slave traders for her plantations was determined by the number of white settlers who were included within her boundaries for protection against possible servile insurrections. For the same reason, it was urged that the Catawba Indians should be included in South Carolina. To improve commercial relations between the two colonies, North Carolina insisted on the adoption of the Pee Dee River as the line in order to give her interior inhabitants a free outlet to the sea and prevent the levying of costly and irritating customs duties by the southern government on goods transported down that stream.

The effect of the controversy on Indian relations and policies was marked. The settlers were constantly at odds with their Indian neighbors on account of the absence of a definite boundary line. The Catawbas were infringed upon, and they often resisted. South Carolina encouraged them in their violence, though in 1745 she urged the Board of Trade to have the line determined for the professed reason of quieting the Catawbas in their possessions. The Board was later warned that further failure to run the line would mean an alienation of the Indian tribes which would be fatal to the colonies. When in 1757 Governor Dobbs made a similar request regarding the Catawbas, the Board of Trade revealed their Indian policy of procrastination and delay when they replied that the Catawba question should await the adoption of a general Indian policy, presumably at the end of the Seven Years War. The two colonies realized soon thereafter that a mutual agreement regarding the Catawbas was impossible. They therefore agreed to defer all efforts toward a solution until the boundary was definitely located. However, this policy was later altered, after South Carolina had broken the agreement.

Service in the militia in the two colonies was also affected. Settlers in the disputed territory, particularly in Anson County, organized militia companies, claiming to have authority for their action from South Carolina. North Carolina Assemblymen charged that the southern government was actively and openly encouraging these organizations.

With all the complications, disorder, and confusion connected with the controversy, a spirit of ill will developed between the two colonies which had an important bearing on all their relationships. With the settlers fighting over lands, the governors threatening to use force, inhabitants in some of the disputed sections organizing militia companies with the supposed encouragement of South Carolina officials, and with the governors corresponding in the bitterest terms and charging each other with doing everything possible to promote disputes, it may be readily seen that tension over the boundary had reached a high pitch by the time of the Seven Years War. As will be further shown, bitterness between the governors resulted in the removal of the South Carolina Executive, thus seriously affecting one branch of a colonial government. Even in the relations of the different branches of a particular government, an irritable and non-cooperative spirit occasionally developed, as in the friction between the South Carolina Governor and Assembly over the appointment of commissioners for the early surveys. The same condition will re-appear in strength before we reach the period of the Revolution in the course of this study.

This unfortunate attitude and its accompanying disturbance of peaceful relations very probably affected the degree of cooperation so necessary between the two colonies in crises of war. For example, during the Cherokee War, when the two colonies were seriously endangered by the hostilities of the Indians in 1760, the militia of North Carolina refused to leave the province to aid South Carolina. The general antagonism toward the latter colony which had existed for years over the boundary dispute probably played a part in this refusal. But this is anticipating a topic—the Seven Years War—which will be treated later in this study. The bitterness does not appear to have developed sufficiently by 1739 to have hindered cooperation in the War of Jenkin's Ear, however, for the two provinces sent aid to General Oglethorpe in the expedition against St. Augustine, and also aided in the fighting in the West Indies.

Wars in the colonies had the general effect of checking the progress of extending the line between the two provinces. As the colonies were absorbed in the more important problems of self-preservation, the boundary issue was allowed to subside during the continuance of hostilities. This was true during King George's War and the French and Indian War, as will appear later. In addition to the preoccupation of the two governments with war measures, the British authorities could not be persuaded by the colonial agents to consider boundary questions during the stress of war. During the latter war referred to above, the Board of Trade simply reported to the Crown that they would make recommendations for a settlement of the boundary question as soon as the war was terminated. In the meantime, the two governors, who had been prevented by the war from submitting proposals for a line, were directed by the Board to cooperate in preserving peace until the war had closed and the King could carefully consider proposals and determine on a permanent line. It will be seen in the following section that no attempt at a survey was made until after the signing of the Treaty of Paris in 1763.

Thus it is seen that the situation relative to a boundary between the colonies at the close of the reign of George II revealed an incomplete survey northwestward from the seacoast, supposedly to the thirty-fifth parallel, and both colonies agitating for further action on the question. South Carolina had pursued a consistent policy since the early surveys, insisting upon an alteration of the line more to her advantage. North Carolina had reversed her policy of defending the early surveys by advocating the adoption of the Pee Dee River and Winyaw Bay line as a permanent boundary. With this situation in view, we now turn to a more detailed account of the war, as it served to check the progress of the division of the provinces at the close of and immediately following the reign here considered.

Section III

EXTENSION OF THE LINE TO THE MOUNTAINS

Progress in the extension of the boundary line was delayed on account of war, as it had been during King George's War. The French and Indian War having broken out in 1754, followed by the general war from 1756 to 1763, the minds of the authorities both in the colonies and in England were directed largely toward the successful prosecution of hostilities. At the opening of the war, North Carolina furnished Virginia a commander-in-chief of her military forces, a year later Pitt gave Governor Dobbs directions "relative to putting the Province in a proper state of Defense in Case of War," and North Carolina raised troops, equipped and trained them, erected batteries, built forts, enlisted Catawba and Cherokee Indians, and cooperated generally with the British forces. Governor Dobbs became anxious that William H. Middleton, the new Governor of South Carolina, should arrive in order to secure better cooperation on the boundary question from the southern Government.[140] However, South Carolina was also busy in support of the war, having issued over £300,000 of currency from 1755 to 1760, most of which was used for war purposes.[141]

In the meantime, there had been some effort toward the extension of the line. In 1749, the South Carolina authorities were protesting to the Board of Trade that the surveys of 1735 and 1737 were not run parallel to the Cape Fear, according to royal instructions. The Board was requested to issue new instructions to the Governor of North Carolina in accord with Article 36 of Glen's instructions,[142] which merely called for the old Cape Fear parallel line. The South Carolina Council, through Charles Pinckney,

[140] *C.R.*, V, 125, 560, 608, 610, 611, 640, 786, 787.
[141] McCrady, *South Carolina under Royal Government*, pp. 275-7.
[142] Glen to Board of Trade, July 19, 1749. *S.R.*, XI, 113.

later sent a memorial to the Board of Trade urging action on the boundary as a means of quieting the Indians in their possessions.[143]

The Board by this time was drawing away from its old position regarding the location of the line. In the draught of their instructions to Arthur Dobbs, the new governor, in 1754, they omitted the article relative to the boundary contained in the instructions to Governor Johnston,[144] as a line had been run in consequence of it but not in exact conformity to it. The Board stated to the King that complaints of many inconveniences arising from it had been filed with them. Dobbs was instructed to enquire into the proceedings of the commissioners who ran the line and report any instances of non-conformity to their instructions and the resulting inconveniences to North Carolina. He was also directed to communicate with the Governor of South Carolina as to the location of a line which would be to the best advantage of both provinces.[145] Eighteen days later, while attending a meeting of the Board of Trade, Dobbs was directed to "inquire into the state of the proceedings" regarding the boundary as soon as he arrived in North Carolina, to consult with the governor of South Carolina on a "proper line," and report his opinion fully to the Board.[146]

After Dobbs arrived in his province he soon saw through the situation. Writing from New Bern in the fall, he stated in reply to his orders that he would inform himself with regard to the desired changes and urge South Carolina to state to the Board her reasons for insisting on alterations, but would await Glen's removal, because he was "too opinionated and self-sufficient to have any dealings with him."[147]

In the winter of 1754, Dobbs prepared a plan of a proposed line with "reasons to support it," and requested South Carolina to prepare a similar one. He planned to send both "sentim[ts]" to the Lords of Trade. Knowing that agreement between the two

[143] Pinckney to Board of Trade, July 5, 1754. *C.R.*, V, 483.

[144] The old instructions were later withdrawn, as shown by the following expression from Dobbs: "I am pleased to hear that Instructions have been given to the Governor of South Carolina to withdraw the former Instructions about the Frontier Line. . . ." Dobbs to Board of Trade, March 15, 1756. *C.R.*, V, 574.

[145] Draught of instructions submitted to the King, June 17, 1754. *C.R.*, V, 1105.

[146] Board of Trade in Conference with Dobbs, July 5, 1754. *C.R.*, V, 171.

[147] *C.R.*, V, 148.

governments was virtually impossible, he requested royal orders and declared it was "absolutely necessary that a line should be immediately determined."[148]

South Carolina had approached the northern government regarding the boundary as soon as information was secured of Dobbs' arrival, terming it a subject of great consequence to the welfare "and even to the peace of this Province." A copy of the instructions of July 19, 1739, was inclosed.[149]

On February 10, 1755, Glen received a communication from Dobbs, containing a copy of his new instructions to enquire into the status of the whole boundary question, consult with South Carolina as to a proposed line, and report his opinion. After reading them the South Carolina governor was shocked. He ridiculed the instructions, comparing them to some memorandum "copied from your Copy book." He declared there certainly must be more of them.

Dobbs notified Glen that he would send a proposal for a line to the Board of Trade, and urged him to make recommendations also. He added that North Carolina would abide by and carry out the King's commands, whatever they might be.

Glen replied with a positive refusal to deviate from his former instructions, stating that none the Crown might issue could be any more explicit and clear than those of 1739, a copy of which he had previously inclosed. He declined to propose a line to the Lords of Trade, but offered to appoint commissioners to cooperate with North Carolina in carrying his instructions into effect; and he urged Dobbs to appoint representatives from his province "without loss of time." A request was also made for the "entire Instruction or instructions" relating to the boundary line, together with a copy of Dobbs' letter to the Board of Trade.[150]

---

[148] He informed the Board of Trade that if the matter were left to the governments it would lead to "almost infinite delays; and probably we should never agree." Dobbs to Board of Trade, December 19, 1754. *C.R.*, V, 155.

[149] McCrady, *South Carolina as a Royal Province*, p. 79.

[150] *C.R.*, V, 375, 376, 377, Dobbs reported this insulting incident of insubordination to the Lords of Trade and it cost Glen his position. In August, Dobbs received a message from the Board which read as follows: "It gave us concern to find that the communication to Mr. Glen of your Orders concerning the Boundary Line gave rise to so disagreeable an Altercation between you. As that gentleman's administration is now however at an end, we shall decline any animadversions upon his conduct."

After thorough investigation into the situation regarding the boundary question, Governor Dobbs draughted a proposal for a "reasonable" line, with evidence to support it, and submitted it to the North Carolina Council for consideration. The Council approved his suggestions unanimously.[151] On January 4, 1755, he sent the proposal to the Board of Trade, indicating that Governor Glen would also send proposals, and urging that an equitable line be decided upon without regard to previous proceedings thereon.

The governor, supported by the Council, urgently requested that the boundary line be altered from the beginning. Their impressive arguments in favor of alteration were as follows:

1. It would be for the best interests of the Crown because of the great saving in expense through the use of natural boundaries.
2. Conditions have greatly changed in both provinces since the original instructions were given.
3. An alteration would add to the general convenience of both colonies.
4. Georgia has been restored to the Crown since the line was surveyed, making it possible for the King to alter the Savannah River line which cut South Carolina off from the West, thereby necessitating her "pushing" for territory northward to Cape Fear.
5. Lord Granville's eighth share of Carolina and Georgia has been taken entirely from North Carolina since the boundary line was run, when it might have been taken from South Carolina and Georgia as well, giving the greater portion of lands and quit rents of North Carolina to private individuals. The Carolinas extend from 32° to 36° 30′ north latitude, or three hundred and ten miles. If the thirty-fifth parallel is made the dividing line, South Carolina will receive 3° or two hundred and seven miles; North Carolina will receive only 1° 30′ or one hundred and three miles, of which Lord Granville will own sixty miles. This would leave only thirty-nine miles to the Crown with a corresponding proportion of income. It should be more equitably divided.

They express hope that the new governor will show a different spirit, and urge amicable cooperation. Board of Trade to Dobbs, August 6, 1755.

[151] *C.R.*, V, 375. Dobbs was diplomatic in all of his correspondence with authorities in England at this time, almost to the point of flattery. He never failed to emphasize his willingness to abide by any decision they might make. These tactics seem to have increased his prestige and influence in the controversy.

With this array of arguments supporting his position, Governor Dobbs proposed that the line be made the Winyaw Bay and Pee Dee River to 34° 20′ north latitude, thence due westward along that parallel to the Cherokee Mountains, at the same time extending South Carolina west of the Savannah River.[152] He answers South Carolina's "most material" objection to making the Pee Dee River and Winyaw Bay the boundary by stating that revenues from her new fertile territory west of the Savannah would soon far surpass those received from the few settlers on the "hot sands" between the Pee Dee and the Waccamaw. And until such revenues equalled the income from the latter region, South Carolina should be allowed to continue taxing the inhabitants east of Winyaw. Provided, however, that North Carolina should have jurisdiction in all other things, and that her commerce on the Pee Dee should be free from customs duties. Dobbs then added to his previous arguments that the proposed line would give North Carolina a water route to the sea and, therefore, prevent South Carolina from levying such unfair duties. If necessary, in order to secure the water route, he proposed to compromise on 34° 30′ north latitude for the westward portion of the line, thereby giving South Carolina a strip extending about eleven miles further northward. It is plain, therefore, that trade relationships were playing a major part in hastening a settlement of the boundary question.

Indian relations were also involved in these proposals. Dobbs took pains to point out that if the westward portion of his proposed line should be accepted, it would quiet the Catawba Indians by leaving them entirely within the limits of North Carolina.

The North Carolina governor showed considerable foresight and some statesmanship when he suggested that, after the line was extended to the Cherokee Mountains, it might be wise to change its direction and extend it through the mountain passes to a river flowing into the Ohio, possibly the Occabach or river of St. Jerome, making such a stream the North Carolina-South Carolina line. He probably had in mind the Licking River.[153] Dobbs closed the communication with an earnest plea for a decision as soon as South Carolina should submit her proposals. He re-enforced the plea with a veiled threat of actual warfare between the colonies, stating that if the question should be left to provincial

[152] *C.R.*, V, 380-385.
[153] The description of this proposed line is too vague to make possible its location on a map.

commissioners it would continue for many years, "and at last if we desire it to preserve our Rights, the longest sword must carry it."[154] Two months later, with withering logic, he replied to Glen's stubborn contention for the old Cape Fear parallel line regardless of the new instructions. His penetrating paragraph read as follows:

Might we not then with as much equity propose that the boundary Line should run thirty miles north of Santee from the sea coast to its Spring heads, which as Savannah River to its source is at present the Boundary line betwixt it and Georgia, and would consequently by its rising so far to the Northward equally prevent their extending their Settlements beyond the Mountains, would it not be as equitable for this Province to expect the one as for your Province to expect the other upon the Cape Fear River.[155]

Such a line north of the Santee would have fallen in the region of the Pee Dee River, the line for which Dobbs was earnestly contending.

South Carolina put forth strong efforts to prevent acceptance of the North Carolina proposal by the Board of Trade. Soon after receiving notice of that proposal from Dobbs, Glen wrote a letter of protest to the Board, and he stated that Dobbs claimed to have "no reason to doubt that the matter will be determined upon his letters." The South Carolina governor "most earnestly entreat[ed]" that the Board would give his province an opportunity of seeing the proposal and the accompanying arguments, with a full opportunity to reply. He further urged that, until the dispute should be settled, the old instructions be observed by both colonies as nearly as possible.[156]

A committee appointed by the South Carolina Council to consider the correspondence relative to the boundary recommended that, since Governor Dobbs had given reasons to the Board of Trade to support his proposed line, a survey of the Pee Dee, Waccamaw, and Cape Fear rivers be made as soon as possible. As such survey was only for the purpose of impartially investigating the "Truth of Facts," as expressed by the committee, it was further recommended that the governor should urge the governor of North Carolina to appoint surveyors to cooperate in

[154] *C.R.*, V, 387.
[155] Dobbs to Glen, March 12, 1755. *C.R.*, V, 390.
[156] Glen to Board of Trade, May 29, 1755. Pub. Rec. of S. C., XXVI, 199.

the survey. After completion, if approved by both provinces as fair and just, the survey should be transmitted to the Board of Trade, or, if necessary, laid before the King in Council. This, course, it was stated, would hasten action by the Crown or the Lords of Trade. It was further recommended that, in case Governor Dobbs declined to appoint such commissioners, he should be requested to send Governor Glen a copy of the instructions which were claimed to have revoked the original instructions, and to issue orders forbidding interference with their surveyors by inhabitants of North Carolina. The Committee, as directed by the Council, transmitted a letter to James Crockatt, requesting him to "use his best endeavors to prevent any determination" regarding a boundary line by the Board of Trade or the Royal Council until South Carolina could present "a true State of the Case."[157]

After consideration of the report, the Council of North Carolina decided that it would not be proper to appoint surveyors, since the governor had already written to the Board of Trade regarding a line. However, that body could see no "Inconsistency" arising by allowing the surveyors of South Carolina to make true draughts of the said rivers, provided that province should bear the entire expense. It was also agreed that North Carolina settlers should not be allowed to interfere with the progress of the work.[158]

The South Carolina government ignored its former uncompromising position in favor of the line described in the instructions of 1730 and 1739, which had been partially run and marked, and proposed that the Cape Fear River be "re-observed"[159] as the permanent boundary line from its source to the sea. Glen stated that, although "'tis true after his Majesty's purchase of the Soil the Line was removed a little in favor of North Carolina by an Instruction from His Majesty, that a line running parallel with the Course of that River, but at the distance of thirty miles, South

[157] N. C. Council Journals, May 1, 1755. Quoted in *C.R.*, V, 490-491. Crockatt was the South Carolina agent in London. McCrady implies that there was no cooperation between him and Governor Glen. *South Carolina as a Royal Province,* p. 165. The exact aim of the above survey is not clear, unless it was to secure accurate information of the relation of those rivers to the thirty-fifth parallel of north latitude in order to be in an advantageous position for bargaining in the negotiations. The committee were significantly silent on their exact purpose.

[158] *C.R.,* V, 491.

[159] The quotation marks and the term are the writer's. The term is used because it best expresses the sense and spirit of the communication to the Board of Trade.

West of it, should be the Boundary line," the line "in the very Infancy of this Government, was the Cape Fear"; and no one will acquiesce in the line of 1735. He further claimed that nearly all inhabitants in the disputed territory desired to live in South Carolina.[160]

It is quite evident that this proposal to re-designate the Cape Fear as the line was made purely as a diplomatic stroke. If not, it was an insult to the Board's intelligence or to its sense of justice and fair play. Both parties knew that, in rank injustice to North Carolina, Granville's grant extended southward to 35° 41', leaving only 41' between his line and the boundary called for in the original instructions and occupying two-thirds of her territory; and the Board also knew how stubbornly South Carolina had fought to retain the line of 1735. The proposal undoubtedly was made for use in bargaining against North Carolina's move for the Pee Dee and Winyaw line. In view of the second compromise, which will be later described, it may have succeeded.

The Board of Trade ignored the proposal, though thoroughly "convinced" that it was imperative that a line should be determined and run. After Glen was removed in the summer of 1755, Governor Lyttleton was appointed as his successor and the Board hoped for better cooperation from him. They were prevented from making a recommendation to the Crown, they stated, by a lack of proposals from South Carolina for a satisfactory boundary line, which proposals Governor Lyttleton was directed to obtain and forward as soon as possible.[161]

The North Carolina government resumed its efforts toward securing a settlement in the fall of the same year. The executive wrote the Board of Trade that he hoped they had received his "observations" on the great difficulties and disadvantages the colony was suffering on account of the delay in ascertaining the boundary line, over which Mr. Glen "did all he could" to promote disputes between the provinces.[162] A year later he again pleaded for immediate action and informed the Board that the South Carolina Council had appointed a committee of inquiry into former proceedings; and that he had written to Governor Lyttleton earn-

---

[160] Glen to Board of Trade, May 29, 1755. Pub. Rec. of S. C., XXVI, 199.

[161] Board of Trade to Dobbs, August 6, 1755. *C.R.*, V, 415.

[162] Dobbs to Lords of Trade, October 28, 1755. *Ibid.*, V, 440. He had again urged the Pee Dee River line on August 24. *Ibid.*, V, 357.

estly requesting him "to send over their opinion where to fix it. . . ."[163] A line "at least to the Southward of 35°" was urged, as all North Carolina grants were issued to that line upon the faith of the agreement of the original commissioners, and particularly since North Carolina was then at the expense of building a fort to protect the Catawba Indians. Since the Catawba Lands were situated on the thirty-fifth parallel, Dobbs expressed a hope that the Board would establish the line from their southernmost town eastward to the Pee Dee River and westward to the mountains, leaving all of the Indians in one government. To satisfy South Carolina's objections he suggested that the parallel of Charleston be made the line between South Carolina and Georgia, and that the former colony be extended westward beyond the Savannah to that extent, thereby giving to South Carolina "a much greater Country" than would be granted to the northern province. Furthermore, Georgia would still retain more territory "betwixt its parallels" than both of the Carolinas.[164]

The Board of Trade were "entirely convinced" of the necessity of an immediate settlement of the boundary controversy, but action was again delayed on account of South Carolina's failure to come to a decision regarding a definite proposal and her consequent delay in supplying the Board of Trade with essential information. That body informed the government of North Carolina that they were ready to act but could do nothing until the report of the committee of the South Carolina Council, appointed by Governor Lyttleton, was received. They added that they were expecting that document "daily," and as soon as it came they would propose such a line "as shall appear to us to be proper."[165] South Carolina's inaction had caused another delay of two years.

---

[163] Dobbs to Board of Trade, October 31, 1756. *C.R.,* V, 641. As an indication of his straightforward, businesslike methods in dealing with this problem, it is interesting to note his actions at this time in dealing with the southern government. He stated to the Board that, in order to avoid delay, he "informed him (Lyttleton) of the line I had proposed with the approbation of the Council here, and sent him a copy of what I sent to your Lordships that he might at once object to it, and not occasion . . . further delay when our different opinions are laid before your Lordships." *Ibid.,* V, 641. [164] *C.R.,* V, 641.

[165] The Board of Trade to Governor Dobbs, March 10, 1757. *C.R.,* V, 749. On May 30 following, Dobbs complained to the Board that, after having "readily" sent his own proposal for a line to Lyttleton, "they have not been so kind as to let me know the Boundary they have agreed to apply for and therefore must rest it upon your Lordships to fix an

Early in November, 1757, the report was received in London with an "opinion" regarding a line, and the Board of Trade immediately notified the governor of North Carolina of its arrival. They also stated that they would "lose no time" in considering it and making recommendations to the King. They added that, though they would consider Dobbs' recommendation relative to the Catawba Indian Lands, they were of the opinion that a matter of so great importance should be taken up when they took up the matter of Indian affairs in general, looking toward a general plan or policy, which they "were not yet ripe for. . . ."[166] The Indian Agents, however, should soon furnish the necessary information.

The British authorities continued to decline to act at that time despite the definite proposals from North Carolina and the receipt of the report from the Governor and Council of South Carolina, for which they had claimed to be waiting. The Board of Trade informed Governor Dobbs that they were "sensible" of the many advantages which would be derived from the settlement of the boundary dispute between his and the southern province, but did not think it advisable to lay it before the Privy Council at that time, as they had declined to consider boundary questions of other colonies which they had laid before them.[167]

The necessity for action was so imperative, with the sections near the boundary in almost constant turmoil, that the colonies did not long permit pressure on the home authorities to relax. In 1761 North Carolina renewed her proposals by suggesting the addition of all territory from Little River to the entrance of Winyaw Bay, thence along the "east bank" of Pee Dee River "until it reaches our parallel." The phrase "east bank" must be an error in the use of terms. As Dobbs always insisted on a water route by way of the Pee Dee River and Winyaw Bay to relieve North Carolina of paying customs duties to South Caro-

---

equitable Line as soon as possible." Lyttleton had informed him that their Council was almost ready to send their proposal to the Board. However, on August 20 Dobbs informed the Board that he had received a copy of the report of the Council of South Carolina. *Ibid.*, V, 762, 784. The southern government had finally begun to function.

[166] Board of Trade to Dobbs, November 9, 1757. *C.R.*, V, 786.

[167] Board of Trade to Dobbs, June 1, 1759. *C.R.*, VI, 46. Two months later, Dobbs wrote the Board that he was glad to leave the question of the location of the line "entirely" to the King's pleasure, as he realized that both provinces were royal property. Dobbs to Board of Trade, September 11, 1759. *Ibid.*, VI, 58.

lina, he must have meant the middle of the stream as the line instead of the "east bank," a term which he always used. His argument and his terms are clearly inconsistent. By "our parallel" he must have meant 34° 20′ north latitude, the line for which he had been contending. This renewal of the old proposal may have been inspired by inquiry regarding the boundary made by the Board of Trade in the same year.[168]

South Carolina had also reached the conclusion by this time that the colonies themselves could never come to an amicable agreement on the location of the line. Governor Dobbs and Lyttleton, finding the settlement of the Catawba Lands question an impossible one for the colonies, agreed to let it subside until the boundary was definitely located. Thomas Boone, the new Governor of South Carolina, immediately concluded that the colonies could never agree. He expressed the hope that Governor Dobbs would concur with him and his Council in the conclusion that it was "unreasonable, possibly prejudicial, but certainly fruitless to inter into disputes upon a subject that must be determined by other arbiters."[169] The North Carolina Government was requested to use its influence to secure such arbitration.

In furtherance of this effort, the General Assembly of South Carolina instructed Charles Garth, Agent in London, to request the Board of Trade to assist in securing from the King orders for settling and establishing the line. The memorial was read before the Board in November, and described the great confusion prevailing on account of the failure of the inhabitants in some regions to recognize jurisdiction of either colony.[170] Since there was no jurisdiction, there was no law, and the result was disputes, injuries and violence of all kinds among the settlers, and between them and their Indian neighbors. Unless the line was established, it was urged, the results might be "fatal" to both colonies through alienation of the dangerous Indian tribes. It was hoped that the £108,000 sterling spent by the colony in the last two years in suppressing Indian hostilities would "have its due weight on the present application." From the standpoint of Indian relations, a significant statement was made, informing the Board that the report of the Assembly was prepared and agreed to in 1758, but the

[168] *C.R.*, VI, 606.
[169] Boone to Dobbs, July 23, 1762. *C.R.*, VI, 791-792.
[170] Pub. Rec. of S. C., XXIX, 265-266.

outbreak of the Cherokee War "put a stop to an application of this nature" until peace was restored.

The boundary line desired was not specified in the above application. The southern government applied in general terms for an allotment of territory of the two colonies, apparently resigning the whole problem to the authorities in England. The Assembly did add, however, that the ancient boundary was the Cape Fear, changed only by the instructions of 1730; and that if the King wished that line still to be observed, it should be recognized accordingly.[171]

In the month following South Carolina's application for settlement, North Carolina also sent an address to the Crown urging an adjustment by royal action as soon as peace was signed. The general confusion again was described, and the request renewed for the Pee Dee River-Winyaw Bay line. Complaint was renewed against the customs duties levied by the southern government on products passing over that route. Futhermore, it was stated, if the inhabitants northwest of the dividing line as then surveyed were placed in South Carolina, they would be forced to travel over two hundred miles to attend court in Charleston. The address closed with an urgent appeal that the proposed line be approved, or that the old line as run be extended along 34° 38' north latitude to the Savannah River, and remain the permanent boundary.[172]

Following these provincial applications, the Board of Trade made a representation to the Crown based on them, describing the long-continued disputes and violence in the provinces over property and jurisdiction; and it was made plain that the cause of the confusion was the lack of a "certain" and "equitable" dividing line. It was repeated that confusion was so great in 1758 that the Board called for the "sentiments" of the Governor and Council of each province regarding the location of a line, and that it was only on account of the state of war that final settlement was not recommended to the Crown at that time.[173] Instead, the governors were directed to cooperate in preserving peace pending final victory in war when the king would have an opportunity to consider it carefully and determine the location with "certainty and precision." However, as Governor Boone had

[171] Pub. Rec. of S. C., XXIX, 267-269.
[172] *C.R.,* VI, 775-779.
[173] Pub. Rec. of S. C., XXIX, 288.

just reported many evictions of South Carolina grantees by the North Carolina governor and courts, and many land surveys, even on the Catawba burying grounds, they felt it an urgent duty to make the following recommendations for the Crown's consideration:

1. That it was imperative that such transactions be immediately ended for the safety of both colonies.
2. That a definite line be established, both for property and jurisdiction.
3. That the proposals of the respective provinces were so "difficult," a more rapid solution is urgent.
4. That the great acquisition of territory in the southern part of the American continent makes "new objects of consideration arise" with regard to later division or arrangement of the southern colonies.
5. That, because the present situation in the Carolinas would "admit of no delay," the Crown should declare and establish a temporary dividing line to preserve peace until a permanent boundary could be fixed by the King.[174]

After reviewing the work accomplished under the agreement of 1734, the Board of Trade expressed the opinion that, although both provinces had expressed many objections to the line thus established, they saw no impropriety in using it as a temporary boundary until a more equitable one could be established. It was therefore proposed that, until the proposals of the two governments could be carefully examined, the line of 1735 be declared the temporary dividing line.[175]

The Board of Trade was not long beginning the draughting of instructions for the respective governors. On March 12, 1763, a committee of the Privy Council ordered the Board to prepare such instructions and submit them. They were completed forthwith and laid before the Royal Council, March 29.[176]

The instructions provided that, in order to prevent the disputes and confusion regarding the boundary, until a permanent line could be determined by the Crown, the line agreed upon and partially run in 1735 should be observed as the temporary dividing line. If said line had not been run and marked to the thirty-

[174] Pub. Rec. of S. C., XXIX, 289.
[175] *Ibid.*, XXIX, 292.
[176] The Board reported that they had prepared instructions for the governors, "signifying to them his Majesty's Pleasure concerning the immediate Establishment of a temporary Line of Jurisdiction. . . .," S.R., XI, 152.

fifth parallel, the governors were directed to appoint commissioners to continue the survey in the same direction as before to that parallel, thence due westward to the eastern limits of the Lands "claimed by the Catawba Indians."[177] The making of settlements and the exercise of jurisdiction upon those lands were forbidden until the Catawba claims were finally adjusted. The forts west of the Catawba Nation should belong to and continue to be maintained by the province which had erected and supported them.[178]

The instructions were approved by the King in Council, March 30, 1763.[179]

In reply to the instructions of March, 1763, Governor Boone wrote to the Board of Trade that he would earnestly endeavor to carry them out; that he had already heard from Governor Dobbs on the subject, who had promised to take no action until he had visited Charleston, which he promised to do in the near future when the matter would be discussed.[180]

Lack of cooperation between the Governor and General Assembly in South Carolina delayed the execution of the royal instructions. In March, 1764, Governor Dobbs again complained that the line had not been run because of that situation, stating that the Assembly "won't act with Governor Boone, and consequently won't give money to defray the Expense until His Majesty allow it out of the Quit Rents."[181] He also expressed the hope that the line would be fixed farther southward than the thirty-fifth degree of north latitude.

Secretary Pownal of the Board of Trade attempted to improve the relations between the two colonies. He "particularly recommend[ed]" that Lieutenant-Governor William Tryon of North Carolina cooperate with the Lieutenant-Governor of South Carolina in carrying into "effectual Execution" the royal orders for establishing a temporary dividing line.[182] The two executives had

[177] See map, p. 32. [178] S.R., XI, 153. [179] Ibid., XI, 154.
[180] Boone to Board of Trade, September 15, 1763. Pub. Rec. of S. C., XXIX, 366-367; ibid., XXX, 5. Dobbs made the trip to Charleston, referred to above. N. C. Council Journals, October 15, 1763. Quoted in C.R., VI, 1014.
[181] Dobbs to Board of Trade, March 29, 1764. C.R., VI, 1037.
[182] Pownal to Tryon, July 2, 1764. C.R., VI, 1049-1050. Tryon was commissioned Lieutenant-Governor of North Carolina, April 26, 1764. He did not arrive in the province, however, until October 10; hence, was not in position to push the survey in that year. The commissioners had completed the task in September.

already begun to cooperate, however. Late in 1763, in accordance with the advice of their respective Councils, they agreed to appoint two commissioners each for running the line, beginning March 1, 1764. They further agreed that the Governor of South Carolina, in an effort to quiet the settlers, should issue a proclamation containing the substance of the royal instructions and directing the inhabitants to refrain from all acts of violence.[183] Governor Dobbs consented that all process should mutually be stayed and all warrants of survey suspended until an adjustment could be made.

In the meantime, commissioners were duly appointed and met in July at the Boundary House near the seacoast where they proceeded to survey the line as described in the royal instructions.[184] The boundary was extended from the meadow stake, at the termination of the survey of 1737, to the old Salisbury-Charlotte Road, a distance of about sixty-two miles. The work was completed September 28.[185] The line was measured as the survey proceeded, in accordance with the directions of the governors.

It is quite evident that the authorities in England suspected that the surveyors in 1737 had taken inaccurate observations in locating the thirty-fifth parallel. In the instructions of 1763 it was distinctly ordered that "in case it shall appear, that the said Line has not been marked out . . . so far north as the thirty-fifth degree," the governors should appoint commissioners to extend the line of 1737 in the same direction to that parallel, thence due westward to the eastern limits of the Catawba Lands. The commissioners failed to detect the error in the astronomical observations and began at the old marker.[186] The errors of

[183] Pub. Rec. of S. C., XXIX, 405-406; *S.R.*, XI, 207. The commissioners appointed by the two colonies were James Moore, George Pawley, Samuel Wyley, and Arthur Mackay. Executive Letter Book, XIV, 394-395; *ibid.*, XXX, 339.

[184] Boone to Board of Trade, August 20, 1764. Pub. Rec. of S. C., XXX, 183-184; Executive Letter Book, 1833-1835, XXX, 339.

[185] The commissioners were fatigued, and "beg[ged] leave to take some rest." Governor Bull ordered one of them to extend the line until it should strike the "South-West" boundary of the Catawba Lands, while the other commissioners separated. Pub. Rec. of S. C., XXX, 198-199. It was a surprise to all the authorities that the line did not strike the eastern boundary of the Catawba Lands. Cf. *ibid.*, XXX, 225.

[186] Prominent writers again have erred in their factual statements regarding this survey. For example, Professor Kerr states that the line from the end of the survey of 1737 was "re-surveyed in 1764," whereas, it

1737 and 1764 were the cause of future controversies between the two colonies. It appears, however, that the Governor of South Carolina sincerely desired to prevent all disputes over the line after the survey of 1764. He issued a proclamation to all persons who might be concerned in the exercise of jurisdiction, informing them the survey was made and the line marked. They were ordered to observe it carefully.[187] It was hoped that the relations of the two colonies would become normal as a result of this policy.

The authorities in both provinces, as well as the British officials, were conscious of the immediate need of a complete and permanent solution of the dangerous boundary problem, regardless of policies of conciliation. In the midst of the survey of 1764, Lieutenent-Governor Tryon was instructed to communicate an opinion relative to a "proper final Boundary."[188] He was ordered by the Crown to accept the dividing line as run and marked in that year, until a permanent one could be established or further instructions were issued. After having been in the province only five days, Tryon promised the Board to submit proposals for a permanent line at his earliest convenience.[189] He drew up a plan of a line which he proposed to the Board early in 1766. It provided for the extension of the line of 1764 from its termination to the Saluda River, a computed distance of 106 miles.[190] The governor also stated that the North Carolina settlers along the line were "very desirous" of having the line altered so as to extend along the Winyaw Bay and Pee Dee River to the line of 1764, thence westward along that survey.[191] The aim was to

---

had never been surveyed. See his *Geology of North Carolina*, I, 2. He further states that the line followed the old Salisbury-Charlotte Road to the southeast corner of the Catawba Lands at that time, but it was not extended directly to the "corner" of said lands until 1813. Cf. Pub. Rec. of S. C., XXX, 198; XXXIII, 44-45; *C.R.*, VIII, 560. Maps of the surveys of 1772 and 1813 are in the N. C. Historical Commission collection, Raleigh, N. C. The U. S. Geological Survey makes the same error by quoting Kerr. See Henry Gannett, *Boundaries of the United States*, p. 101; Edward M. Douglas, *Boundaries*, p. 131.

[187] Pub. Rec. of S. C., XXX, 225.
[188] Pownal to Tryon, July 2, 1764. This instruction was given even before Tryon left England. C.R., VI, 1050.
[189] *Ibid.*, VI, 1054.
[190] Tryon to Board of Trade, January 27, 1766. *Ibid.*, VII, 155, 156.
[191] Hereafter referred to as the people's line.

secure a water route for the Yadkin and Rocky rivers to the sea. Tryon then surprised and disappointed his own province. He threw off all narrow, selfish provincialism and rose to the rank of a statesman. He frankly opposed the adoption of the proposed line on the ground that colonial interests must be looked at broadly, and that such a line "would too much contract the sea board of the south government, and in a future day, might be of more prejudice to that province than of real advantage to this." He was intent on securing the adoption of his own suggested line as the more desirable, renewing his proposal in April and July, 1767, and in October and December, 1768.[192] It appears that he had the support of South Carolina in this plan of settlement. He always claimed that Governor Montagu, the new Governor of South Carolina, told him that he felt the southern government "could have no objections to that line [of 1764] being extended."[193]

With regard to a permanent boundary, Tryon advised the Board of Trade that, on the whole, he was of the opinion that the line as run from the coast to the Salisbury Road was the best for a final boundary. During the following week, he sent all available information regarding the boundary question to the Board in order to hasten action in London by enabling the Lords of Trade to reach a decision on a permanent line of division.[194]

In the meantime, South Carolina had been working for a line more to her own advantage than the temporary one then run. In December, 1764, Lieutenant-Governor Bull proposed to the Board of Trade a boundary line extending from the termination of the survey of that year, along the Salisbury Road to Twelve Mile Creek; thence along the southern limits of the Catawba Lands; thence eastward, northward, and westward around the said tract to the east bank of the Catawba River; thence up said river to its source "in or near Cherokee Mountains."[195] A week later, he attempted to hasten action on his proposal by informing the Board of the great confusion among the northwestern settlements of South Carolina, and stated that the disorder was

[192] *C.R.*, VII, 155, 448, 510, 860, 876.
[193] Tryon to Lord Hillsborough, October 27, 1768; Tryon to Montagu, December 11, 1768. *C.R.*, VII, 862, 876.
[194] Tryon to Board of Trade, February 1, 1766. *C.R.*, VII, 159, 197.
[195] Bull renewed this proposal in July, 1768. Pub. Rec. of S. C., XXXII, 17.

caused by a lack of a dividing line west of the Catawba Lands.[196] In reply to Bull's proposal, Hillsborough stated that, as the Lieutenant-Governor had only mentioned the South Branch of the Catawba without explaining his "Ideas" of a line, he could make no definite proposal to the King, though he realized the "absolute necessity" of extending the line in order to stop the prevalent violence.[197]

South Carolina was inconsistent and unsettled regarding her desires for a location of the line at this time. Later in the same year in which Bull made his proposal as to a Catawba River line, it was urged that the boundary be established along the west bank of the Cape Fear River to its forks, thence along its northwest branch to the thirty-fifth parallel, thence due westward.[198] Such indecision and changing of proposals weakened her case before the British authorities for a time.

North Carolina would not even consider the adoption of the above proposal for a Cape Fear River-thirty-fifth parallel line. Governor Tryon protested vigorously to the Board of Trade against it on the grounds that it would injure North Carolina by "shutting out" four whole counties: namely, Brunswick, Bladen, Cumberland, and Anson; that it would increase smuggling of goods in both provinces. Probably the proposal was only a repetition of Glen's tactics in bargaining for a favorable line.

The Board of Trade, however, took the proposal into their consideration in the summer of 1765 and sent a communication to Governor Montagu of South Carolina. They were either dishonest or ignorant with regard to proceedings relative to the line. They "lament[ed]" the fact that it was left "unfinished by the Commissioners appointed to run it in consequence of His Majesty's Instructions"; and they added that the survey seemed to have stopped short of that district where the greatest disputes had occurred and, consequently, where a line was most needed. It will be recalled that the commissioners were forbidden to extend the line west of the Catawba Lands. The Board expressed the hope that the great divergence of views regarding a proper boundary would not prove irreconcilable, and added that they would

---

[196] Bull to Board of Trade, December 10, 1764. Pub. Rec. of S. C., XXX, 225, 299.
[197] Ibid., XXXII, 42.   [198] C.R., VII, 156.

endeavor to bring about an agreement;[199] but nothing of consequence was done.

In 1768, the officials of both provinces put increased pressure on the home authorities for immediate action on the line. Lieutenant-Governor Bull of South Carolina wrote to the Secretary of State for the Southern Department urging that the question receive the most careful attention. He stated that the western region had become very populous, and "the Jurisdiction of the Courts, Collection of Taxes and . . . Quit Rents, surveying of Lands, Militia and other duties are all in a state of uncertainty" which causes great inconvenience to the settlers and many disputes between them and the officials, as well as serious controversies between the colonies.[200] Three months later, Governor Tryon urged the necessity of an extension on the same official and emphasized the loss of just taxes by North Carolina, the contempt for courts and officers, the general use of the region as a refuge for criminals, and prevailing confusion through duplication of land grants. Tryon added: "On these grounds I beg leave to submit to his Majesty the expediency of closing up the limits between this province and South Carolina."[201] He might have stated further that lack of a definite boundary line was preventing the permanent location of a provincial capital.[202]

To the previous proposals of his province, Governor Montagu then added a plan of his own for a proper boundary. He proposed that the line as run from the seacoast to the Salisbury Road be continued along that road to the southeastern boundary of the Catawba Lands; thence around those lands, as surveyed in 1764, to the Catawba River; thence along the middle of that stream to its southern branch; and along that branch to its source "in the Cherokee Mountains."[203] Montagu urged Tryon to concur in this proposal, confident that a joint appeal to the Board of Trade would practically insure its adoption. It will be seen that the proposal was not original with Montagu, but that it was practically identical with that of Governor Bull.

North Carolina immediately filed strong protests against this proposal. Her objections were pointed and usually reasonable. They might be summarized as follows:

[199] Pub. Rec. of S. C., XXXI, 80-82.
[200] Bull to Hillsborough, July 18, 1768. Pub. Rec. of S. C., XXXII, 16-17. [201] C.R., VII, 862-863. [202] Ibid., VI, 878.
[203] Montagu to Tryon, December, 1768. C.R., VIII, 563.

1. That the proposed line would cut off all of North Carolina's trade with the western Indians, leaving only impassable mountains as a frontier.
2. The whole line of 1767 between North Carolina and South Carolina, which was run at a cost of £2,000 would fall within the limits of South Carolina.[204]
3. The last General Assembly of North Carolina established Tryon County west of the Catawba Lands, a territory of 3,600 square miles, which county is justly hers.
4. The proposed line is "prodigiously erroneous" in its location. The south branch of the Catawba River does not flow eastward and westward but only two or three points westward of north. It does not rise in the Cherokee Mountains but is cut off by the Broad River a distance of forty or fifty miles.
5. North Carolina cannot alter her own proposal to the authorities in England.
6. The line would include in South Carolina a portion of Lord Granville's district.
7. It would leave one section of territory as open to both governments as then existed.
8. The Catawba tract of fifteen miles square could be of no great profit to either province, since the Indians are likely to leave within ten years.
9. The settlers west of Catawba River greatly prefer to remain in North Carolina, since their land grants were issued by this government, and they were enjoying the advantage of local courts.
10. Such a line would counteract a number of the established laws of North Carolina.
11. It would rob North Carolina of over 1,000,000 acres of her best lands.[205]

South Carolina made a reply to the objections offered by Governor Tryon to the South Branch line to the Cherokee Mountains. Governor Montagu referred the question to his Council, which appointed a committee to reply in detail to the principal objections.

[204] Tryon had run a temporary line between the colonies in 1767 at North Carolina's expense. *C.R.*, IX, xix.

[205] *C.R.*, VII, 876-877, 879-880; VIII, 5, 10; IX, xix. Tryon wrote to Lord Hillsborough that "I should loose my county and mountain" if Montagu's proposed line should be adopted. Tryon to Hillsborough, January 10, 1769. The North Carolina Council took up the proposal in January 1771, and proposed "to take the most effectual means to prevent it," urgently requesting the governor to block the "pernicious plan." Council Journals, January 24, 1771.

To the objection that such a line would mean the loss of all trade with the western Indians, the Council denied it, asserting that the existence of a dividing line did not preclude trade with the different tribes. South Carolina's constant trade with the Creeks, Chickasaws, and Choctaws through Georgia territory for thirty-eight years was cited to bear out the point.

The Council answered, regarding the expense of running Tryon's line, that it was only the result of Dobbs' fears lest the Cherokee-South Carolina line of 1765 be extended into North Carolina. With deference to his remonstrance, the Lieutenant-Governor of South Carolina had ordered the line discontinued at Reedy River, a natural boundary "far within the undoubted jurisdiction of South Carolina."

With regard to the organization of Tryon County by the North Carolina Assembly, the objection was regarded as irrelevant and without value, since the establishment of a boundary was a prerogative of the Crown and both provinces should have refrained from such action pending a royal decision. This South Carolina did, it was stated, regardless of trespasses even south of the "pretended continuation" of the line of 1764.

The statement that the South Branch of the Catawba was erroneously shown was denied, and any party concerned was referred to a map which Governor Montagu had caused to be drawn especially to clear up the question.

Since a large amount of valuable territory was at stake in the final decision of the Board of Trade as to the location of the line from the termination of the survey of 1764 westward, it will be well to analyze and evaluate the above arguments in order to reach a conclusion as to the justice of South Carolina's claims. Her position with regard to North Carolina's trade with the western Indians appears to have been correct. She could have cited precedents of colonies other than Georgia in support of her contention. Her charge that the running of the temporary line in 1767 was only a result of Governor Dobbs's jealousy of the expansion of South Carolina northwestwardly could not have been substantiated, though it probably played a part. As to the establishment of Tryon County, South Carolina appears to have been on solid ground in her contention that North Carolina should have awaited the decision of the Crown on the boundary line before erecting a county in the disputed territory. Regarding the location and direction of the South Branch of the Catawba, North Carolina was not only correct but she could not have been expected to accept as final proof a map prepared at the instance of Montagu for the admitted purpose of proving his own point. The northern government was justified in desiring a disinterested arbiter. North Carolina's contention that she could not alter her own proposal to the Board of Trade was not sound. Such a proposal was not arbitrary, and had it been shown that another line could have been justly agreed upon, such a line should have been accepted. The northern government's objection that the Catawba line would include a portion of Granville's district in South Carolina, and that it would leave a section from the head of that stream to the Cherokee Mountains still unmarked, was valid. North Carolina's statement that the Catawba Nation would be of little profit to either province because the game was scarce and the Indians would soon be leaving, was not valid because it assumed that, aside from the fur trade, the territory was worthless. She was probably correct, however, in the contention that the settlers preferred to be in the northern colony, since South Carolina allowed the organization of no local courts, and most of the land grants were issued by North Carolina. The claim that 1,000,000 acres of land would have been lost by North Carolina was not legally sound, though just, because the royal owner had not indicated a dividing line to include a definite territory west of the Catawba Lands.

The Council then offered objections to Governor Tryon's proposal of an extension of the line of 1764. They were as follows:

1. The survey of 1764 was erroneous. Repeated astronomical observations by their surveyor had proven unmistakably that the line was run in $34° \ 49'$, or eleven miles south of the thirty-fifth parallel, which was called for in the royal instructions. By that error South Carolina was losing 660 square miles, or 422,000 acres of land, an area equal to some of the counties in England.
2. The proposed extension was longer than that of 1764; hence, if it should be approved, South Carolina would lose almost 600,000 acres. The combined loss would exceed the area of "two not the least Counties in England."
3. Such a line would sever the lands of many settlers, leaving their homes and their lands in different provinces. This would produce untold difficulties in the collection of taxes, in levying executions on lands, and in many other governmental relationships.

4. Should the inaccurate line be extended, it would run several miles south of Fort Prince George, which had been a great expense to South Carolina, and which served as a principal defense against the Cherokees.
5. As Savannah River extends north northwestward, the extension of the survey of 1764 would greatly contract the province on the west.
6. The best region for raising hemp would be lost by South Carolina.[206]

The Council then offered a defense of the proposed Catawba River line, basing their argument "on the principles of general policy." It was stated that, since South Carolina's staples—rice, indigo, naval stores, and hemp—did not rival or interfere with the produce of Great Britain but were very advantageous to her trade, any action which would aid in raising those staples should be taken.

The settlers west of the Catawba River were vital to the safety of South Carolina in keeping down slave insurrections, it was claimed. As the province purchased an increasing number of negroes from British slave traders, it was held absolutely essential that the northwestern inhabitants should be included in South Carolina. North Carolina's white population was "vastly superior" to the number of slaves; hence, that province suffered no such danger.

The Council then argued that the commercial interests of the province were at stake. Transportation down the rivers which rise west of the Catawba Lands, to Charleston, would be much less expensive than by wagon overland. Those rivers should, therefore, be included in the southern province to their sources. If the Charleston market were thus kept open and easy of access to the settlers of the interior for the exchange of their produce for European goods, it would preclude the establishment of manufacturing in the back country of "home materials for home consumption."

South Carolina saved the inhabitants in the northwestern region during the Cherokee War, it was pointed out, by the forts and militia she had established at great expense. Moreover, as many immigrants imported at the colony's expense "may have settled up the Broad River" in the northwestern section, the Council was convinced that the whole of that stream should be in South Carolina.

[206] Pub. Rec. of S. C., XXXII, 137 *et seq.*; C.R., VIII, 557-558.

The Catawba Indians should be under the jurisdiction of the southern colony because of their effective aid in overawing the negroes, as demonstrated in 1766; to compensate for the great expense incurred in building a fort in their territory; and because of the warm attachment for South Carolina which had developed among the Catawbas. It was further emphasized that the southern government fed and clothed the women and children of that tribe during the Cherokee War.[207]

Upon careful examination, it will be seen that these arguments for the most part were untenable. The first point, regarding encouragement of the production of South Carolina staples, was predicated on the theory that South Carolina was the favored province, and therefore her interests and general welfare must be furthered at the expense of North Carolina; hence, the point must be discredited as fallacious. The second point, regarding the danger inherent in the much greater proportion of slaves in the southern province, was effective argument from a practical standpoint, but assumed that North Carolina should sacrifice her own interests in order to support and make safe an unsound economic and social system. The argument relative to river transportation, Charleston markets, and the prevention of manufacturing in the colony was probably an indirect but smart appeal to the selfish merchant and manufacturing classes in England for support in the controversy. It shows, however, a complete lack of vision in the southern colony in regard to future development of methods of transportation. In the statement that South Carolina saved the population during the Cherokee hostilities by means of her forts, the Council claimed credit for an entire service of which the colony had rendered only a part. North Carolina had also built forts in the western region years before. For example, Fort Dobbs had been built near the present site of Statesville in 1755-56 for "a retreat for the back settlers."[208] In 1756 another fort was built on the site of modern Old Fort, North Carolina, near the Catawba River.[209] The argument that South Carolina's immigrants "may" have settled along the upper reaches of the Broad River was puerile under the circumstances of an important boundary dispute. The authorities had done nothing to verify the claim, but were content with men-

[207] Pub. Rec. of S. C., XXXII, 142 *et seq.;* C.R., VIII, 558-560.
[208] C.R., V, xlvii; J. P. Arthur, *Western North Carolina, A History,* p. 69. [209] C.R., V, xlviii.

tioning the possibility of it. The claim of having gone to great expense in building a fort for the Catawbas and in supporting their women and children was accurate. However, the great injustice done North Carolina in the matter of the Granville grant,[210] with her suggestions for recompensing South Carolina west of the Savannah, overshadowed all other arguments and called for an adjustment southward.

The above report of the South Carolina Council was transmitted to Lord Hillsborough and the southern Agent in London and was laid before the King with the hope that it would influence the royal decision as to a location of the line.[211]

The opposition of the northern province to the South Carolina proposal developed to such an extent that the latter appears to have resorted to a diplomatic manoeuvre in an effort to secure a compromise by which the South Branch of the Catawba would be adopted. After having replied to the many objections made to that proposed line, the Council of the southern province modified the former proposal by advocating the adoption of the northern or main branch of the Catawba River to its source "in the Cherokee mountains."[212] In view of the strong opposition to the South Branch line, it is difficult to believe that South Carolina had the slightest hope of securing the adoption of the more northern line.

Meantime, action was taken in England. The Committee of the Privy Council for Plantation Affairs ordered the Board to take into their consideration all available information relative to the boundary controversy. The Board secured all papers bearing upon the subject and called in the Agent of each of the colonies for a defense of their respective proposals. After careful consideration, they recommended to the Committee of the Privy Council a compromise boundary line.[213] It was to extend from the termination of the line of 1764 along the Salisbury Road to the southern boundary of the Catawba Lands; thence along the southern, eastern, and northern limits of said Lands, to the intersection of the Catawba River with the northern boundary; thence up the

[210] *Supra*, p. 62.
[211] Bull to Hillsborough, June 7, 1770. Pub. Rec. of S. C., XXXII, 278-9.
[212] Pub. Rec. of S. C., XXXII, 147; *C.R.,* VIII, 561.
[213] Board of Trade to the Committee of the Privy Council for Plantation Affairs, April 24, 1771. Pub. Rec. of S. C., XXXIII, 44-45; *C.R.,* VIII, 573-574; Connor, *History*, p. 246; Douglas, *Boundaries, Areas, Geographic Centers and Altitudes of the United States and the Several States*, p. 131.

middle of that stream to the confluence of its northern and southern branches; and from thence due west until it should intersect the Cherokee line. It was further recommended that the temporary line as run from the seacoast to the Salisbury Road, and the line therein recommended from the termination of the line of 1764 to the Cherokee line, be declared the final boundary between the two provinces.

The Committee of the Privy Council accepted the proposal and ordered the Board of Trade to draw up instructions to the respective governors incorporating their recommendations. On May 29, 1771, such instructions were issued to Governor Montagu, and to Governor Josiah Martin,[214] of North Carolina, directing them to appoint commissioners to cooperate in running the line as described.

In the following May, Governor Montagu appointed William Moultrie and William Thompson as commissioners for South Carolina, and Benjamin Farrar and James Cook as surveyors.[215]

Opposition developed in North Carolina, however, as soon as the details of the Crown's decision were known. McCulloh, her Agent in London, protested against the decision and requested that final action be postponed until his government could file its objections to any deviation from Tryon's proposed line. The request was refused and instructions prepared, which the Agent refused to take from the office and for which he refused to pay the fee of £35, 16 sterling. He informed the Committee of Correspondence in North Carolina that he would pay the fee only if so instructed.[216]

The people in the province displayed "great alarm" when the rumor was circulated that the Crown had determined on a line favorable to Montagu's proposal. They felt "much injured" by the loss of such a great extent of "flourishing" country.[217] When

[214] Pub. Rec. of S. C., XXXIII, 55-57; *C.R.*, VIII, 611-612. Martin was commissioned Governor of North Carolina, December 19, 1770, to succeed Tryon. *C.R.*, VIII, 267. Their instructions regarding the boundary were identical. They were re-issued to Martin June 10, 1771. *S.R.*, XI, 234-235.

[215] *The South Carolina Gazette*, Thursday, May 21, 1772; Montagu to Hillsborough, July 27, 1772. Pub. Rec. of S. C., XXXIII, 166.

[216] McCulloh to Committee of Correspondence, July 10, 1771. *C.R.*, IX, 11.

[217] Governor Martin to Hillsborough, November 10, 1771. *C.R.*, IX, 48-49. Martin opposed the location chiefly because he lost his fees on land grants in the transferred territory.

the sheriff of Tryon County experienced difficulties in the exercise of his office following the circulation of the report, the North Carolina Council advised him to continue observing the old line.[218]

The North Carolina Assembly was resentful, particularly toward the British authorities. Governor Martin informed the members in December, 1771, of the receipt of the royal instructions for running the line, and requested an appropriation to defray the expenses to be incurred. It was immediately ordered that the message should lie on the table.[219] Four days later, the Assembly replied that it was greatly concerned over the injury the province would suffer from such a dividing line, and stated that the only recourse was an application directly to the King for redress. The governor was earnestly requested to make such an application in the name of the colony, describing the "numberless injustices" the line would occasion and urging that the old line which was so costly to the province should be made the permanent boundary. They proposed to put forth in the meantime every possible additional effort on their own part to obtain such redress from the King. The Assembly then declined to burden the people with further expense, since they had financed one "equitable" dividing line, to run another which was so injurious to the interests of the colony. That reason alone, they declared, was accountable for their declining the governor's request for funds.[220] The House then took steps to obtain the desired redress. A committee was appointed, consisting of Cornelius Harnett, Maurice Moore, and Robert Howe, to prepare an address to the King petitioning for an alteration of the instructions in accord with North Carolina's interests.[221]

All opposition proved unavailing, however, and Governor Martin, after receiving assurance from Governor Montagu that South Carolina would bear the whole expense of the survey,[222] proceeded to appoint as commissioners, John Rutherford and William Dry; and as surveyors, Thomas Rutherford and Thomas Polk. The southern governor appointed as commissioners, Colonel Thompson and William Moultrie.[223]

[218] N. C. Council Journals, November 25, 1771. *C.R.,* IX, 56.
[219] *C.R.,* IX, 191-192.
[220] Assembly to Martin, December 21, 1771. *C.R.,* IX, 211-212.
[221] *C.R.,* IX, 212.
[222] Martin to Lord Dartmouth, April 20, 1773. *C.R.,* IX, 638.
[223] Executive Letter Book, XI, 14; *C.R.,* IX, 302. J. W. Moore implies that Abraham Alexander and Thomas Polk were the commissioners, but this is an error. See his *History of North Carolina,* I, 150.

This action did not decrease the Assembly's bitterness, however. Governor Martin notified Governor Montagu in April, 1773, of their second refusal to appropriate funds, regardless of his warning that their reasons for such refusal were "ill received by the King."[224] They had given as additional reasons for their refusal the fact that the line greatly favored South Carolina, and the heavy indebtedness of £60,000 incurred in the suppression of the Regulators. Lord Hillsborough wrote to Governor Martin the previous year that he was sorry the King's decision disappointed the North Carolina Assembly, but that it was "proper I should observe to you the indecent manner in which they express themselves to you upon that subject has not escaped his Majesty's notice."[225] The soil was being richly prepared for the revolutionary events of three years later. With regard to the needed funds, the North Carolina Assembly had firmly told the governor that, since South Carolina was reaping all of the benefits while their own province suffered all of the injustices of the survey, the former could meet the expense.[226]

Following the appointment of commissioners and surveyors by the two governments, there was a delay in procedure which was due to a lack of cooperation between the governors. Martin complained to Hillsborough that he waited in vain for two months for Montagu to act on his request to appoint a time and place of meeting for the commissioners, and, as the hot season was rapidly approaching, he finally notified Montagu that the North Carolina commissioners would meet his at the Catawba Town on April 20 and proceed with the survey of the line according to the royal instructions.[227] Such failure to cooperate often exasperated the British authorities and became a serious handicap to the extension of the line.

The governor of South Carolina seems to have ignored this arbitrary appointment. The North Carolina commissioners appeared at the Catawba Town according to notice but found no southern commissioners. After waiting several days, they learned that Montagu was at Camden "on a Tour of amusement."[228] When William Dry, one of the northern commissioners, visited him and

---

[224] *C.R.*, IX, 563.
[225] Hillsborough to Martin, April 1, 1772. *C.R.*, IX, 276.
[226] *C.R.*, IX, 77; Connor, Unpublished Lectures.
[227] *C.R.*, IX, 279-280.
[228] Martin to Hillsborough, June 5, 1772. *C.R.*, IX, 299.

urged that he send his commissioners to meet them immediately, he replied that he did not expect North Carolina to appoint commissioners until South Carolina had agreed to bear the whole expense of the survey. This must have been a policy of studied evasion on the part of Montagu. After being urged two months to appoint a time and place of meeting for the commissioners, he must have been fully aware of the appointment of the North Carolina representatives. He also seems to have been playing false regarding his former agreement that South Carolina would bear all of the expense of the survey, if Martin's report to that effect was accurate.[229] He further informed Dry in the above related conversation that he could not appoint commissioners until he had returned to Charleston and consulted the King's instructions, which would certainly delay the meeting at the Catawba Town until May 20. Governor Martin reported to Hillsborough that he had done everything possible to carry out his instructions and hoped that the survey would not be delayed more than a month.[230] Montagu's motive in this case is difficult to account for, unless he hoped to see the North Carolina Assembly reverse its attitude and agree to meet part of the expense to be incurred. The line was to be located in South Carolina's favor and would naturally have been pressed to a conclusion by South Carolina officials.

The actual survey was begun around May 20, 1772.[231] The line was continued from the termination of the survey of 1764, along the Salisbury Road, around the Catawba Lands to the forks of the Catawba River, thence due westward (supposedly) to the Cherokee Mountains, as directed in the instructions. It was about sixty-five miles in length. The survey was completed and the southern commissioners had returned to Charleston by the middle of June, 1772.[232]

By this survey South Carolina gained the district between the thirty-fifth parallel and the line from the forks of the Catawba to the Cherokee boundary, and extending from the Catawba River and Catawba Lands to the Cherokee line. Its soil was very fertile, producing indigo, hemp, tobacco, and all English grains in abundance. It had an estimated white population of more than

[229] *Supra*, p. 85. [230] *C.R.*, IX, 299.
[231] The exact date is not given in the *Colonial Records*, but the *South Carolina Gazette* for May 21, 1772, announced that the South Carolina commissioners had gone to meet the North Carolinians.
[232] Pub. Rec. of S. C., XXXIII, 166.

5,000. The region was called the New Acquisition until 1785, when the portion lying east of Broad River was organized into the County of York, and the section west of the river became Spartanburg County.

The compromise of 1772 amounted to a trade between the colonies. South Carolina had never become reconciled to the loss of the territory occasioned by the error in the surveys of 1735 and 1737. North Carolina was protesting angrily against the line ordered to be run in 1771. South Carolina had lost eleven minutes latitude in the former surveys and North Carolina had lost eight minutes as the line was supposed to have been run, but the difference in length of the two districts almost balanced the amount of territory exchanged. North Carolina was slightly favored. However, it was then estimated that she had lost 470,000 acres of land as the result of the surveys of 1764 and 1772.[233] Even then the extent of North Carolina's loss was not appreciated. Instead of running the line in a due westward direction from the forks of the Catawba River, the surveyors extended the boundary slightly to the north of west. As a result, the end of the line near the Cherokee border was lying in latitude 35° 15′ 11″ 33‴, or a variation of 5′ 47″ 53‴ from the latitude indicated by the royal instructions. The northern colony, therefore, lost an additional area of 213 square miles, or more than 136,300 acres.[234]

For years North Carolina refused to recognize the survey which had occasioned such loss of valuable territory. In March, 1773, her Assembly directed the Committee of Correspondence to instruct their Agent in London again to petition the King for a new dividing line.[235] She was sullen and embittered, particularly against the British and South Carolina, but against all who were in any way connected with the procedure on the line. When Thomas Polk, one of her own surveyors, petitioned the Assembly in 1773 for his salary as surveyor on the line it was refused on

---

[233] Report of the collectors of the royal revenue in North Carolina, January 1, 1773. By the survey of 1764, lands falling in South Carolina, 60,000 acres; by survey of 1772, lost by Mecklenburg County, 10,000 acres; by the same survey, lost by Tryon County, 400,000 acres. *C.R.*, IX, 369.

[234] Kindly estimated in square miles for the writer by Mr. George F. Syme, Senior Engineer, North Carolina State Highway Commission, from astronomical observations taken in 1807 by Dr. Joseph Caldwell of the University of North Carolina. Dr. Caldwell's connection with the controversy will be described later in this study.

[235] *C.R.*, IX, 578.

the grounds that the last Assembly "fully exprest the sense they had of the injury that would accrue to this Colony," should the proposed line be run; consequently, they could not consider anyone who had aided in running said line "as servants of this community."[236]

The outbreak of the American Revolution enveloped the interest and consumed the energy of both colonies. With it came the end of the period of colonial agitation and controversy over their respective limits. The next period will begin with the birth of the new States.

It will be of value at this point to summarize the boundary situation at the close of the colonial period. Though the boundary had been extended for a distance of approximately one hundred and fifty miles by the surveys of 1735, 1737, and 1764, the extension of the line had not kept pace with the settlements as they advanced westward. However, the survey made on the eve of the Revolution gave some relief to the settlers, though it gave great offense to the North Carolina Assembly. All of the evil effects attendant upon the uncertainty of a dividing line which were found to have grown up before the reign of George III had been accentuated during the first fifteen years of his reign. The collection of taxes, the granting of lands, judicial procedure, militia service, Indian relations, imperial relations, and normal functions and relations in general were seriously affected by the controversy.

Some new elements had appeared, affecting the progress of a final settlement. As a result of the Seven Years War, Great Britain gained new and extensive territories south and west of the colony of Georgia, and the Carolinas immediately sensed the importance of this accession in connection with a final adjustment of their old dispute. Hence, North Carolina's suggestion that Georgia and South Carolina be extended westward to enable her to escape from the unjust contraction of her territories by the Granville grant.

The uprising of the Regulators in 1771 indirectly affected the progress of the line westward. After their refusal to provide funds for the survey of 1772, the North Carolina Assembly reminded the British authorities that the colony was in debt to the extent of £60,000 as a result of that uprising, adding that this indebtedness was a chief reason for their refusal.

[236] *Ibid.*, IX, 509.

The regions in dispute had become a refuge for criminals after the middle of the century, challenging the authority of the law and reducing those sections to conditions of virtual anarchy. This provided for the two colonies a major governmental problem.

Economic interests and selfish appeals appeared with greater emphasis as the end of the colonial period approached. South Carolina demanded the fertile northwestern region for raising hemp and other agricultural products, and the northwestern rivers to their sources in order to keep the stream of commerce directed toward Charleston. She reminded the British authorities that if they were so located, interior manufacturing would not develop. Her slave system must also be protected by incorporating the white settlers of the disputed region in her limits. North Carolina protested that if the proposed Cape Fear line were established, she would lose four counties and her commerce would be given a serious blow by the growth of the practice of smuggling commodities into the province.

Two encouraging features appeared which gave hope that effective action would be taken to reach a just settlement. The North Carolina governor courageously opposed the adoption of proposals offered by his own province which he felt had entirely ignored the interests of a sister colony. This was a new policy— the substitution of statesmanship for bickering. The second element was a firm conviction on the part of the two colonies and of the British authorities that the controversy was so dangerous in its effects that it must be settled with dispatch.

A more significant development was the increased bitterness between the colonial and British authorities during the last years of the colonial period. It has been illustrated by the action of the Secretary of the Southern Department in denouncing the Assembly of North Carolina for their "indecent" conduct in ignoring royal orders and refusing to pay the costs of the survey of 1772, reminding them that their refusal was "ill received by the King." But North Carolina had no scruples against antagonizing the King and his officials. She even refused for years to pay her own citizens who had aided in the survey. Such antagonism toward the British on the eve of the Revolution no doubt played a part in moulding opinion in the colony on the question of making a bid for independence.

It is possible that the long and bitter rivalry between the

Carolinas hindered them to some degree in their efforts to cooperate against the British after the opening of the Revolution, though it is by no means certain. South Carolina frankly requested military aid from North Carolina when Charleston was threatened with attack, expressing the desire that Richard Caswell should command the troops. However, it should be noted that many North Carolinians, including General Allen Jones, vigorously objected, declaring that Caswell had no right to lead the militia out of the State. Though many motives may have been behind these objections, it is possible that the old bitterness played a part. We may well bear this situation in mind as further action by the new-born States is now considered.

CHAPTER III

THE CONTROVERSY RESUMED BY THE STATES

Section I

FRUITLESS NEGOTIATIONS

With the birth of independent States and the forming of their constitutions, there came also the question of the boundaries of the new political units. North Carolina faced the problem squarely, while South Carolina either deliberately ignored and postponed the description of her limits, or was too much engrossed in other things to give it attention. The latter State, in convention assembled, did not mention the question of boundaries during the proceedings either of the constitutional convention itself or the general assembly which followed.[1] The constitution drawn up for the State at that time contains no reference to boundaries.[2] South Carolina seems to have been pleased with the survey of 1772, for in apportioning representation for the General Assembly, the convention allotted to the territory acquired west of the Catawba River by that survey ten members.[3]

North Carolina was more active concerning her boundaries, probably because of her determined opposition to the survey of 1772. In her constitutional convention held at Halifax she adopted a Bill of Rights and a Constitution on December 17th and 18th, 1776.[4] The former document, which was incorporated as a part of the State Constitution, described in detail the boundary lines. Section XXV reads as follows:[5]

---

[1] Journal of the Provincial Congress & General Assembly of South Carolina, November 1, 1775-March 26, 1776, (MSS.), *passim*. These MSS. are in possession of the South Carolina Historical Commission, Columbia.
[2] *Ibid.*, pp. 4-11.
[3] In the proceedings for March 26, 1776, the following entry appears: "The District called the New Acquisition, Ten Members." *Ibid.*, p. 7. This certainly refers to that strip, because it is so designated on maps in possession of the South Carolina Historical Commission.
[4] Journals of the Constitutional Convention, quoted in *C.R.*, X, 973, 974.
[5] *C.R.*, X, 1005; *S.R.*, XXIII, 977-978.

The property of the soil in a free government being one of the essential rights of the collective body of the people, it is necessary, in order to avoid future disputes that the limits of the State should be ascertained with precision; and as the former temporary line between North and South Carolina was confirmed and extended by commissioners, appointed by the Legislature of the two States, agreeable to the order of the late King George II in Council, that line, and that only, should be esteemed the southern boundary of this State, that is to say, beginning on the sea at a cedar stake, at or near the mouth of Little River (being the southern extremity of Brunswick County), and running from thence a northwest course through the boundary house, which stands in thirty three degrees fifty six minutes to thirty five degrees north latitude, and from thence a west course, so far as is mentioned in the Charter of King Charles II to the late proprietors of Carolina.[6]

Thus it is seen that North Carolina ignored all previous surveys, except so much of them as extended from the seacoast toward the thirty-fifth parallel, and reverted to the original agreement entered into between the colonies in 1735. She was willing to return to South Carolina the strip of territory between 35° and 34° 49', gained as a result of the surveyors' error of 1737,[7] but demanded the thirty-fifth parallel of north latitude to her extreme western limits—that is, her ancient charter rights. This would have included within her limits the northern corner of the Catawba Lands, all of the strip gained by South Carolina by the survey west of the Catawbas, and extended North Carolina's western frontier to the Mississippi. Such a line was made unalterable, except by consent of the State Legislature, when the convention inserted the following provision: "any partial Line, without the consent of the Legislature of this State, at any Time thereafter directed or laid out in any wise, notwithstanding."[8] This policy was faithfully adhered to six years later when the Cherokee land question was under consideration by North Carolina, South Carolina, and Virginia. The North Carolina commissioners were ordered to "suffer" no cession of lands, within the State's boundaries "to any other State or person whatsoever."[9] By 1784, reference

[6] That is, to the "South Seas." F. N. Thorpe, *Federal and State Constitutions*, V, 2763.

[7] This statement is based on the assumption that North Carolina was then aware of the probability of the error, as the British authorities had intimated it and South Carolina had emphatically pointed it out.

[8] *C.R.*, X, 1005.

[9] Governor Martin to General McDowell, Colonel Sevier, and Waight-

was being made to "the old line claimed by South Carolina,"[10] which shows that the State had completely repudiated the recent surveys.

The boundary question had an important bearing on the attitude of North Carolina toward the Articles of Confederation, serving to delay her acceptance of them for a time. A motion was made to the effect that, in order to render the confederacy perpetual, it was essential that the limits of each of the States should be ascertained by the Articles of Confederation; hence, it was recommended to the Legislatures of the various states to lay before Congress a description of their boundaries, with a summary of the "grants, treaties and proofs upon which they are claimed or established."[11] When the vote was taken, both of North Carolina's representatives who were present voted in the negative.[12] On the same date, they voted against a proposition giving Congress power to fix even the western boundary of the States claiming territory to the "South Seas."[13]

These votes were cast for North Carolina only four years after the State had refused to pay the salary of even her own citizen for assisting in surveying the line from the forks of the Catawba River to the Cherokee border.[14] She would not tolerate

---

still Avery, September 20, 1782. Executive Letter Book, 1782-1785, V, 177-178. See also, "An Act to Establish a Company for Opening the Navigation of the Catawba Rivers" [sic]. A provision is inserted providing that nothing in this act shall be construed to operate against the claim regarding the southern boundary of the State as set forth in section 25 of her Bill of Rights. This act was to become effective only after South Carolina had enacted a similar law. Laws of North Carolina—1788, Chap. XVI. S.R., XXIV, 961-962.

[10] Laws of North Carolina—1788, Chap. XXIII. S.R., XXIV, 236.

[11] *Journals of the Continental Congress*, October 15, 1777; Worthington C. Ford, ed. (Washington: Government Printing Office, 1907), IX, 806. Dr. J. F. Jameson, Chief of the Division of Manuscripts, Library of Congress, who kindly examined the "Papers of the Continental Congress" for the writer, states that the parts bearing on the origin of the Articles shed no more light on North Carolina's part in the origin of the boundary article than do the *Journals*. Letter from Dr. Jameson to the writer, dated January 14, 1933.

[12] *Journals of the Continental Congress*, IX, 807. John Penn and Cornelius Harnett cast these votes. Thomas Burke, the third member from North Carolina, had left for home a few days before this action. *Letters of Members of the Continental Congress*, Edmund C. Burnett, ed. (Washington: Carnegie Institution, 1923), II, 527.

[13] *Journals of the Continental Congress*, IX, 807.

[14] *Supra*, p. 88.

the idea of filing with Congress a description of a boundary line which she consistently refused to recognize.

A fortnight later, a motion had been made to give Congress power of "deciding all disputes and differences now subsisting or that hereafter may arise between two or more states concerning boundaries, jurisdiction, or any other cause whatever. . . ." A motion was then offered to strike out this provision and instead thereof to insert the words, "the United States in Congress assembled, shall also be the last resort on appeal in all disputes and differences now subsisting, or that hereafter may arise, between two or more states concerning boundary, jurisdiction, or any other cause whatever"; and Congress shall act only on request of a State concerned.[15]

North Carolina's vote on the amended form was unanimous in the affirmative.[16] It is evident that it was satisfactory only after the clause was so worded as to leave the State in complete control of her own boundary adjustments unless voluntarily submitted to the arbitration of Congress.

The final adoption of the Articles of Confederation in this revised form seems to have precluded any controversy in North Carolina herself regarding ratification, which was carried out by the Legislature. Both houses ratified the Articles unanimously.[17]

In the case of the proposed Federal Constitution of 1787, there was no direct discussion of its provisions in their relation to the boundary controversies during the constitutional convention which was held at Hillsborough in the following summer.[18] However, the point was stressed that the Federal Court "should have cognizance of controversies between two or more states; between a state and the citizens of another state, and between citizens of the same state claiming lands under the grant of different states."[19] The fact that such a provision was included in the proposed constitution[20] evidently was satisfactory to the Convention, for in

[15] *Journals of the Continental Congress*, October 27, 1777, IX, 841-2.
[16] *Ibid.*, IX, 843.
[17] N. C. Senate Journals, April 24, 1778. Quoted in *S.R.*, XII, 599. Professor Connor states that, after the Articles were submitted to the Legislature, they were "promptly ratified." *History*, p. 497.
[18] Jonathan Elliott, ed., *The Debates in the Several State Conventions on the Adoption of the Federal Constitution, as Recommended by the General Convention at Philadelphia*, in 1787. 4 vols. (Washington, 1836), IV, *passim.* [19] Elliott, *op. cit.*, IV, 167.
[20] "Constitution of the United States," Article III, section 2.

effect the clause offered the same opportunity for settlement by Federal arbitration which was demanded and secured in the case of the Articles of Confederation. It is significant also that only ten years after North Carolina had discussed this clause, adopted the Constitution, and become a member of the Federal Union, she proposed to take her boundary dispute with South Carolina to the United States Supreme Court for final settlement.[21]

As the Cherokee boundary line played an important part in the State boundary question, particularly after the revolution, it is thought necessary to state briefly the important changes of that line.

The constant raids and murders committed by the Cherokees in retaliation for encroachments on their lands by the western settlers forced upon North Carolina and the adjoining States a settlement of their boundaries with that tribe. In addition to the line run by Governor Tryon from Reedy River to Tryon Mountain in 1767, an extension was made in the following year at the Treaty of Hard Labor from Tryon Mountain to Chiswell's mine in Virginia, thence extending northwestward to the mouth of the Great Kanawha, or to Point Pleasant at the confluence of the Great Kanawha and Ohio rivers;[22] in 1770, by the treaty of Lochabor it was altered to extend from the intersection of the previous line with the Virginia line due westward to the north fork of the Holston River, and thence northward to Point Pleasant on the Ohio.[23] Important changes in the line began again in the year following independence. Governor Caswell appointed Waightstill Avery, William Sharpe, Robert Lanier, and Joseph Winston as commissioners for North Carolina and they met the Cherokees at Long Island on Holston.[24] After prolonged negotiations, they agreed on a boundary line.[25] It was to extend from the point of intersection of the southern boundary of Virginia (to be extended) with the Cherokee-Virginia line; thence to the north bank of Holston River at the mouth of Clouds Creek; thence directly to "Chimney Top"; thence to Camp Creek or McNamies Creek on the south bank of Nollichucky River; thence southeast-

---

[21] *Infra*, p. 105.
[22] *C.R.*, VII, 851-855. See footnote no. 30, p. 97.
[23] Max Farrand, "The Indian Boundary Line," *American Historical Review*, X (1904-05), 788.   [24] *S.R.*, XV, 704.
[25] Executive Letter Book, 1777-1779, I, 160.

ward to the mountains which divide the hunting grounds of the middle settlements from those of the Overhill Cherokees.[26]

North Carolina did not run the line promptly, as promised the Indians, but in 1783 Governor Martin laid the matter before the Legislature. In the previous year, he had instructed the commissioners to demand of the Cherokees formal cession of all lands in North Carolina's chartered bounds to the Ohio and Mississippi rivers, to reduce them to circumscribed limits similar to the Catawbas, and to make a treaty accordingly.[27] However, the Legislature only authorized the governor to procure presents for the Indians to be distributed in exchange for the right of North Carolina inhabitants to settle as far west as the French Broad River, "which we propose to be the boundary line between you and us."[28] Martin then ordered McDowell and Sevier to drive off all settlers on lands west of the French Broad, which was to be a temporary line until another cession could be secured.[29] The northern portion of the line continued to move westward as successive cessions were obtained while the southern end served as a pivot, until the line extended almost east and west by 1799.[30]

North Carolina initiated efforts in 1784 toward securing recognition of the boundary line as described in her Bill of Rights. Governor Martin requested action by the General Assembly in the following words: "The Boundary line with our Sister State of South Carolina, claimed in our Bill of Rights, is now a proper subject for your consideration, to ascertain which with precision becomes daily more interesting."[31] The State felt more confident of a general adjustment of the boundaries of the Carolinas and Georgia at this time on account of the effect of the Treaty of

[26] Journal of the Commissioners, July 20, 1777. A copy of the journal will be found in *The North Carolina Historical Review*, VIII (1931), 58-116. The line is described on page 108. See also Executive Letter Book, 1777-1779, I, 333. The Indians reserved the island, and it was confirmed to them by Act of Assembly. Letter Book, 1782-1785, V, 112. *S.R.*, XIX, 201.

[27] Executive Letter Book, 1782-1785, V, 381.

[28] Governor Martin to the Cherokees, May 25, 1783. Executive Letter Book, 1782-1785, V, 212.

[29] Martin to Governor Harrison of Virginia, July 12, 1783. *Ibid.*, V, 94.

[30] An excellent map showing all the Cherokee lines may be found in the "Annual Report of the Bureau of Ethnology," 1883-84. *House Miscellaneous Documents*, 49 Cong., 2 sess., vol. 10, following last page.

[31] Governor's message to General Assembly, April 20, 1784. Letter Book, 1782-1785, V, 229.

Paris, closing the war with England. Hugh Williamson called to the attention of the governors the fact that Georgia received a great extent of territory "by the way our bounds were settled" in the treaty of 1783.[32] That treaty provided that the southern boundary of the United States from the Mississippi River eastward should be the thirty-first parallel of north latitude and the present southern boundary of Georgia.[33] This enlargement of Georgia territory, it was felt, made an extension of South Carolina westward a logical consequence.

Early in May, 1784, a House committee to whom was referred the Governor's message, recommended that a bill be passed appointing commissioners to extend and establish the North Carolina-South Carolina line.[34] The Legislature was showing unusual interest in the boundary question at that time. A similar bill was reported in the Senate in November and passed the first reading.[35] The House bill was rejected on the second reading,[36] but that body passed the Senate bill through the first reading immediately after it was endorsed and sent down by the Upper House.[37] The bill apparently failed of final passage, for the Lower House passed a similar bill through its first reading in November.[38]

All efforts to secure legislative action failed to produce an act, however, and thirteen months after his previous message, Governor Martin again "Remind[ed]" the General Assembly of the "necessity" of having the boundary line as specified in the Bill of Rights ascertained with precision at "the earliest opportunity." He made the urgent request on the grounds that the settlers should know to which State they belonged, from which they derived their land titles, and to which they should pay their taxes.[39] The Assembly did not act and Martin's administration closed with the boundary question still open.

[32] Williamson to Governor Martin, September 30, 1784. Letter Book, 1782-1785, V, 761.
[33] William MacDonald, *Documentary Source Book of American History, 1606-1913* (New York: Macmillan Co., 1916), p. 206; J. B. MacMaster, *A History of the People of the United States, From the Revolution to the Civil War*, 5 vols. (New York: D. Appleton & Co., 1883-1900), I, 3.
[34] House Committee Report, May 3, 1784. *S.R.*, XIX, 547.
[35] Senate Journal, November 8, 1784. Quoted in *S.R.*, XIX, 429.
[36] House Journal, May 29, 1784. Quoted in *S.R.*, XIX, 666.
[37] House Journal, November 8, 1784. *S.R.*, 768.
[38] House Journal, November 11, 1784. *S.R.*, XIX, 789.
[39] Governor Martin's message to General Assembly, October 26, 1785. Executive Letter Book, VII, 2.

In March of the following year, South Carolina took definite action looking toward a settlement. Her General Assembly passed an "ordinance" appointing commissioners and giving them "full and absolute power" to settle differences and fix a boundary line with North Carolina. Their acts were to be "forever binding" on South Carolina; provided always, that North Carolina commissioners be given powers fully as extensive.[40] In the summer, Governor Moultrie sent a copy of the act to Governor Caswell,[41] who promised in return to lay it before the General Assembly in November and inform him of the results.[42] The governors of the two independent States were cooperating fully in an effort to reach an agreement and a final settlement.

Bills for appointing commissioners and extending the line were frequently proposed to the North Carolina Assembly in 1789 but never reached the third reading.[43] The Assembly was not in the same spirit of cooperation which was shown by the two governors. Its members were not satisfied with South Carolina's attitude toward the constitutional provision relative to the boundary. Finally, on December 26 of the same year, a bill similar to those proposed earlier in the year was "laid over" until the next General Assembly convened, and a resolution was substituted providing that, as the Assembly had been informed of the appointment of commissioners by South Carolina to cooperate in extending the line, North Carolina should join in the plans; hence, as soon as "proper stipulations and agreements" could be made in accord with the ancient charters and the Bill of Rights, commissioners should be appointed. The governor was requested to inform the Governor of South Carolina of this action.[44]

This move later influenced the Assembly to take definite steps to cooperate with the southern government. Early in 1792, a bill was passed in accord with the above resolution, providing for appointment of commissioners to "extend" the line. Reverend James Hall, William R. Davie, Alfred Moore, and Joseph McDowell, Jr.,

[40] Executive Letter Book, 1785-1787, VII, 214; Legislative Papers, January 16, 1792; S.R., XVIII, 675. The commissioners were C. C. Pinckney, Andrew Pickens, and Pierce Butler.
[41] Richard Caswell had succeeded Martin as Governor of North Carolina in 1785.
[42] Caswell to Moultrie, September 18, 1786. Executive Letter Book, 1779-1786, II, 307; ibid., VI, 389.
[43] See House and Senate Journals for December, 1789; S.R., XXI, 346-655, passim.   [44] S.R., XVIII, 376-377.

were designated in the bill as commissioners. They were empowered to "settle and compromise" all differences existing between the two States regarding boundaries and "to fix and establish permanently" the line as far as the eastern boundary of the territory ceded by North Carolina to the United States in 1789.[45] Provided, however, that such extension did not affect the titles of any lands entered in either State. North Carolina would "ratify and confirm" whatever the commissioners should do in the matter and their actions "shall be ever binding on this State"; provided further, that section 25 of her Bill of Rights was not violated.[46]

This act caused a complete reversal of South Carolina's policy in regard to the whole question. A joint committee of her Assembly which was appointed to consider the act submitted a report in December, 1792, consisting of a review of the history of the dividing line, including the adoption of section 25 of North Carolina's Bill of Rights and the act of 1792 forbidding its violation. The committee then stated that it would be "nugatory" for South Carolina to appoint commissioners when "all discussion of right" was prohibited. It was further declared that, to appoint commissioners to act under such a provision would be to concede North Carolina's claims, and might terminate in the surrender of considerable territory of South Carolina. The governor was then requested to inform the northern government that the Assembly would not appoint commissioners until North Carolina should appoint others with "full powers" to negotiate.[47] The report was adopted as the official action of the legislative body. North Carolina's constitution had become a serious obstacle to any adjustment of the boundary problem. In his communication, Moultrie declared that the survey of 1772, in which he was a commissioner, was ratified by North Carolina, referring Governor Spaight, the new governor, to the records of 1771 and 1772, but Spaight re-

---

[45] The cession line in the region of the boundary extended along the Unaka Mountains, thence across the Hiawassee River, and thence due southward for some distance.

[46] North Carolina Legislative Papers, January 16, 1792. The preamble of this bill states that it was being passed in order to prevent disputes, and because South Carolina's act of 1786 showed a genuine desire to settle the question.

[47] Moultrie to Spaight, January 11, 1793. Executive Letter Book, 1792-1795, XI, 14. A copy of the committee's report may be found in North Carolina Legislative Papers, House of Commons, 1792; ibid., 1798, Box No. 154. Letter Book, XVII, 319.

plied with a denial of such ratification.[48] His claim was correct; the survey of 1772 was never ratified by North Carolina until 1803, as will be later shown.

It is seen, therefore, that by 1793 the two governments had assumed positions which were in direct conflict with each other, and the impasse in the negotiations resulted in a temporary check in the progress toward an agreement. In his annual message to the North Carolina Assembly in December, 1793, Richard D. Spaight merely submitted the facts contained in Governor Moultrie's letter of January 11 and made no recommendation as to a future policy for the State.[49] The General Assembly, however, showed interest in the matter, expressing a desire to have the dispute "amicably settled." From the arbitrary position maintained since the framing of her constitution, North Carolina was veering toward a policy of accommodation and compromise. The Assembly influenced the governor to enquire of South Carolina in what manner she would be satisfied to have the line extended, and what were her objections to having it extended as provided in the Bill of Rights. With such information and a knowledge of South Carolina's claims, it was stated, the Assembly could decide whether it would "with justice" to itself and to the State, agree to extend the line in a way satisfactory to the southern government. The governor added his own confident opinion that, "on a fair and cool investigation of the subject all controversy may be avoided" and the line extended to the mutual satisfaction of the States.[50] He also requested all documents relative to the survey of 1772, feeling that they "may perhaps throw some light on the subject."[51] Moultrie sent them, with the exception of the report of the commissioners, which he promised to send "at some future time."[52] This reply appears at first glance to indicate a refusal to cooperate and a desire to withhold information from the North Carolina authorities, but this does not seem to have been the case. The South Carolina governor was in Charleston at the time of writing and the report was in Columbia; hence, it seems that he was sincerely endeavoring to give all possible aid

[48] Spaight to Moultrie, March 18, 1793. Executive Letter Book, 1792-1795, XI, 28.
[49] Executive Letter Book, 1792-1795, XI, 133, 228.
[50] Spaight to Moultrie, June 4, 1794. *Ibid.*, XI, 228.
[51] Executive Book, 1792-1795, XI, 228.
[52] Moultrie to Spaight, July 22, 1794. *Ibid.*, XI, 254, 270.

to the northern governor. With regard to a satisfactory location of the line, however, South Carolina declined to commit herself. In reply to the request for such a statement, Moultrie only sent the available documents desired by North Carolina authorities and ignored the question of his State's position in the controversy.[53] Governor Spaight and the Assembly then adopted a waiting policy until the following year.

The General Assembly, with a strong desire to "expedite" a settlement, again took up the problem in 1796 and passed an act appointing commissioners to cooperate with South Carolina commissioners, should they be appointed, in establishing the line "permanently."[54]

Samuel Ashe, Governor Spaight's successor, who seems to have been very optimistic regarding the prospects of an agreement, transmitted the act to the Governor of South Carolina, expressing implicit confidence in the "ready concurrence and cooperation" of their Assembly in its purposes. There appears to be no doubt that his optimism was genuine for, after requesting that the act be immediately laid before the Assembly of the southern province, he stated that his commissioners would notify those from South Carolina of a time and place of meeting.[55] This would indicate that the northern government sincerely expected to obtain full cooperation and practical results.

Governor Ashe was to be disappointed; South Carolina would not cooperate. She only ignored his communication, and he renewed the request. He stated that North Carolina was anxious to settle the boundary issue "speedily," and that her commissioners were actively preparing to proceed with the survey. He requested information as to what had been done by the government in the matter.[56] The North Carolina Council also had begun to take an active interest in the controversy in the meantime.[57]

[53] Governor Spaight's message to General Assembly, January 7, 1795.

[54] North Carolina Legislative Papers, 1797, Box No. 149. Davie was re-appointed as one of the commissioners. Journal of the Council of State, 1796-1820 (MSS.), entry for August 15, 1798; J. G. deR. Hamilton, "William Richardson Davie: A Memoir" (James Sprunt Historical Monographs, 1907, no. 7), p. 17. Alfred Moore and Jonathan Price were also appointed commissioners. Executive Letter Book, 1799, XIII, 159.

[55] Ashe to the Governor of South Carolina, June, 1798. Executive Letter Book, 1796-1799, XII, 12; Legislative Papers, 1797, Box No. 149.

[56] North Carolina Legislative Papers, 1797, Box No. 149, entry for August 15. Letter Book, 1796-1799, XII, 16.

[57] Journals of the Council of State, 1796-1820 (MSS.), entry for August 15, 1797.

As a result of these concerted efforts, the South Carolina Assembly took the question into careful consideration, but strictly adhered to the State's old policy of refusing to act. In December, 1797, they adopted a committee report regarding the request for appointment of commissioners in which it was stated that it would "not be advisable to go into such an appointment." For reasons causing this decision, they wished to refer the North Carolina authorities to the resolution of December 19, 1792, which they desired to reiterate.[58]

Despite this curt reply, North Carolina continued for a time to pursue a policy of compromise. The State was not only anxious to maintain amicable relations with her southern neighbor and keep the negotiations on a dignified plane, but she was handicapped by her inability to locate the necessary documents bearing on the controversy. In 1798, after her governor had urged action in his message to the General Assembly, it was recommended that, since they could not locate the papers and "ancient documents" supposedly filed in the office of the Secretary of State, and were therefore unable to determine the grounds for North Carolina's claims, the governor "enter into a friendly discussion of our rights" with the Governor of South Carolina and lay the results before the next General Assembly for consideration.[59]

Pursuant to the wishes of the Legislature, Governor William R. Davie endeavored to carry out a policy of conciliation and mutual agreement. But his desire for conciliation did not prevent his being firm or even impatient at times with South Carolina's attitude, especially since the unfriendly resolutions were passed in December, 1792. In March, 1799, he wrote to the Governor of South Carolina reviewing the conciliatory laws of the respective States in 1786 and 1792, and comparing them with the resolutions of the latter year, which he declared were "apparently predicated upon views evidently different from those which dictated the former measure, and which seem to be calculated to create difficulties and to form obstructions" to the attainment of the object which South Carolina had so much at heart in 1786.[60] Regardless of the past, however, he urged a friendly compromise for the following reasons: first, the authority under which South Carolina

[58] Governor Charles Pinckney to Governor of North Carolina, December 26, 1797. Legislative Papers, 1797, Box No. 149; *ibid.*, No. 154.
[59] North Carolina Legislative Papers, 1798, Box No. 154.
[60] Executive Letter Book, 1799, XIII, 41.

based her claim to the line had never been admitted by North Carolina; second, the entire lines of 1764 and 1772 had been held inaccurate by both states; and, third, as a large part of the line (from the end of the survey of 1772 westward) had never been extended, an agreement was obviously necessary. He expressed a keen desire to aid in "any manner in my power" in effecting an object of "so much importance to both states." Thus the new governor of North Carolina both saw the great importance of a settlement and was willing to go to any reasonable length to bring it about. The situation again looked hopeful.

Governor Davie proposed as an "amicable" beginning that the commissioners ascertain the latitude of the line then claimed by South Carolina and that called for by the charter of Charles II and the Constitution of North Carolina, which information would make the nature and extent of the respective claims "perfectly understood" and, doubtless, easily settled. As shown above, the charter would extend the State's boundary to the "South Seas" and the constitutional provision would make the thirty-fifth parallel mandatory for her southern boundary. Davie added that, if necessary and proper, a provisional line might be established which could later be ratified by North Carolina. He then showed his determination to have such a provisional line run by stating that, when his commissioners had set a time and place of meeting to take observations, he would notify the South Carolina governor who, if he desired, might appoint a person to attend and thus be convinced that the observations made by the commissioners were accurate and their proceedings correct.[61]

After long patience and fruitless efforts to secure a cooperative survey, Davie, who was acting in the dual capacity of commissioner and governor, informed the North Carolina Council of the status of the controversy. He reported his inability to persuade South Carolina to proceed with the line or even to appoint commissioners, stating that "they have . . . evaded the measure on some pretense or other," and therefore the commissioners felt it their duty under the act to proceed alone, secure accurate information regarding the line and thus enable the Assembly, if deemed wise, to make some definite proposal to the southern government for settling the dispute. He also stated to the Council that his

[61] Governor Davie to the Governor of South Carolina, March 22, 1799. Executive Letter Book, 1799, XIII, 41.

duties as governor were incompatible with those of a commissioner and suggested that a commissioner be appointed in his stead.[62] The Council recommended such an appointment. About the same time, Davie appointed Wallace Alexander as commissioner in the place of Alfred Moore, resigned.[63]

North Carolina, impatient with evasion, adopted a stronger policy and displayed an increasingly more independent attitude. Davie and Price agreed to proceed to take the desired readings alone in the fall of 1799 in order to enable them to state the facts "precisely" to the Legislature or to "any tribunal," in case it became necessary to take "compulsive measures" with a sister state.[64] This was a veiled threat to take the dispute to the United States Supreme Court. Inability to secure proper instruments in time, and other causes, however, prevented them from proceeding in the fall as planned.

The North Carolina Assembly again took up the question and passed a resolution to appoint an agent to manage the case for the State. They had lost the valuable services of Davie. Before his term expired in 1799, he resigned as governor and went abroad as Commissioner to France, under appointment of President Adams. Benjamin Williams succeeded him.[65] Measures relative to the boundary had failed during Davie's absence abroad, and on his return Governor Williams requested him to accept the above agency.[66] Davie accepted the position.[67]

Governor Williams pursued the same policy adopted by his predecessor, that of independent action with an invitation to the southern government to cooperate. He accordingly notified Governor John Drayton of South Carolina that the commissioners planned to meet on March 18, 1800, at the termination of the survey of 1764 near the Salisbury Road; that they aimed to determine accurately the thirty-fifth parallel and carry into effect the act of 1796. Drayton was invited to appoint persons to attend,

[62] Davie to Council of State, August 15, 1799. Journals of the Council of State, 1796-1800.
[63] Executive Letter Book, 1799, XIII, 159.
[64] Governor Davie to Wallace Alexander, August 27, 1799. Executive Letter Book, 1799, XIII, 159.
[65] Ibid., 1800-1802, XIV, 329; J. G. deR. Hamilton, "William Richardson Davie: A Memoir," pp. 18-20.
[66] Williams to Davie, January 22, 1800. Letter Book, XIV, 329.
[67] Legislative Papers, November 18, 1801, Box No. 189.

that his State might be convinced of the correctness of the proceedings.[68]

Drayton was embarrassed by the flagrant neglect of his predecessor, Rutledge, to exercise the common official courtesies toward North Carolina authorities. The latter had refused even to submit the dispute to his Legislature. Drayton tried to excuse this ungenerous refusal to cooperate on the grounds of Rutledge's failing health, pressing duties in organizing the South Carolina courts, and "other accidents of humanity."[69] The truth was plain, however, though Drayton sent papers in an attempt to prove that their Assembly had "always been ready to consider this business." He declared that the government would adhere to the policy pursued ever since the Revolution, and that the decision had been "calm & accommodating." He frankly stated that the decision made in December, 1786, would "direct my conduct on the present occasion."[70] Nevertheless, he declared, South Carolina was anxious to adjust the dispute on grounds of "mutual justice" and "perfect harmony"; and commissioners should be appointed with full powers as soon as those of North Carolina were given powers of "equal plenitude." Until then, he added, the South Carolina authorities "must & do" insist on the present boundary, and under no circumstances should they allow it to be encroached upon or altered by any State or power whatever.[71]

North Carolina adhered tenaciously to the claims expressed in her Bill of Rights. It was repeated that this document simply stated the facts contained in the charter of Charles II, which was all North Carolina was asking. Governor Williams complained that the dispute had been "less regarded by the State of South Carolina than is conceived the magnitude of the question merited."[72]

By the close of the century there seems to have been considerable confusion in North Carolina in regard to the charter of Charles II to the Proprietors. It had been referred to so often regarding the western limits of the State that the impression was rather general that it specified the thirty-fifth parallel as the dividing line; whereas, it contains no reference to that parallel, as

[68] Governor Williams to Governor Drayton, January 25, 1800. Executive Letter Book, XIV, 32.
[69] Drayton to Williams, February 8, 1800. *Ibid.*, XIV, 40.
[70] *Ibid.*, XIV, 40.
[71] Drayton to Williams, February 8, 1800. Executive Letter Book, 1800-1802, XIV, 40.
[72] Williams to Drayton, February 21, 1800. *Ibid.*, XIV, 66.

has been shown. The charter should have been examined with meticulous care. The State's claim would have been much more effective had it been based on the agreement of 1735, which was made by commissioners of both provinces, accepted by both governments, and approved by the British authorities. It specified the thirty-fifth parallel as the line "to the South Seas" and could have been cited as the action of both governments, just as they were now taking action. It appears that, in the haze of years, the significance of this mutual agreement had been lost sight of. It is true that the surveys of 1764 and 1772 were also mutually made, but they involved errors of latitude, which errors would have been effectively emphasized in the requests for an adjustment. North Carolina authorities had nothing to gain by referring to an old charter which was wholly inapplicable to the case.

At this point North Carolina, in her anxiety to reach a friendly solution, modified her claim. The State disclaimed any desire to encroach upon South Carolina territory and expressed a disposition to acquiesce in the boundary as far as it had been run, "whatever its loss of territory may be." It was the undetermined portion of the line which the State desired to have established, it was said, in doing which, in accord with the charter rights, there need be no fear of encroachment. For both States it must eventually extend from the thirty-fifth degree due westward. This, of course, would necessitate an extension of the line in a southerly direction from 35° 13', the latitude of the western termination of the survey of 1772, to the thirty-fifth parallel. Governor Williams refused to grant a request to postpone the meeting of the commissioners until the Legislature of South Carolina met in regular session on the grounds that a delay would be against the State's interest.[73]

Even after Williams's proposal to accept the surveys as already made and run southward to the thirty-fifth parallel, the North Carolina commissioners expected the deadlock to continue and the southern commissioners to refuse to attend the meeting. Jonathan Price, one of the commissioners, said, "I have little reason to expect" the South Carolinians to attend.[74] Prospects for a mutual agreement were dark. South Carolina likewise was giving up hope of reaching an adjustment through negotiations be-

[73] Williams to Drayton, February 21, 1800. *Executive Letter Book,* 1800-1802, XIV, 66.
[74] Price to Governor Williams, February 28, 1800. *Ibid.,* XIV, 87.

tween the States, and was turning to a new policy. She decided to cut off all negotiations for an agreement until North Carolina should alter the objectionable section of her constitution. "Until that time," the governor made plain, "it will be a matter unattainable; and even unpleasant to persist in."[75]

Drayton then attacked the most pregnable part of Williams's argument—the relation of the charter of Charles II to North Carolina's claim to the thirty-fifth parallel. With regard to chartered rights to that line, he denied that they existed and declared the rights of his own State to the line of 1772 from the forks of the Catawba. The basis or the claim was described on various grounds. In the first place, the royal instructions of 1730 authorized a survey, and they were given after purchase of Carolina by the Crown; North Carolina was accepting the surveys of 1735, 1737, and 1764, which were run under authority of said instructions; the survey of 1772, which North Carolina was contesting, was made under the same authority—why was it not as acceptable? Secondly, Georgia was separated from Carolina by authority of the Crown, although within the limits of the charter of Charles II, and the legality of that separation had never been questioned—why should not the line of 1772 be equally settled? It was sanctioned by the King in Council while the Carolinas were still under his jurisdiction. Thirdly, the commissioners of both provinces signed their names to the plats which were interchanged. Fourthly, South Carolina had constantly enjoyed governmental rights to that line ever since 1772 in all branches—granting lands, holding elections, serving processes from courts of justice, and a variety of other acts of ownership and jurisdiction. Hence, "nothing of it can be surrendered, or even called in question but by the Supreme power of this State, or by such other power, as the Constitution of the United States hath appointed. To that alone it can only be refered," unless section 25 of the Bill of Rights is repealed and the commissioners thereby given a free hand.[76] The suggestion to

---

[75] Drayton to Williams, February 28, 1800. *Ibid.*, XIV, 79.
[76] Drayton to Williams, February 28, 1800. Executive Letter Book, XIV, 79. This letter is one of the strongest written during the history of the controversy, approaching that in which Governor Dobbs taught Governor Glen of South Carolina that North Carolina was no longer a mere appendage of the southern government. Drayton had penned a masterly letter until in the latter part he lost his head and engaged in undignified threats and abuse which somewhat compromised the effect of

appeal to the United States Supreme Court for a final decision was a new policy for South Carolina, though North Carolina had already considered such action, as shown above.

With South Carolina's arbitrary stand, North Carolina altered her method of obtaining an adjustment of the dispute. In his annual message to the General Assembly, Governor Williams reviewed the correspondence with Governor Drayton, describing it as void of a "single trait of an accomodating disposition," and recommended "a resort to the Constitutional Tribunal" as the best means of settling the dispute.[77]

The State then definitely committed itself to settlement by judicial processes instead of negotiation. The Legislature followed the Governor's advice and passed a resolution requesting him to take measures for immediately bringing the matter before the United States Supreme Court for "determination." He was fur-

---

his able letter on North Carolina authorities. It shows how disagreeable the relations between the two governments became at times over this controversy. A portion of the heated section, largely paraphrased, ran in the following strain: "Far more" might be said than you and I might wish to discuss "in matters of such contested nature." If North Carolina is determined to proceed in contesting our boundary, I request that it be done in the manner provided in the Constitution of the United States, and not by sending her commissioners *ex parte* to run a line through "our State." ". . . no encroachment of this kind will be allowed. And I am now reduced to the unpleasant necessity of hereby giving you notice, that should your Commissioners attempt to enter the Territory of this State for the purpose of running a Line, they and all persons aiding or assisting them will be repelled from the same. . . . In candor I think it proper to give you this information; & farther to inform you, it will be so done, in consequence of my particular orders to that effect." Hence, I hope North Carolina will not "provoke a conduct on our part, and in our own State, which may lead to much michief; and by which your commissioners may Suffer in their persons. . . ." The North Carolina authorities will "undoubtedly" be held "accountable to the peace of the Union." Executive Letter Book, 1800-1802, XIV, 85. Governor Williams replied that the manner in which the South Carolina governor had stated his demands "superceeds" the necessity of any remarks from himself on Drayton's observations and conclusions. He simply notified the governor that he would postpone the meeting of the commissioners who were to act with any appointed by South Carolina, and advise resort to the court rather than to "embroil ourselves with a Sister State however unaccomodating her conduct. . . ." Williams to Drayton, March 10, 1800. *Ibid.*, XIV, 97-98. Governor Williams declined to "hazard . . . the dignity of the State," and deferred the meeting of the commissioners until the next Legislature.

[77] Annual Message to North Carolina General Assembly, November 19, 1800. Executive Letter Book, XIV, 272.

ther requested to appoint a "principal Manager" to conduct the case, with power to employ assistant counsel.[78]

On the same day, in Charleston, the South Carolina Legislature took action remarkably similar to that of North Carolina. After again declining to appoint commissioners for the same reasons as formerly, the governor was requested to invite the North Carolina executive to institute suit in the United States Supreme Court for final adjudication. Authority was given to appoint a competent commissioner to defend the State's interests in any suit the northern government might bring, and, if necessary, to prosecute any suit against North Carolina. Power was also given to employ assistant counsel.[79]

Governor Drayton transmitted the information to Governor Williams as requested, with the invitation to institute suit. His communication, however, contained a note of conciliation when he renewed his offer to appoint commissioners at any time North Carolina would give her own representatives full power to negotiate. He added that the dispute had already continued too long between friendly States.[80]

It is difficult to understand why the contestants did not take advantage of a practical condition stated in section 25 of the Bill of Rights. It provided that no alteration should be made in any portion of the line "without the consent of the Legislature."[81] Much of the heated argument and unfriendly correspondence could have been averted had both States been willing to allow their commissioners to have negotiated an agreement, with mutual concessions, if necessary, providing that its stipulations were of no force or effect until considered and formally ratified by the Legislatures of the two States. The fact that no other method than prior agreement could produce an adjustment by mutual consent had been fully demonstrated by the close of the century, and the two States should have resorted to negotiation and tentative agree-

[78] *Ibid.*, XIV, 304. This resolution, definitely altering the State's policy on procedure, was adopted December 20, 1800.

[79] North Carolina Legislative Papers, 1800, Box No. 171; Executive Letter Book, XIV, 328. It was also directed that the Attorney-General take steps to "perpetuate" the testimony of General Moultrie, the only surviving South Carolina Commissioner on the survey of 1772. Generals Pinckney, Pickens, and Anderson, Colonel Hunter, Mr. Dessausser, Major Pierce Butler, and Mr. Falconer were appointed to defend the State's claims.

[80] Drayton to Williams, December 31, 1800. Executive Letter Book, XIV, 312. [81] *Supra*, p. 93.

ment pending legislative action, rather than for each to have demanded full concession of the other's claims prior to consent of the Legislature.

Ex-Governor Davie, who had consented to act as the State's agent, followed the policy of instituting suit in the Supreme Court. He endeavored to collect all documents on the question in order to determine whether the evidence was sufficient to present the case effectively before a judicial tribunal, even contemplating procuring additional records from Great Britain.[82] Governor Williams thoroughly appreciated the important issues at stake. When commissioning Davie as "sole manager" to conduct the case before the Supreme Court, he reminded him that the territorial rights, reputation, and dignity of the State were involved in the controversy.[83]

General Davie approached the problem with intelligence and courage. His plan for establishing the truth in regard to the whole westward line was logical, scientific, and thorough. He proposed, since it was generally supposed that the commissioners in 1764 had not reached the thirty-fifth parallel, that observations should be made at three vital points: namely, at the eastern end of the survey of 1764, at its termination on the Salisbury Road, and at the forks of the Catawba River where the survey of 1772 was begun. He further stated that the commissioners in 1764 were supposed to have inclined considerably southward as they proceeded westward, and he was positive they inclined too far northward in 1772 in ascending the Catawba River to its forks.[84] It was absolutely necessary, he declared, to know the exact difference between these erroneous observations and the time readings before the territorial claims of the State could be effectively stated before a court. It was therefore suggested that two of the North Carolina commissioners be directed to make observations at the three points suggested. Davie recommended that, if they were

[82] Davie to Governor Williams, February 2, 1801. Executive Letter Book, 1800-1802, XIV, 337.
[83] Williams to Davie, February 24, 1801. *Ibid.*, XIV, 361.
[84] Davie to Governor Williams, March 13, 1801. Executive Letter Book, 1800-1802, XIV, 377. Davie was under an erroneous impression as to the survey of 1764 inclining slightly southward. Dr. Joseph Caldwell took observations to determine the facts and he made no reference to a southward incline. See his report of 1807, Executive Letter Book, XVI, 233. Moreover, all modern standard maps indicate that the survey inclined slightly northward. Davie was correct in regard to the line of 1772, however.

incapable, Harris of Halifax, a competent scientist, should be employed.[85] General Davie further revealed a plan to go to South Carolina in order to secure all possible information bearing on the controversy, a mission which later revolutionized the policy of North Carolina relative to the boundary question.

The North Carolina Governor then took up the boundary question with energy and determination. He ordered the commissioners to carry out Davie's wishes regarding the ascertaining of latitudes and to meet at the first point suggested in May, 1801, as "no delay or postponement whatever can be admitted, under the existing circumstances of this business." Governor Williams expected both Davie and the commissioners to meet with stubborn resistance and obstructions on the part of Governor Drayton, Williams gave Davie a letter for use in case Drayton "now objects even to the making the observations with respect to the latitude."[86] The commissioners were told that if "any difficulty [should] arise" they must report it. Great tact was employed in an effort to prevent such difficulties. Williams wrote Drayton that the desired observations were essential if North Carolina was to be able to state her case clearly and fully, presumably before the court. The South Carolina Governor was invited to send commissioners also if he so desired.

Williams' suspicions of resistance by the southern authorities must have been unfounded, for it appears that Drayton not only raised no objections to the plans, but promptly prepared to send commissioners to attend the proceedings.[87]

Preparations to proceed with a settlement were earnestly made by Governor Williams and General Davie. The latter set out to establish the fact of approval of the agreement of 1735 by the British authorities from evidence in the Raleigh documents. However, he reported failure, though he was convinced that, since the

---

[85] Charles Wilson Harris, graduate of Princeton, Professor of Mathematics and Astronomy at the University of North Carolina from 1795 until his then recent establishment of the practice of law at Halifax. H. M. Wagstaff, ed., "The Harris Letters" (James Sprunt Historical Publications, XIV, 1916, no. 1); Kemp P. Battle, *History of the University of North Carolina from its Beginning to the Death of President Swain*, 1789-1868, 2 vols. (Raleigh: Edwards & Broughton, 1907, 1912), I, 50, 168. The governor authorized Davie to engage Harris' services. Executive Letter Book, XIV, 382.

[86] Williams to Davie, March 20, 1801. Letter Book, XIV, 380.

[87] See Letter Book, XIV, 401-2.

province endeavored to carry it out as late as 1764, the King in Council had certainly approved it.[88] He was also unable to find documentary proof of the official appointment of Wyley, Mackay, Pawley, and Moore, commissioners of the two provinces on that survey. Upon such proofs, he said, rested the State's claim to the line of 1764.

With regard to the appointment of these commissioners, it was not so important in 1801 whether or not the Legislatures of the two provinces formally appointed or approved them. The fact remained that the governors had received royal instructions to appoint commissioners to extend the boundary, had appointed them with the advice of their respective councils,[89] and both provinces had joined in bearing the expense of the survey. Tryon had been instructed by the Board of Trade before leaving England to cooperate in the survey of 1764. Though Tryon did not arrive in the province in time to cooperate in the survey, he accepted the finished work and advised the Board of Trade that the line as run thus far was the best for a final boundary.[90] The British authorities accepted this view. Davie was correct regarding formal approval of the commissioners by the respective governments; however, the whole procedure was in nature official. It must be borne in mind that for half a century before 1776 the Carolinas were royal property.

But technicalities aside, there were more fundamental reasons for the difference of opinion regarding the boundary surveys. By 1800 North Carolina had progressed too far in her political philosophy to think of her territory in terms of Crown property long enough to concede the proper weight to pre-revolutionary royal acts. Those acts were valid in law, but to North Carolinians at the close of the century that which had not been done or approved by the sovereign people could rightly be called in question. South Carolina, on the other hand, had been the favored province and it was easier for her to defend British acts. Moreover, she was right in her theory that a royal province was subject to royal orders.

North Carolina, through Davie as agent, was contesting the whole proceedings of the survey of 1772 on the grounds of ille-

[88] The agreement of 1735 was approved in London, as has been shown. *Supra*, p. 39.
[89] *S.R.*, XI, 207; Executive Letter Book, XXX, 339.
[90] *C.R.*, VII, 156.

gality. Documents were not to be found of any description authorizing this survey.[91] At the same time, the State was eagerly looking forward to receiving the facts which her commissioners were soon to procure at the designated points. Disappointment and delay again resulted, however, when Commissioner Price of North Carolina failed to appear with the necessary surveyor's instruments in time to make the observations in May, thus "put[ting] a stop to the business for the present."[92] The State had her own representative to blame for the loss of this opportunity of accurately locating the line with the cooperation of South Carolina.

By mid-summer, the southern government had reversed its policy of cooperation in determining the true latitude at the three proposed points. The North Carolina authorities were informed that the latitude was not the "matter" on which South Carolina's claim was based, but upon a "stronger tenure"; and that she would not cooperate in the work unless the Supreme Court so directed. Hence, any observations thereafter made "will only be considered by this State as Exparte; and by no means as binding upon this State, in the trial of the Cause." It was then pointed out that the commissioners appointed by the South Carolina Legislature were not authorized to ascertain and fix the boundary line "but only to take care of her Interests, & to defend her against any suit North Carolina might bring," or to prosecute any necessary suit against her relative to boundary. The South Carolina governor expressed a strong desire to hasten the hearing before the United States Supreme Court.[93]

While preparations were being made to make the proposed observations,[94] Davie went to South Carolina for the purpose of collecting all available documents bearing on the controversy. He planned to return in December, when he would desire to inform

[91] Davie to Williams, March 25, 1801. Executive Letter Book, XIV, 394. The Secretary of State reported lack of evidence that an Assembly was held from 1771 to 1773 (*Ibid.*, XIV, 405-407), and the Clerk of the House of Commons stated that he did not have the records and papers of the Assemblies held before the Revolution. *Ibid.*, XIV, 422.

[92] Williams to Price, April 2, 1801. Letter Book, XIV, 398. It was then planned to take the desired observations early in the summer.

[93] Drayton to Williams, July 16, 1801. Executive Letter Book, XIV, 428, 432. Governor Williams sent this letter to Davie to read and plan his next step.

[94] Harris of Halifax was now expected to take the readings. *Ibid.*, XIV, 438.

the Legislature, through a confidential committee, of all the facts obtained relative to the dispute. He desired to secure the approval of his plans and future policy by such a committee before proceeding further.[95] In the following month, on request of the governor, the Legislature appointed the desired committee, leaving to its discretion the question of guarding the information.[96]

In the meantime, South Carolina was making strenuous efforts to build up the strongest possible case for presentation before the Federal tribunal. All evidence in the State in any manner bearing on the dispute was collected, and the governor then turned to the British records. He procured from London certified papers, instructions to governors, statements from colonial agents, and various other materials calculated to support the position of his State. He then reported to the Legislature that he had collected materials which would "go far, in establishing the claims of this State. . . ."[97] The governor, apparently impatient, informed the Legislators that they had appointed too many commissioners, which resulted in delaying action. He closed by predicting that the Supreme Court would order a new survey.

The researches of General Davie in South Carolina resulted in the discovery of documentary sources which produced a complete reversal in the policy of North Carolina. He convinced the above-mentioned legislative committee that, by the agreement of April, 1735, South Carolina could rightly claim all of the territory claimed by both the Catawba and Cherokee Indians; and that the same agreement became the basis of North Carolina's territorial rights and all later proceedings relative to the line. He submitted documents relative to the survey of 1772, particularly the royal instructions of June 7, 1772,[98] which were "peremptory

[95] Davie to Williams, October 26, 1801. Executive Letter Book, XIV, 438.

[96] Legislative Papers, 1801, Box No. 182. Ashe, Spaight, Moore, Lacy, Alexander, and Bloodworth composed the committee. Davie had then returned from South Carolina.

[97] Governor's Message to South Carolina Legislature, November 23, 1801. S. C. "Executive Journal, September 18, 1801-1802 Inclusive," p. 20. Drayton was handicapped as were the North Carolina authorities with regard to materials in his own State. In this message he complained to the Legislature that there had been no preservation of Executive Journals in the State since the Revolution, but added that he was filing his own; and he implied that he hoped it would be continued by his successors. Many papers in the office of the Secretary of State, he said, had been lost through carelessness.

[98] Davie later found the record of protests of the North Carolina As-

and conclusive," declaring the line thus far surveyed and that to be run in the same year to be the final boundary. He further convinced the committee that it was under that order alone that the State had been entitled theretofore to claim the whole of Tennessee, as well as a large portion of its western frontier. The committee also considered the royal orders as conclusive and were satisfied it was to the best interest of the State to recognize and support those orders.

In the face of these facts and thus convinced, the committee decided on two major aims: first, to lead the Legislature to alter the plan adopted by the previous Assembly of appealing to the Supreme Court; and second, to seek a settlement at the least possible expense, namely, by endeavoring to substitute the Catawba River as the line from the Waxhaws to its forks instead of the old and vanishing Salisbury Road and the various directions of the Catawba Indian boundary. They proposed then to extend the line of 1772 westward to the Cherokee boundary.[99]

The report sufficiently impressed the Legislature to lead to the adoption of a conciliatory resolution as a foundation for settlement by negotiation. Davie had convinced his State she was wrong, both legally and from the standpoint of her own interest; and though it meant embarrassment, the Legislature courageously reversed its stand. A bill to repeal the first section of the act of 1796—that referring to a suit in the Federal court—was passed ten days later.[100]

The resolutions were laid before the Legislature of South Carolina by the governor with a suggestion that the State should not compromise.[101] Five weeks later, he informed Governor Williams of his action, but added that no law or resolution had been adopted, nor did he believe there would be until the objectionable section of the Bill of Rights was repealed. He then renewed the request to proceed with the case in the Supreme Court, expressing a conviction that it was the only method by which the dispute

---

sembly to Governor Martin in regard to the survey of 1772. Davie to John Steele, January 22, 1806, Kemp P. Battle, ed., "Davie Letters" (James Sprunt Historical Publications, no. 7), p. 63.

[99] Davie to Williams, February 4, 1802. North Carolina Legislative Papers, 1802, Box No. 192; Executive Letter Book, XIV, 537.

[100] N. C. Legislative Papers, 1801, Box No. 184.

[101] Governor's Message to the Legislature, December 10, 1801. S. C. Executive Journal, September 18, 1801 to 1802, inclusive, p. 65; Executive Letter Book, XIV, 518-519.

could be adjusted. Drayton again lost his temper and angrily exclaimed: "As to any compromise, this State will have nothing to do with it: for it knows its rights to the boundaries in question; and is prepared to support the same. . . ."[102]

Governor Williams maintained his self-control and the dignity of the office by simply commenting to Davie concerning the letter that the "manner and substance of it are such as I had ceased to expect; at this stage of our business with them." He added that an amicable settlement was hopeless and asked Davie's opinion as to further steps, "if indeed it can now . . . be proper to take any." Davie was then advised that, if he also felt that further efforts were useless, to submit his account for payment.[103] It appeared that the controversy would be dropped for a time, but Davie replied encouragingly. He advised the governor not to allow Drayton's letter to worry him—that it was just like some of his former heated and ill-advised ones. Furthermore, South Carolina probably declined to act on North Carolina's latest resolutions until her Assembly could learn what was thought were the "real views" of the State.[104]

The refusal of the South Carolina government to take advantage of the concessions and the spirit of compromise contained in the latest resolutions of the North Carolina Legislature, while professing anxiety to compromise, plainly irritated the latter, and their attitude was correspondingly reflected for a time. Even Governor Williams became more firm and wrote Governor Drayton that a "decent respect" for a sister State prevented any remark on the propriety or consistency of such unexpected conduct by South Carolina. In reply to the suggestion to hasten the case to the Supreme Court, and to the refusal to have anything to do with a compromise, Williams gave notice that North Carolina would adopt such means as she deemed proper; that she was sole judge of what was best for her own interests; and that the mode and time of acting "will not perhaps be connected with any views of accommodation as it respects South Carolina" who had through you "unequivocally disclaimed every sentiment of that kind." It was lamentable, he said, that such a dispute should be left for

[102] S. C. Executive Journal, January 9, 1802.
[103] Williams to Davie, January 22, 1802. Executive Letter Book, XIV, 536.
[104] Davie to Williams, February 4, 1802. Executive Letter Book, XIV, 527-529.

settlement by a method in which the conciliatory spirit "may have the least share in the transaction."[105]

Time cooled the passions of the two States, however, and by the close of the year 1802 proceedings were more calm. The governor's annual message to the South Carolina Legislature contained no reference to the boundary dispute,[106] and on the following day, in a brief special message, Drayton simply submitted all correspondence with Williams relative to the controversy.

In North Carolina, after the governor had advised new efforts at conciliation, the Legislature defeated an attempt to secure the adoption of a resolution authorizing the governor to appoint two competent commissioners "to discuss, adjust, and finally settle" the contested line with any representatives South Carolina might appoint.[107]

In the fall of 1803, proceedings were initiated which resulted in the passage of an act which afforded the possibility of a settlement. The spirit of South Carolina's actions and correspondence was changed. Her Legislature instructed the new governor, James B. Richardson, to broach the northern governor anew with the boundary question and to assure him of the "ardent desire" of the State to have the dispute "amicably adjusted" with her sister State; and that it was hoped North Carolina would provide for commissioners who would be entirely free to negotiate, since the Bill of Rights had theretofore precluded such negotiation. Assurance was given that South Carolina would respond heartily.[108] Governor Turner[109] submitted this communication to the General Assembly, as requested, stating that he would "be glad if the General Assembly can fix on any mode by which this matter can be finally adjusted."[110] It was plain that his policy would be one of accommodation. The Legislature, appreciative of South Carolina's apparently friendly communication, passed an act appointing commissioners.[111] The act summarized was as follows:

[105] Williams to Drayton, February 4, 1802. *Ibid.*, XIV, 548-51; Legislative Papers, 1802, Box No. 192.
[106] Annual Message to South Carolina Legislature, November 23, 1802. S. C. Executive Journal, September 18, 1801 to 1802 inclusive, pp. 225-233.
[107] North Carolina Legislative Papers, 1802, Box No. 192.
[108] Executive Letter Book, 1803-1805, XV, 80.
[109] James Turner was elected governor in the fall of 1802, after John B. Ashe, the governor-elect, died before taking office.
[110] Annual Message to N. C. Legislature. Letter Book, XV, 150.
[111] Governor Turner states that South Carolina's changed attitude was the cause of this action by North Carolina. Turner to Richardson, December 18, 1803. *Ibid.*, XV, 195.

Whereas, all former laws have failed to secure a settlement of the boundary question:

I. Be it enacted, that three commissioners shall be appointed by the Legislature and commissioned by the governor to cooperate with commissioners appointed by South Carolina, at such time and place as the governors shall mutually agree upon and direct. They shall have all power to settle all disputes, differences, and claims existing between the two States, and to establish permanently and mark their mutual boundary line to the eastern border of the territory ceded by North Carolina to the United States. Provided, however, that such extension of the line shall not affect land titles entered in either State. This State will ratify and confirm all acts of said commissioners, which acts shall be binding on the State.

II. Said commissioners shall receive forty shillings a day and traveling expenses.

III. The governor shall be empowered to fill vacancies in said commission; he shall also transmit a copy of this Act to the Governor of South Carolina, with a request that the State cooperate without delay in effecting the above purpose.

IV. The governor shall issue warrants on the Treasury to carry this Act into effect.

V. All former Acts regarding the said boundary are hereby repealed.[112]

Thus was enacted a law which was neutral and silent regarding section 25 of North Carolina's Bill of Rights. It gave Governor Turner "great and wellgrounded hopes" that it would be the means of a friendly settlement. He requested Governor Richardson to lay it before the South Carolina Legislature immediately, enabling them to make any necessary provisions for joining in carrying out its purposes. After such action, he said, he would cooperate in setting a time and place of meeting for the commissioners. He added that he had appointed William R. Davie, James Wellborn, and John Moore as commissioners.[113]

Cooperation from South Carolina was not immediate, however. Richardson ignored the communication but finally after a second request, replied that he would lay it before the Legislature

---

[112] *The Public Acts of the General Assembly of North Carolina*, 2 vols. (Newbern: Martin & Ogden, 1804), II, 214-15. It will be noted that the Acts of 1791 and 1796 were repealed by this Act.

[113] Turner to Richardson, December 18, 1803. Executive Letter Book, XV, 195. Their commissions may be found in *ibid.*, XV, 197.

at the extra session in the following May. He expressed perfect confidence that measures then would be taken to "close the difference of boundary."[114]

A new issue entered into the proceedings at this point which served to obstruct the progress expected under the Act of 1803. It was the appearance of a new boundary dispute between North Carolina and the State of Georgia over territory in the same general section. This controversy will be treated later in this study, but as it forces itself upon the attention of the Carolinas at this point in their own dispute, it is necessary here to introduce the subject in its relation thereto. Suffice it to say that Georgia had acquired the territory along the southern border of North Carolina in the region of Buncombe County.

At the beginning of the year 1804, a prominent citizen of Buncombe County wrote to the Governor of North Carolina expressing fear that the law of 1803 for extending the line of 1772 would prove "ineffectual" in its purpose because Georgia had intercepted a portion of the line by organizing a new county called Walton, in the southern portion of Buncombe.[115] Since the North Carolina commissioners could proceed only in cooperation with the South Carolina commissioners, according to the act, he saw no possibility of an extension of the line farther than the southern commissioners would agree to go.[116]

The North Carolina Legislature, reminded by the governor of the old dispute,[117] recognized the difficulty and took immediate action. The Act of 1803 was amended to empower the governor and his successor to enter into any "compact or agreement" with the legislative or executive authorities of South Carolina and Georgia for establishing and running the dividing line between said states and North Carolina.[118] Nothing in this amended act was to affect that of 1803, however, except to extend its scope.

[114] Richardson to Turner, May 17, 1804. Executive Letter Book, XV, 276, 257, 263.

[115] Walton County was organized by the Legislature of Georgia, December 10, 1803. Georgia Journals of the House of Representatives, 1803-1805 (MSS.), pp. 95-121, entries for December 7 and 10, 1803. These manuscripts are in the Department of Archives and History, Atlanta.

[116] Joshua Williams to Governor Turner, January 30, 1804. Executive Letter Book, XV, 230.

[117] Governor Turner's Message to Legislature, November 19, 1804. *Ibid.*, XV, 384.

[118] *Laws of the State of North Carolina*, 2 vols. (Potter, Taylor and Yancey, eds., 1821), II, 1013.

NORTH CAROLINA BOUNDARY DISPUTES 121

This provision is very important, for its aim undoubtedly was to leave in the act the clause protecting land titles.

The South Carolina Legislature, during the special session in May, took no action on the Act of 1803, as promised by the governor, even if the act was considered.[119] At the regular session of that year, however, the Legislature passed an act in December providing for the appointment of commissioners by the governor to adjust the differences between the States through conference with commissioners of North Carolina. Any settlement reached was to be "binding and obligatory" on South Carolina when ratified. It was provided, however, that nothing in the act should impugn South Carolina's "right" to any disputed territory until the objectionable section 25 of the Bill of Rights should be altered to enable the North Carolina Legislature to ratify any agreement made by her commissioners.[120]

After reminding the southern governor that, unless the boundary was adjusted "that harmony which ought to subsist between Sister States" would ultimately vanish, Governor Turner sent a copy of the Act of 1804 and suggested a meeting of the commissioners at Charlotte, North Carolina, or either Chester or Lancaster, South Carolina.[121] Lancaster was agreed upon, and after a delay of seven months on account of Governor Hamilton's inaction in appointing commissioners, October 28, 1805, was set for the meeting.[122]

At the very time when arrangements were nearing completion for negotiations, General Davie resigned as a commissioner for North Carolina.[123] By his resignation, North Carolina lost the services of the ablest man connected with the survey since the days of Burrington and Johnston. Diligent and thorough, he had acquired a broad knowledge of both sides of the dispute and had a better grasp of its significance than other men. He resigned with regret, frankly saying: "I know that the origin and nature of our boundary disputes with South Carolina are not generally

[119] Governor Turner assumed that they did not even consider it. See his Message of November 19, 1804. Executive Letter Book, XV, 383.

[120] *South Carolina Statutes at Large*, 13 vols., 1682-1866 (Columbia, 1836-1875), I, 414-16; Governor Hamilton of South Carolina to Governor Turner, February 28, 1805. Executive Letter Book, XV, 484, 488.

[121] Turner to Hamilton, December 26, 1804. Letter Book, XV, 431.

[122] Hamilton apologized late in the summer for his negligence. Letter Book, XV, 568, 580.

[123] Davie to Turner, October 1, 1805. Executive Letter Book, XV, 585.

understood." The causes of his resigning were probably varied. He owned an estate, Tivoli, near Lancaster, South Carolina,[124] and had long desired to move to it for the purpose of supervising its costly management.[125] Doubtless the dilatory and procrastinating tactics of the South Carolina authorities had borne on his patience. But the chief cause appears to have been inherent in his character. North Carolina, through him, was challenging the whole survey of 1772 as unauthorized because documentary materials were not available. Davie had discovered the royal instructions of June 7, 1771, and he was convinced. His state was wrong and he knew it; hence, he was unwilling to attempt to defend a position in which he did not conscientiously believe. With his resignation he sent an official copy of the above instructions and advised that they be given to his colleagues, adding that the document must have a "decided influence" in the dispute with South Carolina. He warned that without it his colleagues would be surprised by South Carolina's producing it and "by the conclusions they will unquestionably infer from it." He was positive it settled the question of the survey of 1772.

By Davie's unexpected resignation, the State's plans, in the view of the governor, were badly disarranged. It left the commission greatly weakened on the eve of the meeting with the South Carolinians, but Governor Turner acted with promptness and within two weeks he had appointed a successor of outstanding ability—John Steele of Salisbury.[126] He was given all documents, laws, and correspondence bearing on the boundary and soon became well informed on the facts. He sensed the key to the dispute instantly, writing the governor four days after the date of his appointment that the North Carolina commissioners must be prepared to answer South Carolina regarding the royal instructions of 1771.[127] The scientific thoroughness with which he endeavored to collect additional documents which would go to the heart of the dispute reminds one of Davie's methods and approach.[128] Cor-

[124] Wagstaff, *op. cit.*, p. 89 n.
[125] Davie to Haywood, June 9, 1805. Battle, "Davie Letters," p. 56.
[126] H. M. Wagstaff, ed., *The Papers of John Steele*, 2 vols. (Publications of the North Carolina Historical Commission, 1924), 455; Executive Letter Book, XV, 589.
[127] Steele to Turner, October 19, 1805. *The Papers of John Steele*, I, 593. (Cited hereafter as *Steele Papers*.)
[128] See, for example, the last-cited letter.

respondence clearly shows that Steele became the spokesman for North Carolina in the proceedings.

Regardless of his immediate and careful consideration of the instructions of 1771, Steele held to the old position of his State in defense of the line described in the Bill of Rights. He felt that that line was the "true one" and should not be hastily abandoned.

The commissioners for both states met at Lancaster Court House in South Carolina on the appointed day.[129] After protracted conferences, though nothing tangible was completed, they "made some progress," for they "at least stripped the business of a sort of mystery and ambiguity which hung about it and prevented a proper understanding of the case." And the South Carolina commissioners appeared to leave "with much less elevated notions of the validity of their claims, than they had met us with . . . and of course more disposed to put the business on the footing of mutual concession and compromise."

These statements are taken from the account of the meeting given Governor Turner by Steele. The North Carolinians were under serious handicaps in the negotiations. Steele complained in the same report that, because they failed to obtain the essential documents requested, they literally had to "feel our way in the dark." Hence, he felt they had done well under the circumstances.[130] Governor Turner seems to have had the same feeling with regard to the results accomplished for the State.[131]

Before closing the conference, the commissioners mutually agreed to resume negotiations at Charlotte, North Carolina, on the third Monday in January, 1806. General Davie was still intensely interested in the outcome, and sent from South Carolina every document he could "lay [his] hand upon" for use of the North Carolinians at Charlotte.

At the Charlotte conference, the North Carolina commissioners, under the leadership of Steele, appear to have taken even a firmer stand in favor of the line as described in the Bill of Rights and to have been persistent in their arguments. However, they did not have the support of their governor in this position. Gov-

[129] Only two members from South Carolina attended. "Mr. Purcell" of that commission was prevented from attending by illness. The conference continued for a week, from October 28 to November 2. Steele to Turner, November 8, 1805. Executive Letter Book, XV, 611.
[130] Executive Letter Book, XV, 611.
[131] See his Message to the Legislature, November 19, 1805. *Ibid.*, XV, 624-626; Legislative Papers, House of Commons, November 20, 1805.

ernor Turner had become converted to Davie's view that nothing remained to be settled regarding the line thus far surveyed except the portion from its termination westward.[132] Consequently, the commissioners were forced to drop the point.

Nothing was accomplished by way of an agreement at Charlotte and the North Carolinians came away discouraged, feeling that nothing valuable or final could be hoped for from the southern commissioners relative to recognition of "our just and . . . indisputable territorial rights."[133]

Governor Alexander, Turner's successor, after careful study of the situation, referred to the "total failure" of the Charlotte conference with a feeling that further negotiation with the Governor of South Carolina would be fruitless. However, he urged the Legislature to adopt such measures as were deemed best for settling the long-pending dispute. An adjustment was held essential, as it might lead to an understanding with Georgia; for the dispute with the latter State was "bottomed upon the same principle" as that with South Carolina.[134]

The situation was discouraging in 1806. A generation had passed since the last survey was made and the proceedings during that period had consisted largely of fruitless bickerings. Laws had been passed by both States and a constitutional description of the boundary had been drawn up and adopted, all of which were vigorously challenged by one or the other of the governments. New settlers were going into the disputed regions, making the situation more precarious. North Carolina had lost the very valuable services of General Davie, but had enlisted the talents of another very capable citizen in John Steele. Conferences and negotiations had amounted to nothing except to bring the controversy out into frank and open discussion, with both sides laying all of their cards on the table. But the darkness of discouragement was soon to be followed by the dawn of understanding and mutual agreement. On the more agreeable task of discovering the grounds on which the two states, through concessions, could amicably compromise their conflicting claims, we may now center our attention.

[132] John Haywood to Steele, March 16, 1806. *Steele Papers*, II, 470-71.

[133] Steele to Governor Stone of North Carolina, April, 1810. Executive Letter Book, XVII, 268.

[134] Governor Alexander's Message to the North Carolina Legislature, 1806. Legislative Papers, House Journals, April 20, 1806; Senate Journals, April 20, 1806; Letter Book, XVI, 48.

NORTH CAROLINA BOUNDARY DISPUTES

Section II

A Basis for Settlement Reached

Soon after the abortive conference at Charlotte, North Carolina authorities began forming plans to bring about further negotiations. In the fall of 1806, her Legislature passed a resolution which showed an "earnest solicitude . . . for an amicable adjustment of our territorial differences." In transmitting the resolution to the southern government, Governor Alexander added that, if there remained a probability of accomplishing this aim by again convening the commissioners, kindly to inform him.[135]

Knowing that the boundary question would continue to disturb the peaceful relations of the two States until a permanent settlement was reached, Steele set out soon after the failure of the Charlotte conference to secure every document obtainable in London on the subject. Through the governor, he secured the services of United States Senator James Turner in requesting James Monroe, Minister to England, to secure the documents. He requested authenticated copies of the letter of the Board of Trade to Governor Burrington, dated August 16, 1732; the order separating the Carolinas in 1729; and a copy of all orders relative to the boundary given previous to 1776.[136] Through Monroe, Steele procured the documents and a map of the line.

Steele, who had resigned but had been persuaded to resume his duties,[137] proposed a meeting at Earle's tavern, near the termination of the line of 1772, on April 20 following. He expected the aid of Dr. Caldwell in ascertaining the thirty-fifth parallel. His aim was to begin immediately where the commissioners discontinued the line in 1772. A special messenger was sent to Columbia to receive the reply of Dr. Blythe, the Chief of the South Carolina commission, to this proposal.[138] Delays

---

[135] Governor Alexander to Governor of South Carolina, January 6, 1807. Executive Letter Book, XVI, 71.

[136] Governor Alexander to James Turner, January 6, 1807. Executive Letter Book, XVI, 72. Turner persuaded Nathaniel Macon, then in Congress, to correspond with Monroe concerning the required documents. Turner to Alexander, January 12, 1807. *Ibid.*, p. 102. For Steele's very valuable work in this direction he was told, the "Researches you have made on this subject abundantly entitle you to the Thanks & gratitude of our State." John Haywood to Steele, May 25, 1808. *Steele Papers*, II, 552.

[137] In the meantime, John Moore was assuming leadership for North Carolina in the negotiations. *Steele Papers*, II, 493.

[138] Steele to Blythe, April 7, 1807. *Ibid.*, I, 499. The North Carolina Act of 1806 had deprived the governor of the power to set a date and place, a move of which he complained.

occured which prevented this meeting from taking place, among which was a tragedy in which one of the South Carolina commissioners was involved.[139] A meeting set by Governor Charles Pinckney of South Carolina to be held at Columbia in August, 1807, was declined by North Carolina because her commissioners were then engaged on the North Carolina-Georgia boundary.[140]

There was still some doubt in the mind of Governor Alexander whether or not South Carolina really intended to make any compromise, regardless of strong professions to that effect by Pinckney. To satisfy himself on this point, Alexander sent General Moore to Columbia during the meeting of their Legislature to confer with the governor and other leaders.[141] In his letter introducing Moore, Alexander informed Pinckney of the recent favorable agreement made with the Georgia commissioners and expressed a hope for similar results with South Carolina, which would be the case if compromising attitudes were maintained.[142] If, after competent and reasonable commissioners were appointed, there should appear to be no possibility of reaching an agreement, Alexander felt it would be better for North Carolina at once to refer her claim to the Federal authorities "than to temporize any longer."

In order to make sure of North Carolina's claim, Dr. Caldwell was requested to accompany Moore as far as the Waxhaw section and determine the exact latitude of the end of the line of 1764. Having taken various observations, Caldwell reported that the mean readings at that point were 34° 48' 16" 26''', or 11' 43" 34''' south of the thirty-fifth parallel; the line at its intersection with the forks of the Catawba River, 9' 34" 7''' 20'''' north of the parallel.[143]

After a "desultory" conversation between Moore and Gov-

[139] Dr. Blythe killed a negro and fatally wounded a white man for trespassing on his rice lands, creating great popular anger, and for which crime he was indicted by the Supreme Court of South Carolina. Montfort Stokes to Steele, April, 1807. *Steele Papers*, II, 500-501. This incident probably was chiefly responsible for the failure of Steele's plans to materialize.

[140] Governor Alexander to Governor Pinckney, July 4, 1807. Executive Letter Book, XVI, 124.

[141] Alexander to Moore, November 12, 1807. *Ibid.*, XVI, 195.

[142] Alexander to Pinckney, November 12, 1807. *Ibid.*, XVI, 197.

[143] Report of Dr. Caldwell to Governor Williams, December 7, 1807. *Ibid.*, XVI, 223. Benjamin Williams was then governor for the second time.

ernor Pinckney in December, the latter made Governor Alexander's letter of introduction the subject of a message to the assembled Legislature. After due consideration, the Legislature took the position that, since they had found that the South Carolina commissioners had failed to make a report of the results of the Lancaster and Charlotte conferences, the General Assembly had nothing to do with the subject—that it was entirely in the hands of the Executive and the commissioners. Pinckney then fell back on his resources and he and the South Carolina commissioners suggested that Moore should set a date and place for the next conference. Yorkville, South Carolina, and the third Monday in March were agreed upon.

Policies and concessions were then broached with the governor. Pinckney carefully avoided committing himself with regard to any compromise.[144] The Legislators personally were opposed to making any concessions. They were "almost universally opposed to giving up a single foot of territory" which South Carolina then held. Most of them, however, especially from the southern part of the State, told Moore they did not understand the nature of the boundary dispute. General Moore was so discouraged over the prospects that he declined to "flatter" Governor Williams with the hope of a settlement unless North Carolina should yield what she regarded as her just rights.

Progress of a settlement was then checked temporarily by dissension between the governor and his commissioner. Williams was displeased that Moore had set a date and place of meeting, basing his objection on the ground that his predecessor's intention was that another meeting should be agreed upon only in case Moore saw a chance of compromise, which his report indicated was far from the case. Moreover, Williams had "not received a line" from Pinckney. As he regarded the prospects of compromise as gloomy, he declined to require the other North Carolina commissioners to keep Moore's appointment.[145] Moore resigned in

[144] His reply was that of the typical politician. He "universally expressed a sincere wish that our territorial differences should be amicably settled to the satisfaction of both States," and appeared conscious of the necessity of such accomodation, always pledging his best efforts to effect "so desirable an object." Moore's Report to Governor Williams, January 2, 1808. Executive Letter Book, XVI, 247.

[145] Williams to Moore, February 1, 1808. Executive Letter Book, XVI, 265.

protest, though later persuaded by Williams and Steele to continue to serve.[146]

By this time, Steele had decided to offer concessions, and apparently expected Williams to do likewise. Not having learned that Williams had defeated Moore's plan for a meeting, Steele asked the governor for instructions as to the course to pursue—points to yield without equivalents, and those which might be insisted upon.[147] Williams, however, still insisted on the observance of the provisions of the Bill of Rights.

It was generally agreed to hold a conference in Columbia on July 1, 1808. During these sessions North Carolina was to evince a milder policy, though it was to be revealed diplomatically. The commissioners were instructed to negotiate on the most "liberal and friendly principles," but to use the "points and principles" contended for at Lancaster and Charlotte in 1805 and 1806 as a basis for any convention they might then enter into. They were referred to the grounds taken in Davie's report of February 4, 1802, while Agent for the State,[148] and the provisions of the Bill of Rights, from the "letter and spirit of which . . . neither you nor I can depart," unless—and herein was the germ of the compromising spirit—by provisional agreement which could be effective only after a subsequent act of the people of North Carolina, declared by their representatives.[149] Williams was reverting to the provision in the Bill of Rights which forbade an alteration of the line as agreed upon in 1735 except by consent of the Legislature, a clause which should have been employed long before. However, Williams was ignoring his own power. The governor had been authorized in the Act of 1804 to enter into "any compact or agreement" with the authorities of South Carolina or Georgia relative to establishing a permanent line, and by the provisions of the Act of 1803 which were still retained in force and effect, whatever was done through his commissioners should be binding on the State.

At Columbia, the North Carolina commissioners met Dr.

[146] Governor Williams acted illegally in this case. The Act of 1806 had taken from the governor the power to fix a date and place of meeting, and had given it to the commissioners themselves. *Supra,* p. 125. Moore had acted within the limits of his authority.

[147] Steele to Williams, February 7, 1808. Letter Book, XVI, 299.

[148] *Supra,* p. 116.

[149] Governor Williams to Steele, Moore and James Wellborn, commissioners, May 20, 1808. Executive Letter Book, XVI, 320.

Blythe and Thomas Sumter, Jr.; the third member, Allston, never appeared during the entire conference.[150] South Carolina was fortunate in the selection of their chief commissioner, Blythe. With the exception of William R. Davie, he was probably the best commissioner employed by either government during the entire history of the controversy before the Civil War. Though strong in his convictions, he was judicious and fair and always sought after the truth. However, he faced the chief of the northern commission, Steele, who was at least his equal in diplomacy.

The commissioners "formed a board" and began the proceedings. The arguments used by the South Carolinians were almost the same as those presented at Lancaster and Charlotte, with one difference; on those occasions they relied chiefly on the prerogative of the Crown, but they now relied on the prerogative plus certain Indian treaties. They attempted to give to them and to the Agreement of 1735 a construction which would give South Carolina a "vast deal more" territory even than she then claimed to possess. But Steele convinced them that their claims under the convention of 1735 and the royal prerogative were founded on opposite principles, hence could not stand together. After the most careful consideration of the Indian treaties, the North Carolina commissioners denied that the terms of any one or all of them together "had the slightest bearing upon the case." They took even a broader position on this point; admitting for the sake of argument that the terms of those treaties could be construed as the South Carolinians desired, they denied that an instance could be adduced in the entire history of American colonization where a dispute concerning jurisdiction had been decided on authority "so crude and so liable to be affected by considerations, and attended with circumstances different from those which usually influence civilized nations."[151]

After a week of prolonged discussions, an agreement was reached. The forces which were at work making an adjustment imperative were: the conviction that the dignity and interests of both States would be promoted by a friendly, equitable solution; the consciousness that in accepting appointment as commissioners, it imposed upon each of them the obligation to lose sight of purely

[150] Steele's preliminary report to Governor Williams, July 27, 1808. *Steele Papers*, II, 811-20.
[151] Steele's preliminary report to Governor Williams, July 27, 1808. *Steele Papers*, II, 812.

local views and interests and approach the problem "as citizens of the same national commonwealth" whose paramount duty was to preserve the peace and harmony between the States.[152] Thus actuated by sentiments of liberality and conciliation, the commissioners agreed to terminate all disputes and dissensions which had ever existed between the two States regarding their mutual boundaries on the following terms:[153]

Art. 1st. The line beginning at a cedar stake on the Atlantic Ocean, and running thence northwest and west to a point at the Salisbury road, near the Catawba lands, as described in the plans of survey begun in 1735 and ended in 1764, shall be, and remain the same in its whole extent as heretofore established.

Art. 2d. From which point at the said Salisbury road, mentioned in the preceding article, instead of following the road to where it enters the Catawba lands as at present, shall be run and marked in direct course to the southeast corner of the said Catawba lands, at Twelve-Mile creek, which line is hereby established in lieu of the said road; thence along the line of the said Catawba lands, pursuing its different courses to where the Catawba river enters the said lands on the northwardly, to the confluence of the northern and southern branches thereof, and from thence due west along the line as run and marked by commissioners in the year 1772, to the termination of said line.

Art. 3d. And from the termination of the said line of 1772, a line shall be extended in a direct course to that point on the ridge of mountains which divide the eastern from the western waters, where the thirty-fifth degree of north latitude shall be found to strike it nearest to the termination of the said line of 1772, thence along the top of said ridge to western extremity of the state of South-Carolina; it being understood that the state of South-Carolina does not mean by this arrangement to interfere with claims which the United States or those holding under the act of cession to the U. States may have to lands which may be, if any there be, between the top of said ridge and the said 35° of north latitude.

The contracting parties, for their mutual benefit and convenience,[154] agree to adopt and confirm the lines of boundary as described in the preceding articles, and to renounce respectively to each other every right, claim and pretention which may be inconsistent with the true meaning and purpose of this agreement, which is to establish between the states of South-Carolina and

[152] Preamble to the articles of Agreement, July 11, 1808. *Ibid.*, II, 798-9.

[153] The complete text of this agreement may be found in Executive Letter Book, 1805-1808, XVI, 349 *et seq.* and in *Steele Papers*, II, 798-800.

[154] This article should be noticed very carefully; it became the basis of a final settlement, though often modified.

North-Carolina, a permanent and unalterable boundary. Provided nevertheless, that in case at any time this agreement shall be contested or not conformed to, after the ratification of it by the legislatures of said states, all the rights claims and pretentions herein intended to be renounced and conveyed, and all other rights and claims in relation thereto, shall revive and exist in the same force and effect as they did before the signing these presents, in favour of the state which shall conform thereto.

Article 1, confirming the line from the coast to the Salisbury Road, had been insisted upon at Columbia by North Carolina because of South Carolina's dissatisfaction with the survey of 1764 on account of the error in latitude. North Carolina felt she must counterbalance her own loss in 1772.

Article 3 was deliberately worded so as to admit of two different constructions because of the existing ignorance of the topography of the western section. It was felt by the North Carolina commissioners that, if the thirty-fifth parallel should fall south of the Blue Ridge, the territory intervening would have to be ceded back to South Carolina to satisfy the settlers who would otherwise have to cross the mountains to attend court; and if the Blue Ridge should prove to be south of the parallel, Georgia should cede the intervening territory to North Carolina by ratifying the Convention and supplement agreed to between her commissioners and those of North Carolina in June, 1807.[155] If Georgia should ultimately decline to ratify, the point of intersection of the thirty-fifth parallel with the Blue Ridge would have to be adopted as the western extremity of South Carolina in order to secure the essential natural boundary.[156]

This agreement was again a compromise. Steele stated in his preliminary report that it was simply a matter of mutual concession or of indefinitely continuing the dispute. North Carolina was contending for the thirty-fifth parallel while South Carolina stood firm for the line of 1772, or 35° 9' 23". The rectangle within these lines, however, was divided diagonally, according to the agreement, which called for a line extending from the end of the survey of 1772 to the point where the thirty-fifth parallel struck the Blue Ridge nearest the line of 1772.[157] In addition to these

[155] *Infra*, pp. 185, 187.
[156] Steele's preliminary report. *Steele Papers*, II, 815-7.
[157] Since the survey of 1772 inclined too far northward the above diagonal also began too far northward at its eastern end, at North Carolina's expense.

concessions, North Carolina agreed that the line from the end of the survey of 1764 at the Salisbury Road should extend directly to the southeastern corner of the Catawba Lands, thus ceding to South Carolina considerable territory and "a number of inhabitants." This is an important point, in view of some historically inaccurate statements made by South Carolina, which will be treated later in this study. The question of land titles was also raised by South Carolina but, as the North Carolina act appointing commissioners provided that such titles should not be affected by the extension of the line, her commissioners refused to agree to any provision regarding them.

North Carolina, through her Legislature, ratified the Agreement in the fall of 1808.[158] The line described was declared to be the "permanent and unalterable line," with such limitations as were contained in the convention itself.

South Carolina was not so prompt in ratification. When the Agreement came up for consideration, a committee of her Legislature reviewed the respective claims as to the location of the line, stating that the State had invariably protested against and always refused to acquiesce in any other lines than those established by royal authority. When they attempted to review the history of those surveys, however, they made a gross factual error. It was stated that the surveys of 1735 and 1737 were made according to an agreement "entered into between the respective executives"; whereas, it will be recalled that the agreement was made by the commissioners with the advice of Governor Gabriel Johnston.

It was then stated that North Carolina accepted the line to the Salisbury Road on the grounds that it was ratified by the General Assemblies of both provinces. Serious doubt was then expressed as to the fact of such ratification, on the grounds of the absence of a record of such action.

The conflict in argument and the inconsistency of the committee's position should be noted. Regarding ratification by the respective Legislatures, the argument constituted an unconscious admission that, if the record of the action had been at hand, it would have been sufficient proof of North Carolina's claim; whereas, it had just been declared that South Carolina recognized

[158] *Laws of the State of North Carolina*, 2 vols. (1821), II, 1131; *Steele Papers*, II, 574; Executive Letter Book, XVII, 81. The act of ratification quotes the provisions of the Agreement.

NORTH CAROLINA BOUNDARY DISPUTES   133

the line only where it was based solely on royal action. The two statements cannot be harmonized.

It was stated that the inhabitants of both States had always regarded and "acted upon" the line of 1772 as the legal boundary This claim was true in many cases but there had been many disputes between the citizens, particularly with regard to land titles. It was further claimed that the royal instructions of 1732, the agreement of 1735, and express Indian treaties between the Cherokee Nation and the Crown, had all allocated the Cherokee territory to South Carolina; the North Carolina-Cherokee boundary was therefore intended by the Crown at that time to be the dividing line between North and South Carolina. Hence, it became legally the boundary, since ratification by colonial assemblies was not regarded as necessary to establish a boundary line at that time. This was one of South Carolina's strongest arguments. It was logical, and was recognized by Davie before South Carolina began to capitalize on it.

With regard to the line from the end of the survey of 1772, the committee admitted difficulty in deciding "how and where the state of South Carolina ought in strict propriety and equity, to contend the boundary line . . . should run," though South Carolina strongly felt it should be a simple extension of the line of 1772.

The committee recommended that the Legislature should ratify the Agreement of Columbia and that a bill be prepared "forthwith" to that effect; that such bill contain a clause providing that the extension of the line should in no wise affect the titles of any persons to lands entered or located in either State.

The Legislature declined to pass the bill ratifying the Agreement. Their reasons were various. The western members stated that, as North Carolina knew, the line would give her more territory than the South Carolina commissioners were apprized of; hence, they desired first to have the thirty-fifth parallel ascertained on the Blue Ridge.[159] Apprehension concerning private titles to lands which would be transferred by the survey was a further cause of hesitation.[160] A resolution was adopted by both Houses December 17, 1808, directing the State's commissioners to proceed

[159] General Wellborn to Governor Stone, April 22, 1809. Executive Letter Book, XVII, 72. David Stone was governor of North Carolina from December, 1808, to December, 1810.
[160] Steele to Stone, April 30, 1809. *Steele Papers,* II, 591; Letter Book, XVII, 68.

to ascertain the point of intersection of the parallel with the Blue Ridge at the point nearest the end of the survey of 1772.[161] The Legislature was desirous of this information before ratifying the Agreement.

The commissioners of the two States favored this procedure,[162] but Governor Stone opposed it on the grounds that, since North Carolina had ratified the Agreement of Columbia, she was obligated to approve all acts of her commissioners made under it. Moreover, South Carolina would be free either to approve or reject the survey.[163]

The South Carolina government determined to have the above point of intersection located independently if necessary.[164] This policy was later carried out, and the State's astronomer supplied the Legislature with the information.[165]

The Legislature again took up the Agreement for consideration in 1809, after the governor had referred to it in his message. A joint committee's action brought about an important change in the Agreement. They reported their "approbation" of the Convention, adding that they would have recommended immediate ratification had they not been informed by local inhabitants of the region that a slight alteration of Article 3 would, for most of its course, give a natural boundary line, and would afford relief to some of their citizens who felt injured by the line as described. They had been further informed that a line from the point of intersection of the Blue Ridge with the thirty-fifth parallel to the Block House[166] in the line of 1772 would run almost parallel to the Saluda Mountains for some distance, intersecting the headwaters of the Saluda River about four miles from its source. As the committee under-

[161] S. C. Executive Journals, July 8, 1809. The South Carolina commission was very uncertain at this time, Thomas Sumter having been appointed to an embassy and Dr. Blythe seriously planning to resign on account of broken health, leaving only Joseph Allston who had never attended a meeting of the commissioners since his appointment. The possibility of having to deal with an entirely new commission was giving the North Carolina commissioners concern.

[162] Blythe to Steele, May 19, 1809. Steele to Stone, June 18, 1809. Executive Letter Book, XVII, 85, 87.

[163] Stone to Steele, July 21, 1809. Ibid., XVII, 88.

[164] See Governor Stone's letter to Governor Drayton, September 12, 1809. Ibid., XVII, 99.

[165] S. C. Journal of the House of Representatives, December 15, 1809.

[166] This term is used so often in the sources at this date to indicate the termination of the survey of 1772, it will be so used hereafter for economy of space.

stood that the inhabitants living on the headwaters of the Saluda River north of said line were separated from North Carolina by the Saluda Mountains which were passable only at one gap, and were still further separated from the Buncombe County Court House by these mountains, they recommended the adoption of the following resolutions:

1. That the South Carolina commissioners be instructed to endeavor by friendly negotiation with the northern commissioners to obtain an alteration of the line described in Article 3 of the Convention of Columbia to cause it to extend from the Block House to the nearest point of the Saluda Mountains, thence along their summit to the intersection with the Blue Ridge, thence along the ridge to its intersection with the thirty-fifth parallel nearest the Block House. If unable to secure this alteration, the commissioners were to urge the adoption of some other similar natural boundary.
2. That if this alteration of the line should be obtained, the commissioners be instructed immediately to notify the commissioners of North Carolina that they were ready to meet them at the Block House as soon as convenient with astronomers and surveyors to determine, run and mark the line as the "permanent boundary in that quarter"; and that South Carolina would ratify the line so determined and marked.
3. That the surveyors so employed should file an accurate plat of the line.
4. That the sum of $3,000 be appropriated for the purpose, and provided in the tax bill.
5. That the governor be requested to take measures necessary to carry out the provisions of these resolutions.[167]

The House merely concurred in the report as adopted by the Senate on the previous day. It will be noted that both the report and the resolutions are entirely silent regarding land titles—the professed reason for not ratifying in the fall of 1808. It is quite probable that, if the desired alteration could be obtained, so much territory would be gained that a clause providing for the security of land titles would be superfluous. Such was probably their line of reasoning, and it was smart maneuvering. Steele charged that these resolutions were passed simply to avoid a settlement by

[167] S. C. Journal of the House of Representatives, December 15, 1809; Executive Letter Book, XVII, 177 *et seq.*; *Steele Papers,* II, 820-23. See also, Battle, ed., "Davie Letters," *op. cit.,* p. 65.

leaving the dispute "up in the wind again."[168] It is most probable that he was mistaken in their motive, however, for later negotiations brought about an agreement for an alteration.

The content of this report demonstrates the fact that the Legislature of South Carolina, though sympathetic with the agreement of July 11, 1808[169] was not in favor of running the line, as were the commissioners of the two states, until the results of their efforts to obtain an alteration were known.[170]

A technical point of law arose in the minds of Governor Stone and Steele as to whether the North Carolina commissioners had power to negotiate regarding an alteration after their State had ratified, unless some prior action by the Legislature was taken.[171] Governor Stone finally concluded that such negotiations would become legal if any agreement reached should be considered by the Legislature and ratified before marking the line. He therefore agreed to instruct his commissioners to meet those of South Carolina near the Block House at a date to be mutually agreed upon,[172] stating that he desired to secure accurate information of the topography of the region, which was so difficult to obtain.[173] He specified, however, that in case the line should be altered to run north of that described in the Convention of Columbia, North Carolina must receive an equivalent area in some other section.[174]

The Legislature of North Carolina, in the winter of 1811, opposed Governor Stone's policy of again entering into negotiations on the third article of the Convention of Columbia. South Carolina was notified by Benjamin Hawkins, the new governor, that the Legislature adhered to its former ratification of the unaltered form of the document and declined to put the dispute again into the hands of commissioners.[175]

[168] Steele to the Governor-elect of North Carolina, November 12, 1810. *Steele Papers,* II, 640.

[169] Hereafter referred to as the Convention of Columbia.

[170] The North Carolina commissioners favored a survey at this time because they felt confident the southern Government would not ratify until after the line was run.

[171] From the standpoint of the wisdom and expediency of such negotiations, Steele was absolutely opposed to them. Executive Letter Book, XVII, 286.

[172] James Kilgore had been appointed as a South Carolina commissioner late in 1809 to succeed Sumter, resigned.

[173] Stone to Governor of South Carolina, March 1, 1810. S. C. Executive Journal, March 31, 1810; Executive Letter Book, XVII, 237.

[174] Stone to Steele, May 10, 1810. *Ibid.,* XVII, 273.

[175] Governor Hawkins to Governor Middleton of South Carolina, January 4, 1812. *Ibid.,* XVIII, 44.

South Carolina then decided to ratify and on August 29 a bill was passed providing for such ratification. It provided that, since North Carolina had ratified the convention, it also should be "forever binding" on South Carolina.[176] The same safeguarding clause was inserted regarding revival of title in case either State should ever contest the line. This revealed the continued presence of fear of North Carolina's constitutional description of the boundary.

If statements by one of the North Carolina commissioners were true, South Carolina had been playing for time for three years in order, if possible, to win her points regarding the agreement. Many influential South Carolinians had told General Wellborn in the winter of 1809 that their Legislature would without doubt ratify as soon as its members saw that North Carolina would refuse to negotiate a new agreement.[177]

After South Carolina's ratification, Governor Hawkins appointed commissioners for North Carolina in 1812. Steele again served and Montfort Stokes and Duncan Cameron were appointed. Cameron resigned and Robert Burton was appointed in his stead. The War of 1812 affected the personnel at this time. General Wellborn had been withdrawn because of the demand for his military services in the conflict.[178]

Arrangements were made for carrying out the convention and the commissioners of both states met near the Block House July 20, 1813, to proceed with the line according to Article 3.[179] After various astronomical observations were made by Dr. Caldwell and Dr. Meigs of Georgia on the thirty-fifth parallel, and, as a consequence of the results obtained, they disagreed as to the "practicability of fixing a boundary line according to the true intent and meaning of the said article." The commissioners therefore met "at McKinney's, on Toxaway river" and entered into an agreement by which they agreed to recommend that their respective Legislatures agree that the commissioners should begin at

[176] *Statutes at Large of South Carolina*, V, 667-669; Letter Book, XVIII, 272.

[177] Wellborn to Governor Stone, April 3, 1810. Executive Letter Book, XVII, 275.

[178] *Steele Papers*, II, 699-700, 709-10; Letter Book, XIX, 38, 115, 283.

[179] The North Carolina commissioners were instructed to negotiate only on the basis of the Convention of Columbia and the acts of their Legislature. Governor Hawkins to Steele, Stokes, and Burton, July 10, 1813. Executive Letter Book, XVII, 115.

the termination of the line of 1772 and run a line due west to the ridge dividing the waters of the north fork of Pacolet River from the waters of the north fork of Saluda River,

thence along the said ridge to the ridge that divides the Saluda waters from those of Green river, thence along the said ridge to where the same joins the main ridge which divides the eastern from the western waters, thence along the said ridge to that part of it which is intersected by the Cherokee boundary line run in the year one thousand seven hundred and ninety-seven; from the centre of the said ridge at the point of intersection, the line shall extend in a direct course to the eastern bank of the Chatooga river, where the thirty-fifth degree of north latitude has been found to strike it, and where a rock has been marked by the aforesaid commissioners with the following inscription, viz. Lat. 35, 1813. It being understood and agreed that the said lines shall be so run as to leave all the waters of Saluda river within the state of South Carolina, but shall in no part run north of a course due west, from the termination of the line of 1772.[180]

North Carolina now felt that the controversy would terminate. In requesting the Legislature to ratify the provisional agreement, Governor Hawkins declared that he contemplated "the approaching just and amicable" settlement of the long dispute "with the utmost satisfaction."[181] The Legislature acted promptly, passing an act ratifying the agreement of September 4. After quoting the text in full, it was enacted that the provisional agreement was "fully ratified and confirmed."[182]

The Legislature of South Carolina also acted with energy and passed an act on December 17, 1813, by which the agreement was "fully and absolutely ratified and confirmed," and was "substituted for, and in the room and stead of the third article of the conventional agreement on boundary, signed at Columbia."[183]

The commissioners proceeded to run the section of boundary between the western termination of the survey of 1764 and the Catawba Lands in conformity to the provisions of the Convention of Columbia. Ignoring the old line along the Salisbury Road,

[180] *Statutes at Large of South Carolina*, I, 417; *Steele Papers*, II, 732-4, 832-4.
[181] Executive Letter Book, XIX, 484.
[182] *Laws of the State of North Carolina* (1821), II, 1280-1282; *The Revised Statutes of the State of North Carolina* (1836-7), II, 86.
[183] *Statutes at Large of South Carolina*, I, 417-418. The clause was again added providing that, should North Carolina refuse to ratify or even contest or call in question the above agreement, all rights and title should again revert to South Carolina.

they ran a direct course eight miles from a red oak on the above road to a gum at the corner of the Catawba Lands, intersecting the old road about midway between the two points.[184]

By this survey, South Carolina gained additional territory. The strip varied in extent from a mere point at the south to approximately two miles at its greatest width. On December 18, 1813, the Legislature of South Carolina passed an act formally incorporating it in the district of Lancaster. In this act the General Assembly of South Carolina grossly erred in its history. The statute provided that

all those parts or portions which have been heretofore under the jurisdiction and supposed to belong to the State of North Carolina, but are found on extending and running out the line between the two states, in conformity to the treaty on boundary of the year one thousand eight hundred and eight, to be included within the limits of the State of South Carolina, shall be taken and regarded to all intents and purposes as forming a part of the said district of Lancaster.[185]

The territory gained by this survey had been North Carolina territory by virtue of the same royal instructions and official proceedings by which South Carolina was uncompromisingly claiming the line of 1772, which instructions declared the whole line from the seacoast as the "final boundary." It was not merely "supposed" to be North Carolina territory, but was legal property. If the territory between the Salisbury Road and the direct line run in 1813 had never really belonged to North Carolina, it follows that South Carolina had never had a boundary west of the Catawba Lands. South Carolina was assuming a contradictory position. It is unmistakeable that the survey of 1813 embodied an outright concession to South Carolina.

The status of the dispute at the close of the War of 1812 was much more hopeful. However, the controversy with Georgia had entered and caused further complications. Disagreement between a commissioner and the Governor of North Carolina also delayed the proceedings momentarily. But the favorable develop-

---

[184] Commissioners for South Carolina on this survey were Joseph Blythe, Henry Middleton, and John Blasingame. *Revised Statutes of North Carolina* (1836-7), II, 86.
[185] *Statues at Large of South Carolina*, V, 697.

ments far outweighed these complications. North Carolina was definitely convinced by Dr. Caldwell's work that the survey of 1764 was erroneous in her favor. This made her more willing to consider granting concessions. Both states had become convinced that they would have to yield on some of their demands, if a friendly settlement could ever be reached. The failure of two conferences had made plain that fact. This consciousness was evident during the later conference at Columbia. As a result, an agreement was made which became the basis of a final settlement. The Convention of Columbia, though topographical conditions in the region forced its later modification, was the means of real progress toward a settlement. It was a compromise, providing that the line should extend diagonally southwestward from the end of the survey of 1772 back to the thirty-fifth parallel, a line for which North Carolina had been fighting for a generation. On the other hand, South Carolina gained territory along the Salisbury Road. Prospects for a final adjustment were the brightest they had been since the dispute originated, just a century before. With this situation in view, the proceedings which brought the dispute to a close until after the War between the States may now be considered.

Section III

Agreements Modified and the Line Surveyed

The alteration of the line at the Salisbury Road constituted a land mark in the progress of the survey. With the completion of that link, the boundary supposedly was settled permanently from the seacoast to the Cherokee line in the western mountains. Furthermore, the two States had formally agreed on a line from the end of the survey of 1772 to the Georgia border.

The governors of the respective States were elated over the propects that the troblesome problem should soon be forever removed as a bar to their friendly and normal relations. Governor Allston of South Carolina expressed great pleasure to Governor Hawkins that the dispute "is at length settled."[186] After reviewing the facts relative to the line before the Legislature, including the mutual ratification of the Provisional Agreement entered into at McKinney's on Toxaway River,[187] Governor Hawkins remarked,

[186] Executive Letter Book, XX, 83.
[187] Hereafter designated as the Provisional Agreement.

"It is a source of gratification that the long disputed question of boundary between the two States is at length nearly settled."[188] It only remained, he added, to run and mark the line from the end of the survey of 1772 according to the Provisional Agreement.

The new governor of North Carolina, William Miller, proceeded to carry out the agreement and the acts and resolutions of the Legislature relating to the boundary. On December 28, 1814, he commissioned General Stokes, Thomas Love, and John Patton to "run, mark, and establish" the line.[189] They had been designated as commissioners by an act of the Legislature of the same year.[190]

South Carolina cooperated fully in the plans for a survey. Her Legislature took action similar to that of North Carolina, but by resolution. The governor was requested therein to inform Governor Miller of their ratification of the Provisional Agreement which was to be substituted for Article 3 of the Convention of Columbia, and to request him to appoint commissioners to join in running the line accordingly. The governor was then given power to appoint such commissioners for South Carolina.[191]

All necessary legal proceedings were completed and the governors began a courteous correspondence regarding time and place of meeting for the commissioners.[192] It was finally agreed that the commissioners should meet at the "Widow Earle's" in Rutherford County, near the end of the survey of 1772, on the second Monday in September, 1815.[193]

Impatient with the long and dangerous quarrel, the commissioners and the people of both States were anxious to see the survey completed. Governor Williams of South Carolina wrote the North Carolina governor that ". . . there exists every disposition here [Charleston] to close this business."[194] The commissioners of the two States met at the time and place appointed and proceeded to run the line as described. North Carolina was

[188] Governor's message to North Carolina Legislature, November 23, 1814. Executive Letter Book, XX, 436. [189] *Ibid.*, XXI, 21.
[190] *Laws of the State of North Carolina* (1821), II, 1315; *Revised Statutes* (1835-7), II, 87.
[191] Governor D. R. Williams of South Carolina to Governor Miller, January 19, 1815. Letter Book, XXI, 46.
[192] Executive Letter Book, XXI, 22, 71, 166.
[193] Governor Miller to Governor of South Carolina, July 3, 1815. *Ibid.*, XXI, 196. The second Monday was September 11.
[194] Williams to Miller, January 19, 1815. *Ibid.*, XXI, 46.

at a disadvantage in the early proceedings by virtue of the fact that she had the services of only two of her commissioners; the third was prevented by illness from joining the group until they reached Saluda Gap.[195] The other commissioners of the two States labored in vain for "several days" endeavoring to carry out their instructions.[196] The "impracticability" of carrying the Provisional Agreement into effect was soon recognized. They found that a line due west from the end of the survey of 1772 did not strike the summit of the ridge dividing the waters of the north fork of Pacolet River from the north fork of Saluda River at the point expected so as to form the natural boundary desired; and that such a westward extension would not leave all of the waters of the Saluda in South Carolina, but would cross three small branches about a quarter mile from Three Springs. Under these circumstances and after various "descriptions," the commissioners held a conference at Greenville, South Carolina, November 2, 1815. They concluded that a modification of the Provisional Agreement was necessary, though deeming it "proper" and "expedient" to adhere as nearly as practicable to that agreement by establishing the natural boundary as far westward as the Cherokee line which was run in 1797. By mutual concessions they agreed to extend the line to the top of the ridge dividing the waters of the north fork of the Pacolet from the north fork of the Saluda, thereby giving North Carolina an area of about 500 acres. They further agreed "to keep the ridge round to the three Springs of Saluda," giving South Carolina an area of about 400 acres.[197]

The relations between the commissioners during these trying days were of the friendliest sort. After the above agreement was reached, they proceeded "with great cordiality and respect" in an effort to complete the task within three weeks. The commissioners from each State furnished an equal number of surveyors, chain carriers, markers, and guides. Stone monuments were erected at

[195] General Stokes to Governor Miller, dated Binson's Gap, Head of Little River of French Broad, October 1, 1815. *Ibid.*, XXI, 253.

[196] The South Carolina commissioners at this time were Dr. Blythe, John Blasingame, and George W. Earle. Executive Letter Book, XXI, 255.

[197] Preliminary report of Stokes to Governor Miller, October 1, 1815. Executive Letter Book, XXI, 253. See also *Laws of the State of North Carolina* (1821), II, 1318-9.

the end of the survey of 1772, at the foot of the ridge between the Pacolet and Saluda rivers, at the junction of the "green River Mountains" with the Blue Ridge, and at various intervening points, to the marked rock on Chatooga River.[198] This rock marked the corner of three States—North Carolina, South Carolina, and Georgia. It was supposed to be directly on the thirty-fifth parallel, but in 1820 Governor John Geddes of South Carolina ordered that observations be taken of various points in the State, one of which was the marked rock on the Chatooga, and the astronomer later stated that its latitude was 34° 59′ 34″.[199] According to his readings, North Carolina received about one-half mile of territory, though neither State was aware of it.[200] The total length of the line from the termination of the survey of 1772 to the rock on Chatooga River was 74 miles and 189 poles. The total cost of the proceedings to North Carolina amounted to $1260.49.[201] The North Carolina commissioners submitted a final report to the governor at the close of the year, with a plat of the line.[202] Governor Miller laid it before the Legislature immediately with a suggestion that, if both States would ratify the work of the joint commission, it would "put an end to this long subsisting difference."[203]

In accordance with the governor's suggestion, the Legislature adopted a resolution to the effect that, as soon as the pending bill was passed for ratifying the agreement of Greenville and the survey made pursuant thereto, the governor should notify the southern executive and request him to lay the North Carolina act

---

[198] Letter Book, XXI, 354-5. Details of the origin of this "Painted Rock" will be described later in this study in the treatment of the Georgia-North Carolina controversy.

[199] James M. Elvard, Astronomical Observations in South Carolina (MSS.), entry of March 22, 1820. These manuscripts are in the office of the South Carolina Historical Commission, Columbia.

[200] The writer assumes no responsibility as to the fact of this claim. The readings are simply stated from the astronomer's official report to the governor. Standard maps would indicate that the line co-incides with the thirty-fifth parallel; if so, the rock was also directly on the parallel.

[201] Report of the Controller, December 15, 1815. Executive Letter Book, XXI, 308,

[202] North Carolina commissioners to Governor Miller, December 8, 1815. *Ibid.*, XXI, 305.

[203] Governor's message to Legislature, December 9, 1815. *Ibid.*, XXI, 306.

before his Legislature.[204] The act was passed declaring the agreement of Greenville "ratified and confirmed," and establishing the line as run and marked as the permanent boundary.[205]

On December 15, South Carolina also took action. Her General Assembly passed an act ratifying and declaring the agreement "forever binding" on the State.[206]

Thus the dividing line between the Carolinas was extended westwardly to its junction with the State of Georgia. One of the chief obstacles to an adjustment of the respective claims from the earliest appearance of the question of a boundary to its final settlement was the topography of the territory concerned. It had dictated the claims of the States; and, even after agreements were made, had often forced their radical modification.

Before the formation of the Union under the Articles of Confederation, South Carolina had little valid argument. As has been shown, she had entirely ascaped the injustice of having her territory given outright to an absentee owner—Lord Granville. On the other hand, North Carolina had been forced to sacrifice two thirds of her domain, with all it meant to the province economically and financially. It must be conceded that justice demanded some sort of compensation, and the only recourse was concession from the southern province, which in turn could be expanded westward with justice to all concerned.

After 1782, however, conditions changed. The advantage was not so preponderantly with North Carolina, though she still had a strong case. In that year, she confiscated the Granville Tract as a consequence of the Revolution. It is almost a mystery why South Carolina never alluded to this fact or took full advantage of it, either in the correspondence of her officials or in the conferences and negotiations between the commissioners. She seems to have failed to realize the changed situation which would have afforded her an effective reply to a point which had commanded the sympathy of fair-minded men from the time it first had been urged. North Carolina evidently was conscious of her changed position as a result of freeing herself from the effects of the gross injustice, and desired to seek a fair solution of the boundary dispute.

[204] Resolution of North Carolina Legislature, December 18, 1815. Executive Letter Book, XXI, 320.
[205] *Laws of the State of North Carolina* (1821), II, 1319.
[206] *Statutes at Large of South Carolina*, I, 419-21.

NORTH CAROLINA BOUNDARY DISPUTES   145

She was more ready to make concessions after having gained possession of this large portion of her territory than while the major portion of her revenues were being collected and appropriated by a British nobleman. Such concessions were made. By mutual compromise, the States were ultimately and permanently divided. To the boundary problem following the War between the States we may now turn.

Section IV

CONFUSION AND A NEW SURVEY

After the settlement of 1815, the North Carolina-South Carolina boundary controversy for over half a century ceased to be an object of concern between the two States. It was never again mentioned in the annual messages of the governors of North Carolina before the Civil War.[207] Governor David L. Swain, in a letter to Joseph T. Cogsdell in 1835, complained of the great injustice done the State in the early surveys,[208] but no action relative to the boundary was taken. After that date, the State was too much engrossed in discussing the issues which led to the War between the States to give the matter attention, even if it had been to the State's interest to have done so. After the War, the tyranny of the invader was the object of popular resentment to the exclusion of all other questions for more than a decade.[209] The same conditions existed in South Carolina, and fellow-sufferers are not inclined to quarrel. At the end of the first national administration after the restoration of home rule in North Carolina, the State again began to shape its policy as to its boundary problem. This was the result of the initiative taken by South Carolina. That State had vaguely described her boundaries in revising her laws in 1873, as will later appear. However, as the eastern portion of the line was becoming constantly more indefinite and uncertain, the Legislature passed an act in December, 1880, to "authorize and require the re-running and re-marking" of a portion of the South Carolina-North Carolina line. The governor was required to employ a surveyor to re-run and re-

---

[207] Executive Letter Book, 1816-1844; Governor's messages in pamphlet form in library of the University of North Carolina, *passim*.
[208] Letter Book, XXX, 339.
[209] See J. G. deR. Hamilton, *Reconstruction in North Carolina* (New York: Columbia University Studies, LVIII, 1914, no. 141), *passim*.

mark the boundary from the seacoast to the end of the survey of 1737, thence westward to the end of the survey of 1764, thence along the old line to the corner of York County, as provided in the Revised Statutes, Part I, Title I. The work should be completed within one year from the date of the act. The governor was required to send a copy of the act to the Governor of North Carolina and request that a similar appointment be made to join in a cooperative survey.[210]

The Revised Statutes, however, did not describe the line as extending along a portion of York County. They were misleading in their provisions. The Statute referred to by the Legislature merely described the line to the end of the survey of 1764 at the Salisbury Road and stated that it shall extend from "thence along the line extending from this point to the Tryon Mountains." This clause gives the impression that the line from the end of the survey of 1764 was a simple extension westward to the mountains, whereas, it turned northward around the Catawba Lands and along the Catawba River to its forks before turning westward; and the Legislature had this old line in mind, regardless of the vague wording of the Revised Statutes.

The South Carolina governor transmitted the Act of 1880 for "running anew" the boundary line, and requested that a suitable person be appointed by the Governor of North Carolina to join in the survey.[211] Governor Jarvis received the document, with the request, and promised in return to lay it before the Legislature, which was then in session.[212] The Legislature adopted a general policy for dealing with boundary disputes, which was enacted into law. An act was passed in 1881 which would meet any contingency that might arise relating to the subject. The governor was authorized to appoint a competent commissioner for North Carolina to cooperate with commissioners who might be appointed by the "contiguous states" of South Carolina, Georgia, Tennessee, or Virginia, to "re-run and re-mark" the boundary line between North Carolina and any of the said States. When

---

[210] *North Carolina Executive and Legislative Documents, Session 1881* (Raleigh: *News & Observer*, 1881), Document no. 2, p. 3.

[211] Governor Hagood to Governor Jarvis of North Carolina, January 24, 1881. *North Carolina Executive and Legislative Documents, Session 1881*, Document no. 2, p. 2.

[212] Jarvis to Hagood, January 31, 1881. *Ibid.*, Document no. 2, pp. 2-3.

such line should be established, the governor was directed to issue warrants for the State's share of the expense incurred. In case of failure of the commissioners to reach an agreement, the governor was empowered to appoint arbiters who were to act with arbiters to be appointed by the other States concerned in the settlement of the true boundary. In case the arbiters could not reach an agreement, the governor was directed to report the fact to the following General Assembly for further action. It was further provided that no survey should be valid until after adoption by the Legislature.[213]

The policy herein set forth became the established practice of the State for a generation. The revised code of 1905[214] and that of 1908[215] continued this general method of handling the problem, and in the following year the law was amended so as to broaden the governor's general powers by authorizing him to "institute and prosecute" legal proceedings to protect the State's boundaries whenever he deemed such action necessary.[216]

The Governor of North Carolina did not appoint a commissioner to act with the South Carolina representative in 1881, though the Legislature passed the general act referred to above. His failure to act was probably because of a clause contained in the South Carolina act of 1880 specifying that the work should be completed within a year from the date of enactment.

South Carolina was determined to have the line run and marked, however, and appointed a surveyor to carry out an independent survey.[217] He ran a portion of the line between his State and Mecklenburg County, North Carolina, and erected a few

[213] *The Code of North Carolina*, 2 vols. (New York: Banks & Bros., 1883), II, 42-43. In 1889 the North Carolina Legislature passed a similar act with the same general provisions, except the Governor was to lay the final report of any new survey before the Council of State instead of the Legislature. *Laws and Resolutions of the State of North Carolina, 1889* (Raleigh: Josephus Daniels, 1889), chap. 475.

[214] *Revisal of 1905 of North Carolina*, 2 vols. (Raleigh: E. M. Uzzell & Co., 1905), II, 482, chap. 113, sections 5315-9.

[215] *Revisal of 1908 of North Carolina*, 2 vols. (Charleston: Walker Evans & Cogswell Co., 1908), II, 2547.

[216] *Amendments to Revisal of 1905, enacted 1907-1915* (Raleigh: n. p., 1915), chap. 63.

[217] Special message of Governor Scales to North Carolina Legislature, February 10, 1887. *Executive and Legislative Documents*, Session 1887 (Raleigh: Edwards, Broughton & Co., 1887), Document no. 19, p. 2. The surveyor is called in the sources, "Mr. Spencer."

monuments; "but it settled nothing and left the people, if possible, in greater trouble than before."[218]

Conditions in Mecklenburg County grew constantly worse. Disputes over the limits of farms were frequent. The State line named in the deeds was simply the recognized boundary of the farms. Finally, in January, 1885, representations were made to the governor by the Legislators of Mecklenburg County, and by other prominent citizens, "pressing upon him the importance of having the line between said Mecklenburg County" and South Carolina re-surveyed and re-marked "so as to relieve the people from great annoyance and vexation, growing out of the fact that the line was not known."[219]

Governor Scales applied to the Governor of South Carolina for a "joint commissioner" but "for want of time" the matter was not brought to the attention of the Legislature, which was then sitting; nor was it brought before the succeeding session, because of "a misapprehension of the facts." The North Carolina governor decided to have made an independent survey, as the southern government had done in 1881. In April, 1886, he appointed a member of the Legislature, S. B. Alexander, as a commissioner to resurvey "and settle, as far as practicable, this line." The surveyors were Arthur Winslow of Raleigh and J. H. Collins of Pineville, North Carolina.

There was great difficulty in locating the line because of the careless surveying done in 1772. The boundary was finally run from Twelve Mile Creek at the southeastern corner of the Catawba Lands, to the northeastern corner; and from the latter point along the old line to the Catawba River. Confusion was more confused. There were now three possible locations for the county line alone, in addition to the line run by Spencer for South Carolina in 1881. A section of the North Carolina surveyors' report will show the three possible locations, with the territory lost or gained. The surveyors' table is as follows:[220]

[218] Special message of Governor Scales to North Carolina Legislature, February 10, 1887.
[219] Governor Scales' special message of February 10, 1887.
[220] This table is taken from the final report of Commissioner Alexander to Governor Scales, 1886. *Executive and Legislative Documents*, session 1887, Document no. 21, p. 3.

	Twelve Mile Creek to N.E. Corner Indian Lands		N.E. Corner Indian Lands to Catawba River		Area	
	True Course	Distance	True Course	Distance	Gained	Lost
1. Present recognized line	N.36¼W.	14⅝ miles	S.54¾W.	7⁷⁄₁₆ miles	0	0
2. Line with courses deduced from map of 1772 and corrected approximately for magnetic variations	N.33 W.	13¾ miles	S.56¾W.	8¼ miles	3338	3080
3. Line with distances corresponding with map of 1772	N.37 W.	13¾ miles	S.53¼W.	7½ miles	5480	0

It will be seen from the above table that North Carolina had been losing the use of over 5000 acres of land. Neither of the possible locations agrees with the Spencer survey of 1881. It was perfectly clear that *ex parte* surveys would never settle the dispute. Consequently, Alexander reached the following conclusion: "The line can only be determined and located by a joint commission, and I recommend that it should be determined as early as possible." He was forced to this urgent recommendation by the fact that disputes "have already arisen, and many constantly arise between the people who live along this line."[221] Governor Scales then reported the facts to the Legislature in his special message, stating at the same time that, with the Act of 1881 in force, no new legislation was necessary in order to enable him to proceed with an adjustment.

Nothing was accomplished, however, because of a lack of cooperation on the part of South Carolina. Governor Scales later informed the Legislature that nothing had been done since his special message was delivered, though he had written to the Governor of South Carolina "several times" asking his cooperation in adjusting the line. He added that there were then two different surveys of the line—one by North Carolina and the other by South Carolina—"and so it must remain until South Carolina will

---

[221] Alexander's report to Scales, 1886.

arbitrate the matter, or join us in a survey."[222] South Carolina was unwilling to participate in such a survey at that time.

Exactly a century had passed since the last joint survey when North Carolina again took action which finally led to an amicable settlement.[223] On March 9, 1915, as a result of vanishing line markers and the accompanying confusion, an act was passed authorizing the governor of the State to appoint a commissioner and chain-bearers to "re-run and re-mark" the boundary line from the Atlantic Ocean to the Waccamaw River, a distance of "about eight miles."[224] Arbitration was again provided as a resort in case the commissioners should fail to agree; and should arbitration prove impossible, the following Legislature was to be so informed. When the purpose of the law should have been carried out and the proceedings of the commissioners approved by the Governor and Council of State, the Governor was required to issue a proclamation to the effect that the new survey was the permanent boundary between the States.[225] The act contained a change in method of meeting the cost of such surveys. The traditional policy was to allow each colony or State to bear half of the total expense; the new policy was to require North Carolina to meet the cost of the proceedings of her own representatives. This departure was a saner method, because it made the State's commissioners responsible directly to their own government and therefore was conducive to economy of expenditure. South Carolina was sufficiently impressed to adopt the same policy, as will later be shown. In North Carolina the statute was re-enacted in March, 1919,[226] and so amended as to extend the scope of the resurvey

---

[222] Governor Scales' message to North Carolina Legislature, 1888. *Public Documents of the State of North Carolina,* Session 1889 (Raleigh: Edwards & Broughton, 1889), Document no. 1, p. 26.

[223] *Journal of the Senate of the General Assembly of the State of North Carolina, Session 1915* (Raleigh: Edwards & Broughton 1915), p. 786; *Journal of the House of Representatives of the General Assembly of the State of North Carolina, Session 1915* (Raleigh: E. M. Uzzell & Co., 1915), p. 952.

[224] *Public Laws and Resolutions of the State of North Carolina* (Raleigh: Edwards & Broughton, 1915), chap. 188.

[225] *Public Laws and Resolutions of the State of North Carolina* (1915), chap. 188.

[226] *Journal of the Senate of the General Assembly of the State of North Carolina, Session 1919* (Raleigh: Commercial Printing Co., 1919), p. 531; *Journal of the House of Representatives of the State of North Carolina. Session 1919* (Raleigh: Edwards & Broughton, 1919), p. 624.

from the seacoast to Lumber River at the "corner of the dividing line between Columbus and Robeson counties."[227]

Nothing was done following the passage of either of the last two acts toward re-running and re-marking the eastern portion of the line, whose lack of definiteness was causing confusion in the counties of Brunswick, North Carolina, and Horry, South Carolina. Confusion so increased in the years following the passage of the last act, however, that individual citizens in the disturbed region began to appeal to the Governor of North Carolina to endeavor to have the eastern portion of the line resurveyed and plainly marked. Over a period of years, "from time to time," many "reputable citizens" filed such requests. Such an appeal came from one C. Edward Taylor of Southport, Brunswick County, North Carolina, the contents of which were given by Governor A. W. McLean to the Governor of South Carolina as an example of the pressure being brought to bear on the government by citizens of his State toward securing a settlement of the renewed dispute.[228] Governor Richards replied to the communication by expressing appreciation for "bring[ing] to my attention the question of the dividing line" near the coast; and he added, "I agree with you as to the importance" of a settlement.[229] It appears, therefore, that throughout the period, authorities of South Carolina were unaware of the occurrence of these frequent disputes; at least they had taken no action, either executive or legislative.

Threatening incidents near the boundary line forced the interested attention of both States on plans for a solution. In January, 1928, a party of North Carolina fishermen were digging clams just off the coast in the region of the old line, but in territory which they professed to believe was within the bounds of North Carolina. It is possible, however, that they were attempt-

[227] *Public Laws and Resolutions of the State of North Carolina* (Raleigh: Commerical Printing Co., 1919), chap. 166.
[228] Governor McLean to Governor John G. Richards of South Carolina, February 4, 1928. South Carolina Governor's Correspondence (MSS.). This correspondence is in the Governor's office, Columbia, South Carolina, and was kindly loaned the writer by Governor Blackwood personally for use in this study.
[229] Richards to McLean, February 7, 1928. N. C. Governor's Correspondence (MSS.). This correspondence may be found in the Governor's Office, Raleigh, North Carolina, and was made available to the writer through the generosity of Governor O. Max Gardner. Duplicates of Governor McLean's letters to Governor Richards are also on file there.

ing to escape payment of the heavy tax laid on clams in North Carolina. At that time, the North Carolina tax was twenty cents per bushel; whereas, in South Carolina it was only eight cents.[230] The fishermen were arrested by the South Carolina Fish Warden, who was "duely equipped with a badge to prove and a gun to enforce his authority," on the grounds that they were digging in South Carolina waters. The fishermen protested vigorously but "the warden and his gun won the argument."[231] While preparing to go to jail, however, the prisoners escaped by a ruse. Nevertheless, the warden had "furnished the spark that rekindled the flame" which had been alternately smouldering and flaring up for more than two centuries. Later offenders were "deposited in a South Carolina jail."[232]

These and similar incidents, which were fast approaching the point of open violence, led the Governor of North Carolina to initiate proceedings which finally led to a settlement. Governor McLean sent the Governor of South Carolina a copy of the Act of 1915, as amended in 1919, and requested that he urge the Legislature of his State, then in session, to provide for cooperation in a new survey, should there be no existing law which so provided.[233] Richards replied with a promise that he would accede to the request and give notice of the response of the General Assembly.[234]

The South Carolina executive was very cooperative. He carried out his promise on the same day. In a message to the Legislature, accompanied by Governor McLean's letter, he warned that "This appears to be an important matter," and is submitted for such action as may be deemed wise and proper.[235]

South Carolina acted with reasonable promptness. Senator Spivey of Horry County—the South Carolina county directly involved—introduced a bill which was passed and concurred in

[230] *Raleigh News and Observer*, March 11, 1928.
[231] *Ibid.*, April 27, 1928. See also, issues of March 4th and 11th.
[232] *Ibid.*, April 27th and March 11th, 1928. The writer attempted to secure facts regarding prison sentences and fines imposed on later prisoners, but the clerk of Brunswick and Horry counties replied that they could not supply the information unless the names of the prisoners were given. The names have not been ascertained.
[233] McLean to Richards, February 4, 1928.
[234] Richards to McLean, February 7, 1928.
[235] Extract from Richards' message to South Carolina Legislature, enclosed in his letter to Governor McLean. See also *News and Observer*, February 10, and March 4, 1928. Cf. McLean to Richards, March 6, 1928.

NORTH CAROLINA BOUNDARY DISPUTES 153

by the House, thus enacting a law on March 1 which was in substance a re-enactment of the North Carolina law. It provided for the appointment of a commissioner and chain bearers by the governor "to re-run and re-mark the boundary line" from the Atlantic Ocean to Lumber River, near "a corner of the dividing line between Columbus and Robeson counties."[236] It will be noticed that the exact words of the North Carolina act are here used. A copy of this act was forwarded with expedition to North Carolina on the day following its enactment.[237] It seems that South Carolina had sensed the danger of further complications over the line, whose location had become vague since it was marked in 1735.

On receipt of the South Carolina act also authorizing the appointment of a commissioner, Governor McLean proceeded to act under the North Carolina law and appointed an exceptionally competent engineer as commissioner for the State in the person of George F. Syme, Senior Engineer of the North Carolina State Highway Commission.[238] In the same month, Governor Richards appointed Colonel J. Monroe Johnson of Marion, a very able engineer, describing him as "one of the outstanding engineers in our State."[239]

In the meantime, Governor McLean became apprehensive lest the frenquent "unseemly disputes" should result in violence before the line could be officially run. Consequently, after having a conference with J. S. Nelson, Commissioner of Fisheries, and Major Wade Phillips, Director of Conservation and Development, he proposed that a temporary line be staked out by the fisheries commissioners of the two States in order to prevent conflicts pending the final establishment of the permanent boundary. This action was "to be without prejudice to the official action in marking

[236] *Acts and Joint Resolutions of the General Assembly of the State of North Carolina* (n. p., n. p., 1928), Statute no. 927. See also a report of this action in the *News and Observer*, May 4, 1928.
[237] Richards' secretery to McLean, March 2, 1928; *News and Observer*, March 4, and April 27, 1928.
[238] McLean to Richards, March 15, 1928; *News and Observer*, March 17, 1928. At the time of his appointment, Syme had had thirty years experience as a civil engineer for various railroad companies, and was appointed by the President of the United States on the commission to locate the proposed Nicaraguan canal. George C. Love of Durham was appointed chief engineer of the North Carolina surveying party.
[239] Richards to McLean, April 12, 1928; *News and Observer*, April 14, 1928.

the line. . . . "[240] The proposal was accepted by Governor Richards.[241] He was at a disadvantage in reaching an agreement as to the location of a temporary line because no charts or drawings of the survey of 1735 had been preserved by South Carolina. Cooperation between the two governors was perfect, however, and Governor McLean had photostatic copies made of the drawings and documents in the office of the Secretary of State, Raleigh, for his use. A temporary boundary line was soon laid off.

At a conference in Raleigh in April between the commissioners of the two States and Governor McLean, plans were finally made for beginning the survey early in the following month.[242] A warm dispute arose soon afterwards between the two commissioners regarding the location of the line. Johnson wished to move it farther northward, presumably to the point called for in the royal instructions of 1730, regardless of the mutual compromise of 1735.[243] Syme refused to join in the survey unless it should again be run through the old boundary house as in the survey of 1735.[244] Governor Richards supported North Carolina's position on this point, stating that the two governments had accepted the old line for a "hundred years or more" and, "therefore, it had become the actual boundary no matter what the two States had contended for long ago."[245] Johnson then cooperated with Syme.

This agreement was expected "to eliminate every controversy." Syme and Johnson publicy "expressed the opinion that this time there was not going to be any row over the line, regardless of who gets a strip of land hitherto claimed by the other";[246] and a leading newspaper expressed the hope that the dispute should soon be "finally settled if the Commissioners can manage to set a new precedent and keep an agreement." However, it further expressed a fear that a part of Brunswick and Columbus counties

[240] McLean to Richards, February 9, 1928; *News and Observer*, February 10, 1928.   [241] *Ibid.*, February 22, 1928.
[242] McLean to Richards, April 26, 1928; *News and Observer*, April 27, 1928.   [243] *Supra*, p. 37.
[244] Mr. Syme stated to the writer in a personal interview that he and Johnson sat in the former's office in Raleigh and "abused one another over this point until we became good friends," and then reached an agreement.
[245] Johnson to Richards, May 4, 1928; Syme to Johnson May 4, 1928. This correspondence is in the office of the Highway Commission, Raleigh. It was kindly supplied the writer by Mr. Syme for use in this study.
[246] *News and Observer*, April 27, 1928.

NORTH CAROLINA BOUNDARY DISPUTES 155

might be "delivered" to South Carolina, for at that time not even the commissioners knew the size and extent of "no man's land."[247]

Arrangements were completed and the representatives of the two States met on the coast at Little River, May 10, 1928, and began the actual survey.[248] Progress on the line was much slower than expected on account of various obstacles and impediments. The commissioners had expected to complete the line by midsummer, but topographical features hindered the work, reminding those informed on the early survey of the tortuous experiences of the early commissioners. Swamps along the Waccamaw and Lumber rivers were almost impassable.[249] Excessive heat was an almost constant and occasionally a prohibitory obstacle to progress. It overcame the subordinates who were cutting through the thick growth along the border, and made the necessary instrumental accuracy impossible to obtain at times.[250] Following the period of intensive heat, came a season of almost constant rains which flooded the swamps and "drenched the men every day and cut their progress at least fifty per cent."[251] Syme reported that Waccamaw Swamp, through which they had to run the line, was flooded with water from three to five feet deep for a cross-distance of two miles. Regardless of these difficulties, however, the line was completed, except for rechecking nine miles near Lumber River, early in September.[252]

The commissioners "reproduced in its entirety, the original State line" between Lumber River and the coast as surveyed in 1735.[253] The last monument was erected on Goat Island December 4, 1928, completing the survey and permanently marking the

[247] *Ibid.*, March 11 and April 27, 1928.

[248] Syme to Johnson, May 4, 1928; Johnson to Richards, May 4, 1928.

[249] Mr. Syme stated to the writer that they encountered a swamp in the region of the Waccamaw which was two and a half miles wide, and another on the Lumber River approximately one mile wide.

[250] Syme to McLean, August 11, 1928.

[251] Preliminary report of Syme to McLean, September 7, 1928. This report is in possession of Mr. Syme, and the governors of the two States have copies on file.

[252] Syme to McLean, September 7, 1928.

[253] As an unmistakable proof that the commissioners resurveyed the line directly in its location, they cut a Long Leaf Pine tree on their line, examined it and found the original blaze made in 1735, with 193 rings from the blaze to the bark. This, it is evident, checks exactly with the date of the last survey, and shows that neither State lost any territory thereby. Blocks of this boundary tree are now preserved in Raleigh and Columbia.

line.²⁵⁴ The line was run from the point of division on the coast in a northwestward direction, having a true meridian bearing of N 44° 26′ 11″ W at the Boundary House monument in latitude 33° 52′ 53.4″ N, and longitude 78° 34′ 37.2″ W, for a distance of 43.08 miles to a granite monument marking the corner of Columbus and Robeson counties²⁵⁵

The relations of the two States during the negotiations and the proceedings were for the most part satisfactory. Aside from the dispute between the commissioners regarding the location of the line, their relations were exceptionally friendly throughout.²⁵⁶ The surveyors quarrelled occasionally, and the subordinates frequently had serious misunderstandings; at times their verbal altercations almost reached the point of physical combat. The citizens along the boundary, with one exception, were calm and cooperative. A land owner of South Carolina, dissatisfied with the location of the line, dug up and removed one of the granite monuments, which the commissioners had to re-set. Governor McLean then issued a proclamation offering a reward of $600 for information leading to the arrest and conviction of any person removing the monuments.²⁵⁷

With official proclamation of the new survey as the permanent line,²⁵⁸ the controversy of more than two centuries was closed justly and amicably. North Carolina had won her contention that the line should not be altered by running farther northward, which change would have brought with it unlimited confusion over land ownership, collection of revenues, and other functions and relationships.

North Carolina re-stated her general policy of handling bound-

---

[254] Syme to McLean, December 7, 1928.

[255] Proclamation of Governor McLean, August 11, 1928. D. L. Corbett, ed., *Papers of Angus Wilton McLean* (Raleigh: Edwards and Broughton, 1931). The final report of the commissioners of the two States prepared by Mr. Syme may be found in the offices of the governors at Raleigh and Coulmbia, and in the offices of the Secretaries of State at the respective capitols.

[256] Personal interview with Commissioner Syme, January, 1932.

[257] Proclamation of December 13, 1928. This document is also in the governor's office, Raleigh. See also, letter from Syme to McLean, November 26, 1928.

[258] These proclamations may be found in the offices of the respective governors. Surveys prepared by the commissioners are preserved by the two Secretaries of State, by the Governor of North Carolina, by Mr. Syme, and by the North Carolina Historical Commission.

ary questions by enacting a law with the same general provisions, giving the governor power to protect the State's boundaries by instituting suit, if necessary, against any State which might contest the lines.[259]

Having thus followed the development of the controversy which arose between the Carolinas, and noted its general effects on the life and history of the two colonies and States down to the present time, we are now in a position to return to the account of the running of the remainder of the State's southern boundary—that portion which divides North Carolina and the State of Georgia—a section over which a dispute developed which, though briefer in its course, involved even more inter-State bitterness and violence.

[259] *The Code of North Carolina* (1931), chap. 124, sections 7396-7400.

PART II
THE GEORGIA-NORTH CAROLINA BOUNDARY DISPUTE

CHAPTER I

ORIGIN OF THE DISPUTE AND EARLY EFFORTS TOWARD SETTLEMENT

The original boundaries of the colony of Georgia reveal the same indefiniteness of description as characterized those of the earlier colonies. The Charter of June 9, 1732, provided that the colony should be bounded by the Savannah and Altamaha rivers, "and westerly from the heads of the said rivers respectively, in direct lines to the south seas."[1] The particular branch of the Savannah River which should be regarded as the "head" of the stream was in no manner indicated.

The independent State seems to have accepted the charter boundary as a matter of course, or to have ignored the obligation to define its boundaries; they were not mentioned in the Georgia Constitution of 1777.[2] The State did not draw up a new constitution from 1798 to 1861; hence, after the former date no constitutional description of the boundary existed during the course of the dispute with North Carolina.[3] In 1783, the Georgia Legislature passed an act in which it was stipulated that the "limits, boundaries, jurisdictions, and authority of the State of Georgia had and did and of right ought to extend from the mouth of the river Savannah along the North side thereof and up the most Northern stream or fork of said river to its head source."[4] The Constitution of 1798 contains a similar provision,[5] adding that the line should follow the Tugaloo River to the Chatooga, thence along that stream to its intersection with the northern boundary of South Carolina; but if the Chatooga did not extend that far

---

[1] F. N. Thorpe, ed., *Federal and State Constitutions*, II, 771. The charter is here copied in full.   [2] *Ibid.*, II, 777-785.

[3] Walter McElreath, *A treatise on the Constitution of Georgia* (Atlanta: The Harrison Co., 1912), *passim;* Thorpe, *op. cit.*, II, 777-85.

[4] Robert and George Watkins, *A Digest of the Laws of the State of Georgia* (Philadelphia: Aitken, 1801), pp. 264, 749. (Cited hereafter as Watkins, *Digest.*)   [5] Article I, section 23.

northward, the line should turn due westward from the head or source.⁶

The ownership of the territory disputed between Georgia and North Carolina was first questioned while claimed by South Carolina. The dispute arose over the interpretation of the term "head" of the Savannah River. The latter State described her claim as follows:

South Carolina claims the land lying between the North Carolina line and a line to be run due west from the mouth of the Tugaloo River to the Mississippi, because, as the State contends, the River Savannah loses that name at the confluence of Tugaloo and Keowee rivers, consequently that spot is the head of Savannah River; the State of Georgia, on the other hand, contends that the source of Keowee is to be considered at [as] the head of Savannah River.⁷

South Carolina instituted suit against Georgia before Congress under Article IX of the Articles of Confederation. She was basing her position on "the general acceptance of the words—Head-Northern-Stream-Savannah River and the sense to be drawn from them as they are conjoined in the Charter."⁸ The disputed area involved ownership of 37,500 square miles, or 24,000,000 acres.⁹

The case was adjourned repeatedly until finally, on September 4, 1786, both States appeared, represented by their agents. A court was appointed to try the case, but no decision was ever rendered in consequence of a compromise reached between the two States. Both governments appointed commissioners with full powers to settle the dispute,¹⁰ who met at Beaufort, South Carolina, April 28, 1787, and drew up an agreement or convention.¹¹ The first

⁶ Oliver H. Prince, *A Digest of the Laws of the State of Georgia* (Milledgeville: Grantland and Orme, 1822), p. 551. (Cited hereafter as Prince, *Digest*.)

⁷ Petition of South Carolina to Continental Congress, *Journals of the Continental Congress*, 1785. Quoted by W. R. Garrett, "History of the South Carolina Cession" (*Tennessee Historical Papers*, Nashville, 1884), p. 9. See also, *C.R.*, V, 382.

⁸ W. Few to the Speaker of the Assembly of Georgia, October 19, 1786. Quoted in *Georgia Historical Quarterly*, XII (1928), 59.

⁹ *Ibid.*, p. 60.

¹⁰ *S.R.*, XVIII, 675; Executive Letter Book, VII, 213; Watkins, *Digest*, p. 390.

¹¹ Called the "Treaty of Beaufort." The commissioners were C. C. Pinckney, Andrew Pickens, and Pierce Butler on the part of South Carolina; representing Georgia were John Habersham and Lachlan McIntosh. Georgia House Journals, February 3, 1787; Georgia Governor's Letter

article provided that the boundary between the two States should be the Savannah River to the confluence of the Tugaloo and Keowee rivers, thence along the Tugaloo to the Chatooga River, and thence along the Chatooga to its source.[12] This convention ceded all of the territory bordering on the present North Carolina and Tennessee line to Georgia, as far as it lay in the power of the two States to convey territory. The convention was ratified by the Legislature of Georgia.[13]

Action of the South Carolina Legislature, which was then in session, altered the situation. On March 8 of the same year, just before the signing of the treaty of Beaufort, that body passed a bill conveying to the United States the territory bounded by the Mississippi River, the North Carolina line, a line drawn along the summit of the Blue Ridge from its intersection with the North Carolina line to the most southern branch of the Tugaloo River, and thence westward to the Mississippi. The congressional delegates of South Carolina were directed to make a deed accordingly.[14]

These inconsistent acts of South Carolina required the confirmation of Congress, according to the Articles of Confederation. They, with the deed of cession, were presented to Congress the same day, August 9, 1787. The cession to the United States was accepted on the same day. The motion to confirm the convention of Beaufort was referred to a committee which, it appears, never reported.[15]

Book (MSS.) (hereinafter cited as Governor's Letter Book) July, 1803. These sources are in the Department of Archives and History, Atlanta. The Georgia records of this period were carelessly kept. In his special message to the Legislature in 1810, Governor Mitchell described the "mutilated" condition of portions of the records for the period of the Revolution and for several years thereafter. He urged that they be transcribed into "good and durable books." House Journals, November 26 and December 11, 1810. The record of the latter date indicates that nothing was done toward better preserving these valuable records.

[12] The State vs. Georgia Railway and Power Company. Opinion by George Hillyer, Arbiter, September 17, 1915, in which is quoted the language of the treaty of Beaufort. *Georgia Historical Quarterly*, I (1917), 155-6; Garrett, "History of the South Carolina Cession," p. 10.

[13] Georgia House Journals, January 31, 1788; Prince, *Digest*, p. 53.

[14] Garrett, "South Carolina Cession," p. 10.

[15] The failure of this committee to report was probably due to the impressive progress then being made by the constitutional convention of 1787, which completed its work in the following month by adopting the Constitution, soon to supplant the Articles of Confederation under which the dispute had been referred to Congress.

The United States thus came into possession of the twelve-mile strip of territory, the northern boundary of which was to become the subject of a serious controversy between Georgia and North Carolina—a dispute which was "bottomed upon the same principle" as that with South Carolina.[16]

The cession of their western lands by the two States brought about another important change in the ownership of the twelve-mile strip. The South Carolina cession of 1787 was followed by that of North Carolina in 1789.[17] Congress accepted the cession and received a deed, executed by the North Carolina delegates in Congress.[18] Governor Martin then issued a proclamation definitely announcing the completion of the cession. Georgia held out until 1802 and used her territory in bargaining with the Federal government for the twelve-mile strip obtained from South Carolina. In April, 1802, she ceded the Mississippi Territory and received in return that portion of the South Carolina cession north of her boundary, $1,250,000, and a guarantee of the extinction of all Indian titles within her limits.[19] Thus North Carolina and Georgia were in possession of adjacent territory, the line of division of which was to occasion more inter-State bitterness and violence than the controversy between the Carolinas.

Georgia took immediate steps to determine the boundaries of her new possessions. On May 7, 1803, her Legislature adopted a resolution directing the governor to take such measures as he might deem necessary "to ascertain and identify that tract of country ceded by the United States to this State," and to direct the Surveyor-General to lay a map of the region before the following Legislature.[20]

Early in December of the same year, after settlers in the region had petitioned Georgia to be incorporated in her government, the State proceeded to provide by law for organizing the territory into a county called Walton.[21] An extract of the law was sent

[16] Governor Alexander's message to North Carolina Assembly, November 20, 1806. Executive Letter Book, XVI, 48.
[17] S.R., XXV, 4-6; Legislative Papers, December, 1799, Box No. 167.
[18] Samuel Johnston and Benjamin Hawkins to Governor Martin. Executive Letter Book, entry for April 11, 1790.
[19] Augustus S. Clayton, comp., *A Compilation of the Laws of the State of Georgia, 1800-1810*. [20] Quoted in Prince, *Digest*, p. 53.
[21] Georgia House Journals, December 7, 1803; Senate Journals, December 10, 1803; Clayton, *A Compilation of the Laws of the State of Georgia*, p. 128.

immediately to Governor Turner of North Carolina.[22] The desire was expressed of having the line between North and South Carolina extended north of the Blue Ridge, since Georgia had acquired the title to the previous South Carolina claims. North Carolina was requested to cooperate in running such a line, beginning at the termination of the survey of 1772 and running a direct course to the point of intersection of the thirty-fifth parallel with the Blue Ridge. From that point the line should follow the summit of the ridge to the intersection of a line drawn due west from the head of Tugaloo River, as described in the Act of Cession of South Carolina.[23] The act was not to become effective until the line was run, provided the survey was made within six months after its enactment.

Governor Turner was requested to lay the question of a survey before the North Carolina Legislature and to expedite action toward a settlement. Delays which he could not prevent, however, interfered with all efforts. South Carolina's attitude was a principal cause. When the six months time limit was about to expire, Turner complained that her quibbling over the North Carolina Bill of Rights and the resulting failure to join in extending the line between the Carolinas had prevented the survey of the North Carolina-Georgia line.[24]

After the organization of Walton County, opposition in North Carolina to Georgia's encroachments became positive and active. Governor Turner was greatly surprised and displeased because the county had been erected before the North Carolina Legislature could meet and consider Georgia's request to join in running the line. He stated that Milledge's request arrived after the Legislature had adjourned.[25] Confusion in the disputed region itself increased steadily. The laws of Georgia "cannot in that quarter be carried into effect, and . . . irregularities are constantly taking place between our citizens, and those of North Carolina," accord-

[22] Governor Milledge of Georgia to Governor Turner, December 15, 1803. Governor's Letter Book, 1802-1809 (MSS.). These manuscripts are in the Department of Archives and History, Atlanta. See also, Executive Letter Book, XV, 214.

[23] *Steele Papers*, II, 905-6. As has been shown above, the thirty-fifth parallel does not strike the Blue Ridge. Ignorance of topography of the region again encouraged a boundary dispute.

[24] Turner to Williams of Buncombe, March 10, 1804. Executive Letter Book, XV, 260.

[25] Turner to Milledge, October 20, 1804. *American State Papers-Miscellaneous*, I, 443.

ing to reports of officials from Walton County.[26] Complaint was made to Governor Turner that "outrages" committed in the region by an armed force "resembled more the doings of men warring against an enemy" than acts of citizens of the same nation.[27] One citizen testified in court that he and nine others had been arrested and taken to the prison of Buncombe County.[28] The Governor of Georgia urged the Legislature to take immediate steps for settling the dispute and thus improve the conduct of the North Carolina citizens near Walton County.

Buncombe County citizens were at the same time filing complaints with their own government against inhabitants of the southern part of Buncombe who "claim[ed] to be" in South Carolina, refused to obey North Carolina laws, and balked at the payment of taxes. When the county sheriff would levy on their property, they would "raise with force & arms, & retake it & threaten our officers." Settlers at the head of the French Broad threatened that if the sheriff should come there again, they "will take him to Louisville, Ga. &c."[29] It was further reported that the inhabitants had "beat and abused officers heretofore," and now it is expected that lives will be lost.[30] An earnest plea for the State's protection was made.

The initiative in legislative action toward securing an adjustment of the dispute, which was constantly growing "more threatening," was taken by Georgia, though such action was the result of a letter from Governor Turner regarding the situation.[31] A bill was passed authorizing the appointment of commissioners to run and mark the dividing line.[32] It appears, however, that no commissioners were appointed at that time, probably because of objection to certain provisions of the North Carolina Act of 1803 relative to land titles.

[26] Governor Milledge to Georgia Legislature, November 6, 1804. Georgia House Journals, 1803-1805.
[27] Milledge to Turner, February 5, 1805. Governor's Letter Book, 1802-1809, p. 152.
[28] Depositions before the Justice of the Peace of Jefferson County, Georgia, February 16, 1805. Copied in *Annals of Congress,* 9 Congress, 2 session (Washington: Gales & Seaton, 1852), p. 985.
[29] Joshua Williams of Buncombe County, to Governor Turner, January 30, 1804. Executive Letter Book, XV, 230.   [30] *Ibid.,* XV, 359.
[31] Governor Milledge to Georgia Legislature. House Journals, November 12, 1804.
[32] Georgia House Journals, December 6, 1804; Senate Journals, December 8, 1804.

NORTH CAROLINA BOUNDARY DISPUTES 167

The Legislature of North Carolina in 1804 amended the Act of 1803 for settling the dispute with South Carolina, to include the settlement of the Georgia question,[33] though Georgia felt that, as she then owned the territory to the Tennessee border, the North Carolina commissioners had power to cooperate with Georgia commissioners under the provisions of the Act of 1803 authorizing a survey to the Tennessee line.[34] The objectionable proviso of the Act of 1803 was retained in the amended Act of 1804. Georgia made strong protest against this clause and her governor declined to request the Legislature to act further while it remained in force.[35]

When transmitting a copy of this act to Governor Milledge, Governor Turner urged the immediate appointment of commissioners and the taking of all necessary steps toward a settlement.[36] He defended the land title clause, which provided that land titles granted by either State should not be affected by the running of the line, on the grounds that it was necessary in order to prevent violence. Furthermore, he said, it was the accepted policy of both States and nations.[37] He was on firm ground in this position.[38]

Georgia objected to the land title clause on the grounds that there were no legal titles to the land held when it was ceded by South Carolina to the United States, claiming that South Carolina had voided all titles in 1786.[39] Governor Turner made a distinction in the types of settlers in the region on the basis of their rights to land. He frankly stated that there were many settlers about whom North Carolina knew nothing, and that if Georgia had extended government over them only, his State would have raised no objection. But he added that there were many others who held North Carolina grants which were legally obtained, and the State would never be so "cruel" as to abandon them and thus invite the violence which would certainly follow. He then took

[33] *Laws of the State of North Carolina* (1821), II, 1013.
[34] Milledge to Turner, April 6, 1804. Governor's Letter Book, XV, 294. Turner had expressed the same opinion as to powers of his commissioners. Turner to Williams of Buncombe, March 10, 1804. Executive Letter Book, XV, 234.
[35] Milledge to Turner, May 23, 1804. Governor's Letter Book, 1802-1809.
[36] Executive Letter Book, XV, 433.
[37] Turner to Milledge, May 8, 1804. Executive Letter Book, XV, 304.
[38] See Douglas, *op. cit.*, and Gannett, *op. cit., passim.*
[39] Milledge to Turner, February 17, 1805. Governor's Letter Book, 1802-1809, p. 157.

a position which could not be successfully answered; and that was, that his government would never acknowledge Georgia's jurisdiction over such regions until the running of the line proved it was her right. Georgia further claimed as proof that titles were void that, as the North Carolina grants were made while the territory was owned by the United States, they could not be legal. The point would have been very effective had Georgia been accurate regarding the facts she assumed. However, she was wrong for two reasons. In the first place, thousands of grants were made after the Federal government had ceded the territory received from South Carolina back to Georgia—that is, after 1802.[40] In the second place, much of the territory claimed by Georgia under the cession from the United States had never been under the jurisdiction of the Federal government, as the astronomers later proved. Nevertheless, with regard to the land titles clause, under the circumstances which she was convinced then existed, Georgia felt that "The injustice of [her] objection presents itself to her too forcibly to be conceded."[41] Governor Milledge then took the position that, if North Carolina declined to run the line unless his State should incorporate a similar provision in her law, action must be deferred until both Legislatures "come to some understanding on the subject."[42]

It is evident that the two States had reached an impasse. In his annual message of 1804 to the Legislature, Governor Milledge merely submitted the correspondence of the governors bearing on the dispute;[43] and on the following day the whole question was referred to the Committee on the State of the Republic. After receiving another urgent request for action from Turner immediately thereafter, Milledge sent a special message to the Assembly.[44] Two weeks later, definite action was taken when a bill which "required" the governor to appoint commissioners passed the Senate.[45] The House concurred in the bill a fortnight later.[46] When transmitting a copy of this act to the Governor of North Carolina, with a request that it be laid before the Legislature,

---

[40] George A. Digges, comp. *Buncombe County North Carolina Grantor Deed Index*, 3 vols. (Asheville: The Miller Press, 1927), v. P-Z, *passim*.
[41] Governor's Letter Book, May 23, 1804.
[42] *Loc. cit.*
[43] Georgia, House and Senate Journals, November 6, 1804.
[44] House and Senate Journals, November 12, 1804.
[45] Georgia, Senate Journals, November 26, 1804.
[46] Georgia, House Journals, December 10, 1804; Clayton, *op. cit.*, p. 189.

Governor Milledge proposed to appoint commissioners as soon as he should be informed of such action by North Carolina.[47] He had already urged haste on the part of North Carolina on account of the six months time limit in the Georgia act.[48]

Pursuant to the powers given him in the North Carolina Act of 1804, Governor Turner designated the commissioners appointed to run the North Carolina-South Carolina line to act also in the Georgia dispute.[49] He proposed that if Georgia had taken action to cooperate in the survey, the two governors immediately proceed to fix a time and place of meeting for the commissioners in order to hasten an "amicable'" settlement and prevent further "serious disturbances."[50]

The old land title question continued to obstruct all efforts at cooperation on the survey. When Turner urged Georgia to send commissioners to the meeting of the North and South Carolina commissioners early in 1804,[51] differences over that question prevented Georgia from participating. Early in the following year, the North Carolina governor again proposed joint action on the terms of the proviso, but stated emphatically that his State could not participate on any other terms.[52] Georgia then advanced new arguments against the land titles proviso. It was argued that, as Georgia had never granted lands in the disputed territory, none of her citizens would have claims to any land in North Carolina when the line should be run; therefore this clause should apply no farther than South Carolina had exercised her patent authority, which was only to the ridge dividing her territory from Walton County; that some of the North Carolina grants were obtained before the Indian titles were extinguished, and some after it was known that Georgia had acquired the region. It was further charged that the titles were obtained by land speculators merely for profit, and not by real settlers who were desirous of developing the region. Georgia also declared that approval of such a

[47] Milledge to Turner, December 11, 1804. Governor's Letter Book, 1802-1809, p. 443; Executive Letter Book, XV, 429; Georgia, Senate Journals, November 5, 1805.
[48] Milledge to Turner, April 6, 1804. Executive Letter Book, XV, 294.
[49] *Steele Papers,* II, 471.
[50] Turner to Milledge, December 26, 1804. Executive Letter Book, XV, 433.
[51] Turner to Milledge, February 25, 1804. *Ibid.,* XV, 234.
[52] Turner to Milledge, January 8, 1805. *Annals of Congress* (Washington: Gales & Seaton, 1852), 9 Congress, 2 session, p. 981.

proviso would not leave a "single acre" at her disposal, as the entire area was covered by North Carolina grants. On these grounds of opposition to the proviso, Georgia firmly "dissent[ed] to the same."[53]

Governor Turner replied directly to these arguments. His points summarized were as follows:[54]

1. The territory was not covered by North Carolina grants. It is 130 miles long and 60 to 70 miles wide, and "abounds, in every part, in unappropriated lands." Allowing a proportionate quantity of lands granted to lie in the section affecting the Georgia claims, she, who abounds probably more than any other State in unappropriated lands, cannot insist upon the establishment of a principle which manifestly tends toward individual oppression.
2. The claim that absentee owners, and not the settlers, are the holders of the North Carolina grants is also erroneous. Very few, "if any," grants were obtained by speculation.
3. Should the Georgia line extend as far northward as demanded, many North Carolina grants will be forfeited, unless Georgia agrees to the proviso.
4. The practice of nations, as well as the "uniform policy" of every State in the Union, except Georgia, in fixing boundaries show that individual property should be protected. As Georgia knew the conditions in the disputed territory when she acquired it, there is no reason why she should depart from general custom.
5. North Carolina only persists in maintaining her position from a consciousness of the justice of her contentions.
6. The proposal to run the line and leave the question of titles to future deliberation of the two Legislatures must be declined because it is against the known will of the Legislature of North Carolina, as well as contrary to propriety. Furthermore, partial proceedings might tend to irritate more than to conciliate.
7. Postponement of the survey, though regretted, is inevitable under North Carolina laws while the Georgia government maintains its present position.

Taken as a whole, this was a strong reply. Georgia's claim that all of the land in the region had been appropriated was incorrect. North Carolina continued to grant lands there for a number of years after this date.[55] Even had it been true, Georgia had

[53] Milledge to Turner, February 17, 1805. Governor's Letter Book, 1802-1809, p. 162.
[54] *American State Papers-Misscellaneous*, I, 447.
[55] Digges, *op. cit., passim.*

received an enormous amount of territory on the south and west by the treaty of 1783 with England, and other treaties with the Indian tribes. Her desire to evict North Carolina grantees was not justified from a standpoint of reason and justice. Nor was the claim that North Carolina landholders as a group were speculators, though it was the State's privilege to have sold all of its western lands to speculators had she so desired, without altering her position with regard to her boundary claims. But admitting for the sake of argument that the point was pertinent to the question of locating the dividing line, the charge was erroneous. North Carolina's land policy at this time is clearly demonstrated in the following table, indicating the size of the first 1,000 grants in Buncombe County from 1790 to 1800:

	Date	1790 to 1800			
No. of Acres	1 to 100	100-200	200-300	300-500	above 500
No. of Tracts	454	282	88	90	86

Total 1000

That is, all but 86 grants were tracts of less than 500 acres. The proportion continues approximately the same through the date the charge of wholesale speculation was made.[56] It is evident, therefore, that North Carolina was not dealing in wild speculation, but was endeavoring to settle her western lands with a large number of small farmers who would make up a stable population. Furthermore, Georgia was leading the States in sordid speculation, as a glance at the history of the Yazoo claims at this time will demonstrate. The accusation against North Carolina simply opened her to attack.

Governor Turner was also correct in his contention that if the line should have been run as far north as demanded, North Carolina would lose all of her land grants in the disputed region. His insistence on protection for individual property on the grounds of both justice and precedent was reasonable, as has been shown. He was also sincere in his declaration that North Carolina was

[56] Digges, *op. cit.*, vol. P-Z, *passim.* See also, F. A. Sondley, *Asheville and Buncombe County* (Asheville: The Citizen Co., 1922), p. 116. Sondley states that North Carolina granted lands in Walton County to people "who had settled there."

conscious of the justice of her claims. The State did not have the slightest doubt that Georgia was in error as to the location of the line. It might be accurately stated that this was also true of Georgia, but it must be remembered that this dispute with North Carolina was only three years old at the time, and the former State had not long been examining the location of the parallels of latitude; whereas, North Carolina had been vitally interested for three quarters of a century and had a better conception of approximate locations than did Georgia.

Governor Turner was not on such safe grounds in his refusal to agree to a survey first and negotiations relative to the land question later. Georgia wishes deserved more consideration in this case than they received when first expressed. North Carolina's attitude was lacking in accommodation.

The governor was taking the only possible position left for him, however, under the State's laws, when he deferred the running of the line while Georgia maintained her position on the proviso.

Governor Milledge urged a prior survey, nevertheless, suggesting that the land titles question be left to the future deliberation of the two Legislatures. If such a course should be accepted, he requested a meeting of the commissioners.[57]

Georgia's case was again weakened by the inconsistency apparent in the statements of her governor and her Legislature. While the former frequently reported general confusion and continued "outrages," the Legislature stated in their act for appointing commissioners that the authority of the State was recognized generally in the territory.[58]

The Georgia government enjoyed the active support of many citizens of Walton County on the issue of the land titles. They drew up an address to the governor in the fall of 1805, urging him "not to accede to the views of North Carolina" in that regard.[59] County grand juries added their influence in support of the government. The Grand Jury of Franklin County, Georgia, moved by the "many Flagetius outrages" committed in Walton County, recommended that the Legislature strongly endeavor to

[57] Milledge to Turner, February 17, 1805. Governor's Letter Book, 1802-1809, p. 162.
[58] Clayton, *op. cit.,* p. 190.
[59] Georgia House and Senate Journals, November 5, 1805.

effect a settlement of the dispute for the relief of "oppressed and defenseless Citizens" in that "distressed County."[60]

The governor submitted the people's address to the Legislature. He also asked the body to request the Legislature of North Carolina to agree to a conference being held by three or more citizens of each State to consider the controversy, with power to "determine the same"; and in case of disagreement, to ballot for arbiters from other States, "whose decision shall be conclusive and binding on both States."[61] On the following day, the matter was referred to the Committee on the State of the Republic.

In the meantime, the "Walton War" had taken on so violent a nature and had become so widespread that the county elections became mere factional fights with no appearance of legality. In the fall of 1805, one Ebenezer Fain appeared in the Georgia Senate and produced his credentials of election. After careful consideration the Committee on Privileges and Elections reported adversely, recommending that his seat be denied on the grounds of open violation of the State's election laws. The body agreed to the report and the seat was formally denied.[62] The House member from Walton appears to have been seated in the following year; "Richard Williamson, Esq." was listed among the members.[63] Walton had no representative in the Lower House when the extra session of 1808 opened;[64] but "John Nicholson, Esq." attended from Walton at the opening of the regular session of the same year.[65] Five days after the opening of the session, a resolution requesting the governor to issue writs of election for Walton County was "laid on the table." The Committee on Privileges and Elections reported that, judging from the election return of Francis Nicholson, they considered that the election was held in Franklin County instead of Walton at a time when Walton County was not in a state of invasion;[66] and even if such conditions ex-

[60] Presentments Franklin County Court, October term, 1805. Quoted in Georgia Senate Journals, November 6, 1805.
[61] Governor's message to Georgia Legislature. House and Senate Journals, November 5, 1805.
[62] Georgia Senate Journals, November 6, 1805.
[63] Georgia House Journals, November 2, 1807.
[64] *Ibid.*, May 8, 1808.   [65] *Ibid.*, November 7, 1808.
[66] The State Constitution of 1798 provided that, in case a county should be invaded or in a state of insurrection at the time of an election, it might be held in another county. Thorpe, *op. cit.*, II, 800. See also, Georgia House Journals, November 9, 1810.

isted, there was not a majority of the county participating in the election as required by the Constitution.[67] It was found that only twenty-two electors actually voted; consequently the committee reported that Nicholson had not been "constitutionally elected." A resolution was adopted to the effect that he should no longer be considered a member of the House.[68] Two days later, he was allowed $84.00 for his "past services" and his seat declared vacant.[69]

Confusion in the county appears to have subsided for a time and normal elections conducted by 1809. Representatives were present and fully recognized in both Houses.[70] At the opening of the regular session in 1810, Walton was represented in the Senate but not in the Lower House,[71] though two claimants of a legal election soon appeared. Nicholson's seat was contested by one Reuben Allen. It was found that Allen's claim was based on the insurrection clause of the State constitution of Georgia, though he and many of his followers admitted living in South Carolina since 1804, claiming they had been forced by terror growing out of boundary violence to leave the disturbed county.[72] Nicholson and all other voters acknowledged paying taxes to North Carolina and performing all other civic duties required of them, upon demand of that State. It was further reported that the officials appointed pursuant to the law establishing Walton County "have never in the smallest manner performed any duties . . . or attempted to carry into effect any of the tax or other laws of this State." Many of the voters supporting Nicholson, it was stated, had long been "utterly opposed to the laws of Georgia," and friendly to North Carolina; and they had actually engaged in expelling "by force and arms" those inhabitants of Walton who supported the laws of Georgia. The committee found that the county was in "a complete state of disorganization . . ." so that there were "none of the most common and ordinary functions of

[67] The Surveyor-General reported that there were 133 heads of families in the county at the time. Georgia House Journals, 1808-1809, p. 38.
[68] Georgia House Journals, 1808-1809, p. 38.
[69] Ibid., November 14, 1808. Nicholson's case must have been reconsidered, with favorable action, for he reappeared in December following, the oath of office was administered and he was seated. House Journals, December 7, 1808.
[70] Georgia House and Senate Journals, November 6, 1809.
[71] Ibid., November 5, 1810.
[72] Georgia House Journals 1810 (Printed), pp. 24-25.

officers, none of the most trivial regulations" normal to any orderly county government adopted, "and in fine the exercise of no duty in contemplation of government" which could entitle the county to equal rights and privileges with the other counties of the State. Hence, it was apparent to the committee that neither Nicholson nor Allen had been "legally and constitutionally elected," and therefore it was recommended that the seat be denied to either. The House acted accordingly.[73]

A month later an effort to defer representation of Walton County in the Lower House failed. The House, in Committee of the Whole, considered a bill to apportion the representatives among the several counties in the State according to the third census, as provided by the State Constitution. Upon resumption of proceedings in its legislative capacity, the bill was reported favorable. Representative Clayton then moved that the act be amended by adding just after County of Walton, the clause, "one member whenever the dispute between this State and North Carolina with regard to boundary, is settled and adjusted in our favor. . . ."[74] The amendment was rejected. The report of the Committee of the Whole was then adopted, "the bill read the third time, and passed under the title aforesaid."[75]

Thus Georgia insisted on representation of the county during the progress of a settlement of the controversy, regardless of all of the prevailing confusion and violence.

In the meantime, Georgia had reversed her entire policy in an endeavor to force a solution in her favor. In his annual message of 1805, Governor Milledge reminded the Legislature that the boundary controversy "is still unsettled," submitted all correspondence with Governor Turner on the subject together with the petition of the Walton County citizens, and urged that a solution be sought.[76] The Joint Committee on the State of the Republic, to whom the whole subject was referred, reported that, as the enactment of the law for appointing commissioners to cooperate with commissioners of North Carolina at the last session had demonstrated a desire "to put a speedy and amicable termination

[73] Committee report, November 9, 1810. Georgia House Journals, 1810 (Printed), pp. 24-25.
[74] Georgia House Journals, December 6, 1810.
[75] Ibid., December 6, 1810.
[76] Governor's annual message to Georgia Legislature. House and Senate Journals, November 5, 1805.

to the controversy and its concomitant evils"; and as the refusal of North Carolina to appoint commissioners, except under a provision which could deprive Georgia of soil rightfully hers by purchase from the United States precluded the probability of an amicable adjustment without congressional "interference," a different policy should be adopted. They therefore recommended that the current Legislature present a memorial to the General Government stating Georgia's claim to Walton County and the "interference" of North Carolina, together with the resulting "oppression and outrages," and calling upon the United States Congress to put the people of Georgia in peaceable possession of that territory.[77] The House adopted the committee report and the Senate concurred. A joint committee was appointed to draw up the memorial to Congress.[78]

A fortnight later, Crawford of the joint committee presented the draft of a "memorial & Remonstrance" for approval of the House, which may be summarized as follows:

1. By the second article of the Articles of Agreement and Cession of April 24, 1802, between commissioners of the United States and the State of Georgia, the United States ceded to Georgia all territory adjacent to the southern boundaries of the States of Tennessee, North Carolina, and South Carolina, lying east of the eastern boundary of the territory ceded by Georgia to the United States in the first article of said agreement and cession; which territory was accepted by Georgia June 16, 1802.
2. North Carolina "had never claimed or exercised jurisdiction" over, nor demanded or received taxes from, the people of said territory. Nor had she "extended the protecting arm of government to them."
3. Georgia, solicitous to give such protection and security, and on the earnest request of "those Selfgoverned people," on December 10, 1803, passed an act to organize the inhabited parts of the territory into Walton County.
4. By the same act, authority was given for the appointment of commissioners to cooperate with other commissioners and "ascertain and plainly mark" the North Carolina-Georgia line from South Carolina to Tennessee.
5. The Governor of North Carolina, acting under a law of 1803, agreed to appoint commissioners to act with Georgia

[77] Report of Joint Committee on the State of the Republic, Georgia House Journals, November 13, 1805.

[78] Georgia House Journals, November 13, 18, 20, 1805; Senate Journals, November 18 and 20, 1805.

commissioners, provided the running of the line should not affect titles to lands held under North Carolina grants.
6. Georgia declined to cooperate until this provision should be removed by legislative action, which was declined by the northern government.
7. Upon this failure to agree, Georgia proceeded to organize Walton County and to extend government to the people. ". . . a few turbulent persons" then attempted to prevent the operation of Georgia laws in the county, alleging that North Carolina jurisdiction extended over the greater part of it.
8. Nevertheless, an election was held there for Representatives who sat in the last Legislature of Georgia.
9. To obviate all difficulties, the Legislature of Georgia at the last annual session passed a second act December 10, 1804, for appointing commissioners. North Carolina also passed an act amending that of 1803 to apply to Georgia as well as to South Carolina, "but clogged with the same provision, as to the legality of their land grants."
10. North Carolina then declared that the line could not be run unless said grants were previously acknowledged by Georgia to be valid. This was regarded as inadmissible; hence, no commissioners have been appointed.
11. The county has recently been invaded and "the most cruel outrages" perpetrated against persons and property, many peaceful citizens having been lodged in North Carolina jails. Many others have had to "fly for refuge" across the mountains.[79] Disorganization is so complete that at present Walton County has no representation in the Legislature.
12. To accede to North Carolina's demand would be "improvident and unjust," as large grants are issued to speculators. After all, very few if any inhabitants hold grants under North Carolina.
13. The Legislature of Georgia have "felt deeply for their unfortunate fellow-citizens," and have made every effort to affect a settlement. All applications have failed.
14. With sincere regret the Legislature feels it is necessary to apply to the "Supreme Legislature of the Union," convinced that is the only method left to pursue, and the only source from which a termination of the dispute can now be expected. The Legislature therefore "entreats" the Congress of the United States to interpose and cause the thirty-fifth parallel to be determined and the line plainly marked.

[79] John Nicholson had been sent by the "exiled inhabitants" to plead their condition before the Georgia Legislature. Georgia House Journals, November 30, 1805; Senate Journals, December 2, 1805.

15. "This will completely terminate the question," as North Carolina does not claim territory south of said parallel and Georgia claims no jurisdiction north of 35°.[80]

Many of the above statements were historically accurate. However, the claim that North Carolina had never exercised jurisdiction or attempted to collect taxes in the disputed territory was incorrect. It has been shown above by testimony of Georgia's own representatives that it was North Carolina's general policy to endeavor to perform all functions of government in the region. It has been shown that the State had been granting lands in the territory constantly, and a State does not issue grants without collecting taxes on them thereafter. The charge regarding speculation has been treated above.[81]

The great contribution made in this document toward a solution, however, was the definite statement that both States would readily accept the thirty-fifth parallel as the line when it should be located with absolute accuracy. This gave the key to a simple but final and amicable solution. One of the North Carolina commissioners caught the significance of this admission immediately and pointed it out in a letter to the leading North Carolina Congressman, Nathaniel Macon, who was then the Speaker of the House. Stating that he had observed Georgia's application to Congress, he added that if their claim extended no farther north than the thirty-fifth parallel, "there can be no difficulty between us[,] for a due west course on the line of that degree is our claim."[82]

The above report was unanimously adopted, after which the House requested the governor to send the memorial and all correspondence to the United States Congress.[83] Governor Milledge carried out the request, adding all documents bearing on the question.[84]

The whole question was submitted to Congress January 13, 1806, and referred to a special committee of five members.[85] The

[80] Georgia House Journals, November 29, 1805.
[81] *Supra*, p. 171.
[82] Steele to Macon, February 26, 1806. *Steele Papers*, II, 1.
[83] Georgia House Journals, November 29, 1805.
[84] Milledge to Georgia's Senators and Representatives, December 20, 1805. Governor's Letter Book, 1802-1809, p. 200.
[85] Annals of Congress, 9 Congress, 1 session, p. 339; Daniel R. Goodloe, "The North Carolina and Georgia Boundry," North Carolina Booklet, III

committee was directed to examine the whole question and report their opinion to the House.

A report was made in February following by Chairman Spalding. It appears that they accepted all of the statements in the Georgia memorial as facts; but the point must not be lost sight of that Spalding was a Georgian. It was stated that, between the thirty-fifth parallel and the northern boundary of Georgia as described in the treaty of Beaufort of 1787, was a twelve-mile strip which belonged to South Carolina until ceded to Georgia by that treaty; that it was owned by South Carolina until ceded to the United States in 1787; and that it was transferred to Georgia in 1802 by the Federal Government.

As her Legislature had formally ratified the "treaty of Beaufort," it was natural for Georgia to hold tenaciously to that line. However, two points are vital in estimating the validity of her claim; namely, no record has been found of formal ratification by South Carolina; and, as her Legislature ceded the territory to the United States one month and twenty days before the signing of the Beaufort convention, it is logical to conclude that the Legislature never did ratify a boundary agreement in which the State no longer had any concern. Georgia did not really have a right to the line she claimed. The State was on sounder ground in stating that land titles granted before 1798 were not valid because it was not until that year that the Treaty of Tellico was signed extinguishing the Indian title.

The Congressional committee felt they "had no right to enter into the feeling of either of the parties," or to "pronounce" upon the justice of the clause relating to land grants. They therefore confined their opinion to the request that Congress should define and mark the thirty-fifth parallel, which both States proposed to accept when accurately located. They were convinced that the United States were "bound in good faith to use their friendly offices" with North Carolina to obtain an amicable determination of the limits of the territory which the Federal Government ceded to Georgia, in all parts where the line was disputed. Hence it was recommended that a resolution be adopted authorizing the

---

(1903-4), 5. The committee members were Spalding of Georgia, Stanford of North Carolina, Campbell of Tennessee, Moore of South Carolina, and Epps of Virginia.

President to appoint a commissioner to act with commissioners of Georgia and North Carolina to ascertain and run the line.[86]

The report was read and referred to a Committee of the Whole House, to be considered on the following Friday.

The question was not taken up for consideration in the Committee of the Whole House on the date designated. It is probable that the report of the special committee appeared biased in favor of Georgia, and that Congress was not willing to act without the arguments in defense of North Carolina's claims.[87] No action was taken, and the matter was dropped. Georgia claimed at the time that the Representatives in Congress "abstained, however, from pressing the affair, on receiving assurances from the State of North Carolina that they would represent to their own State the necessity of meeting on some other grounds the requisition of Georgia."[88]

In the regular session of the Georgia Legislature of 1805, the dispute was again taken up and an act was passed "authorizing and requiring" the governor to appoint two or more commissioners, with full and competent power, to cooperate with commissioners of North Carolina in designating more plainly the boundary line of Walton County.[89]

It appears that the governor did not carry out his duty as required in the act. Continued violence in the territory, however, forced the question on the attention of the two States constantly and led to executive and legislative action. Governor Milledge referred to the controversy in his annual message of 1806, expressing confidence to the Legislature that North Carolina would readily agree to submit the question to the arbitrament of commissioners of both States who, if they should fail to agree, should have power to appoint arbiters from other States to decide the dispute "conclusively."[90]

The message and documents were referred to the Joint Com-

---

[86] *American State Papers-Miscellaneous*, I, 439.

[87] This is the conclusion of Daniel R. Goodloe in his brief sketch on the dispute (N. C. Booklet, 1903-4, III, 8); and a study of the sources leads the writer to the same conclusion.

[88] *American State Papers-Miscellaneous*, II, 72. The writer has not found any evidence of this promise, though it may have been made verbally.

[89] *American State Papers-Miscellaneous*, I, 448-9. The act was dated December 10, 1805.

[90] Governor's message to Georgia Legislature. House and Senate Journals, November 4, 1806.

mittee on the State of the Republic for examination and report. They reported that they had carefully examined the measures taken to organize Walton County and to reach an amicable settlement with North Carolina over the question of jurisdiction, that North Carolina had refused to assent to them unless Georgia agreed to the land title proviso. The refusal of two successive Legislatures to agree to such a clause, on the grounds that it was "impolitic and unjust," was considered "Correct and Just." As Georgia had passed two acts inviting North Carolina to cooperate in a friendly adjustment and had met with refusal, and as the memorial to Congress to have the thirty-fifth parallel accurately determined had been of no effect; therefore, it was the committee's opinion, Georgia might complete the organization of Walton County by establishing courts and providing for the protection of persons and property without incurring the slightest imputation of want of respect for a sister State.

Desiring continued harmony with North Carolina, however, and believing that an amicable settlement would yet be brought about, the committee recommended the adoption of the following resolutions:

1. That the Legislature would by joint ballot elect three commissioners to join such commissioners as might be appointed by North Carolina to ascertain the thirty-fifth parallel and plainly mark the dividing line.
2. That if North Carolina declined to appoint commissioners, or if such commissioners declined to cooperate with those of Georgia; then it should be their duty to proceed alone to ascertain said parallel according to the Articles of Agreement and Cession agreed to between Georgia and the United States on April 24, 1802.
3. That the governor be required to transmit a copy of these resolutions to the Executive Department of North Carolina "as soon as possible."[91]

The House adopted the committee's report, though it declined to agree to the contention of Walton County citizens that Georgia was bound to make good their losses suffered from the "illegal and arbitrary conduct" of adherents of North Carolina. Satisfaction for such losses, it was contended, could be secured through the law courts as soon as the "differences" between the two States had been adjusted.

[91] Committee Report, November 25, 1806. Georgia House Journals, 1806-1807, pp. 185-7.

The Senate having concurred in the report of the committee,[92] the Legislature proceeded to elect as Commissioners, Thomas P. Carnes, Thomas Flournoy, and William Barnett, to ascertain the thirty-fifth parallel and run the line.[93]

The Legislature of North Carolina also took definite action in 1806 to bring about a settlement. Stating that the land titles proviso "can answer no valuable purpose, so far as it respects the State of Georgia, and may be an impediment to an amicable and speedy adjustment and settlement of boundary between the two States," the act provided that such proviso in the Act of 1804 "shall not be construed to extend or have any relation to the State of Georgia. . . ."[94]

Thus North Carolina, for the sake of maintaining harmony with the government and State of Georgia, and to check effectively the confusion and violence prevailing in the disputed region, compromised what she considered a just position.[95] This generous action paved the way for active and friendly cooperation. Keen appreciation was felt in Georgia. John Milledge, who had been appointed United States Senator from Georgia, wrote to John Steele concerning the North Carolina law as follows: "The passing of the act in the way it was done certainly ought to be considered by Georgia as indication of the willingness of North Carolina to remove every obstacle of controversy between the two States."[96] Governor Irwin of Georgia received "a very pleasing letter" from the Governor of North Carolina, with a copy of the act repealing the proviso, and then announced that there existed "the most flattering prospects of an amicable adjustment of our differences respecting boundary."[97]

[92] Georgia Senate Journals, November 29, 1806.
[93] Georgia House and Senate Journals, December 5, 1806; Minutes, Executive Department, September 1806 to February 1808 (MSS.), entry for December 5, 1806. These manuscripts are in the Department of Archives and History, Atlanta. See also, Governor Irwin of Georgia to Governor Alexander of North Carolina, December 10, 1806. Governor's Letter Book, 1802-1809, p. 219; Executive Letter Book, XVI, 64; *American State Papers-Miscellaneous*, II, 72; *The Augusta Herald*, December 11, 1806. This issue is in the Department of Archives, Atlanta.
[94] *Laws of North Carolina*, 1806, chap. IV.
[95] At the time this law was passed, local politicians were leading different factions, electing various sets of officials for the same office and encouraging violence among the inhabitants. Georgia House Journals, November 5, 1806.
[96] Milledge to Steele, January 27, 1807. *Steele Papers*, II, 494.
[97] Governor Irwin to Senator Milledge, January 20, 1807. Governor's Letter Book, 1802-1809, p. 220.

On January 1, 1807, Governor Alexander proposed a meeting of the commissioners of the two States, to be held at Buncombe Court House on April 20 following.[98] Governor Irwin informed his commissioners of the proposal,[99] which was courteously declined as inconvenient. The Georgia commissioners then suggested June 15 as a convenient date, which proposal was conveyed to the Governor of North Carolina[100] and was accepted.[101]

All available useful documents, papers, and surveyors' instruments were collected in preparation for the meeting and the survey which was expected to follow the negotiations.[102] As it was expected that the location of the thirty-fifth parallel "will be the principal subject in debate," the great demand was for able scientists, and the North Carolina commissioners earnestly requested that Dr. Joseph Caldwell of the State University be secured.[103] He was approached and consented to serve.[104] Dr. James Hall also served as a scientist for North Carolina. Dr. Josiah Meigs, President of the University of Georgia, and also a distinguished scientist, was the "artist" for that State.[105] The Legislature, however, directed the Surveyor-General to attend the commissioners also.[106]

The parties of the two States proceeded to Buncombe Court House on the date agreed upon and, after exchanging their credentials, organized themselves into a "Board" for definite work. The most important issue proved to be the question of confirmation of titles to lands transferred by running the line. The North Carolina commissioners based their argument in favor of such guarantee on the following grounds:

[98] *Ibid.*, pp. 222-223. John Steele, John Moore, and James Wellborn were appointed commissioners.

[99] Irwin to Georgia commissioners, January 28, 1807. *Ibid.*, p. 222.

[100] Irwin to Alexander, March 11, 1806. *Ibid.*, p. 223.

[101] Alexander to Irwin, March 25, 1807. *American State Papers-Miscellaneous*, II, 73; Irwin to Georgia commissioners, April 16, 1807. Governor's Letter Book, 1802-1809, p. 225; Executive Letter Book, XVI, 106.

[102] Governor Alexander to John Steele, May 28, 1807. *Steele Papers*, II, 514.

[103] John Moore to Governor Alexander, April 22, 1807. Executive Letter Book, XVI, 108.

[104] John Haywood to John Steele, May 29, 1807. *Steele Papers*, II, 516.

[105] *Ibid.*, II, 817.

[106] The commissioners and surveyors were to receive $3.00 per day for their actual services and $3.00 per 20 miles for necessary traveling expenses, which remuneration the governor was to pay from the contingent fund. Georgia House Journals, December 6, 1806.

1. Precedents established by other States in similar controversies.
2. That Georgia's claim was recent, having begun only in 1802.
3. That North Carolina secured the territory by right of conquest when, just at the opening of the Revolution, an army of North Carolinians under General Rutherford actually reduced that territory and marched into the enemy's country far beyond it.[107] Dates of grants and other authentic documents showed that North Carolina had claimed and exercised an uninterrupted jurisdiction over the area since the close of the Revolutionary War.
4. That as North Carolina got the territory in this manner in her efforts toward establishing American freedom and independence, and conceived to be within her limits by virtue of ancient charters and conventional agreements, to grant lands to individuals could not be justly regarded as an invasion of the territorial rights of any other government. If not so intended, the purchasers from North Carolina should be considered as innocent and, therefore, entitled by considerations of equity to have their entries and grants confirmed.
5. That the lands granted by North Carolina were paid for in certificates obtained for service in the "common cause" of the Revolution, or in money to be applied to the discharge of those certificates; hence, if any grants should fall in Georgia this consideration should have weight and tend to induce Georgia to confirm them.
6. It is manifest from the uncertainty existing on both sides at this meeting as to the true location of the line, that North Carolina never issued a single grant knowing it to be in another State. Thus, whether the number issued be few or many, the principle was the same, and Georgia should confirm them from consideration of a sister State.[108]

In reply to the arguments in support of these general points, the Georgia commissioners "with great candor and liberality admitted the justice and reasonableness of a certain portion of the claims," but decided that their powers were not competent to agree to any stipulations which would bind the State of Georgia to confirm those claims and give them validity in law. However, they expressed willingness to recommend confirmation to their

---

[107] This claim of conquest was accurate. General Rutherford subdued the territory far beyond Buncombe County. *S.R.*, XI, 338.

[108] Steele's preliminary report to Governor Alexander, July 2, 1807. *Steele Papers*, II, 520-2.

government, confident that the Legislature would confirm them in a manner giving adequate relief.

The preliminary discussions then closed and the commissioners divided themselves into two committees; the first to prepare the draft of a convention, and the second to prepare for the departure of the party to the mountains to "search" for the thirty-fifth parallel.

At the suggestion of the North Carolinians, they adopted formal articles of agreement with regard to methods of procedure. They were as follows:[109]

Article I. The territories of North Carolina and Georgia are, and of right ought to be, separated by the thirty-fifth parallel of north latitude; and for preventing in the future all manner of dissensions concerning jurisdiction, the undersigned commissioners will proceed forthwith to ascertain said thirty-fifth parallel, and to run and mark the line accordingly; which line, when ascertained and completed with joint concurrence, shall be the permanent dividing line.[110]

Article II. The commissioners of Georgia do not consider their powers competent to enter into any agreement which should bind their government to confirm land grants heretofore obtained from North Carolina, which land may fall within the limits of Georgia on running the line. But said commissioners promise and agree to recommend a certain portion of such claims in a special manner to the liberality of their government, not doubting that the Legislature will by law provide for the confirmation of said titles in a manner to give adequate relief. To this end said commissioners will recommend the establishment of an impartial tribunal for examining and determining on the merits of the various claims; said tribunal to be composed of three persons, to be appointed and paid by each State. Their meetings should be held in the State of Georgia, and their decisions to be "conclusive."

Article III. The commissioners agree to recommend to their respective Legislatures "in the most earnest manner" the enactment of laws of amnesty and "ob-

[109] These articles are here only summarized. The complete text, dated June 18, 1807, may be found in *American State Papers-Miscellaneous*, II, 74-76. They were signed by all commissioners except Thomas Flournoy of Georgia, who did not attend. [110] See map, p. 32.

livion" for all offenses (under the degree of capital) committed in Walton and Buncombe counties after December 10, 1803,[111] which were related to the boundary dispute between the two States.

After the signing of this agreement, the astronomers proceeded the following day to take observations at Douthat's Gap, a point on the summit of the southernmost portion of the Blue Ridge east of the source of Tugaloo River.

The State surveyors of Georgia had been making observations to ascertain the thirty-fifth parallel of north latitude before the above articles of agreement were signed and before the special surveyors of the two States had taken up their work. The result was inaccurate readings caused by the incompetence of the Georgians. Surveyor-General Sturges of Georgia had taken observations at the home of one Amos Justice, on the route from Asheville to the Blue Ridge, and about three miles from the point of intersection of the ridge with the old road from South Carolina to Kentucky.[112] He had found that point to be the approximate location of the desired parallel. On June 21, Dr. Caldwell and Dr. Meigs took observations at the same point, the average of which was 35° 33′ 32″ 20‴, or a difference of "twenty miles or upwards." The commissioners of Georgia, who "had been taught to believe" that the previous observations were entirely accurate, were "astonished and mortified" at the first readings of the special scientists.[113] Because of their great respect for the latter's ability, however, they "were under the necessity of suspending their astonishment," and proceeded with the survey.

Moving fifteen miles further westward, Caldwell and Meigs again took observations at a point near the mouths of Davidson and Little rivers, which point Surveyor-General Sturges had also found to be the thirty-fifth parallel. Their readings of June 22 were as follows.[114]

North Carolina	35° 17′ 6″ 93‴
Georgia	35° 18′ 10″ 22‴

[111] Date of law establishing Walton County.

[112] This road is shown on a map in the Annual Report of the Bureau of Ethnology, 1883-84. *House Miscellaneous Documents*, 49th Congress, 2nd session, 1886-7, vol. 10.

[113] Preliminary report of Steele to Governor Alexander, July 2, 1807. *Steele Papers*, II, 522-523; Report of Georgia Commissioners to Governor Irwin, July 25, 1807. *American State Papers-Miscellaneous*, II, 73-4.

[114] *Loc. cit.*

These results show a mean difference of 17' 38" 57''', or again a difference of more than twenty miles.

Confident of the accuracy of their observations, they proceeded due southward twelve miles to Ceasar's Head, a point near the summit of the Blue Ridge at its southernmost point. On June 24, the astronomical observations were as follows:[115]

    Georgia . . . . . . 35° 11' 1" 0'''
    North Carolina . . . . 35° 9' 15" 21'''

After these observations were taken, the Georgia commissioners were impressed that the thirty-fifth parallel could not be found on the Blue Ridge and became extremely desirous of deferring further observations until the following October. They were somwhat doubtful of the accuracy of the astronomers' instruments.[116] It was with much difficulty that the North Carolina commissioners persuaded them to continue. The North Carolinians stated that they were not willing to drop the work until the thirty-fifth parallel had been located, which could be done with the instruments they were using; and they pointed out that the readings taken by the astronomers of the two States were very similar.[117]

On June 26 further readings were taken as follows:[118]

    Georgia . . . . . . 35° 06' 20" 24'''
    North Carolina . . . . 35° 07' 21" 11'''

As will appear from these readings, the party was still approximately seven miles north of the desired line.

These observations convinced the commissioners of both States that the thirty-fifth parallel could not be found on the summit of the southernmost point of the Blue Ridge. Hence they negotiated articles supplementary to those signed at Buncombe Court House, and signed them on June 27, 1807. They contained the following provisions:

[115] Preliminary Report, July 2, 1807. *Steele Papers*, II, 524.

[116] Letter from the Georgia commissioners to North Carolina commissioners, dated Douthat's Gap, June 25, 1807. Copied in *The Minerva* (Raleigh), July 30, 1807. See also Steele's preliminary report, July 2, 1807. *Steele Papers*, II, 524.

[117] Letter from North Carolina commissioners to the Georgia comissioners, dated "Near Douthard's Gap of the Blue Ridge," June 26, 1807. *The Minerva*, July 30, 1807.

[118] *American State Papers-Miscellaneous*, II, 76.

Article I. The commissioners of Georgia, speaking for their State, admit after receiving numerous careful astronomical observations, that Georgia has no claim to the soil or jurisdiction of any part of the territory north or west of the Blue Ridge, and east or south of the present temporary boundary line between the white people and the Indians. And that they will recommend to their Legislature the repeal of the act establishing Walton County, at the next session, and to abrogate all proceedings for the organization thereof.

Article II. The North Carolina commissioners promise and agree to recommend to their government, and particularly to the civil and military officers in Buncombe County, to execute mildly and with clemency the laws concerning forfeitures and penalties, and in every other respect where the State may be concerned (under the degree of felony), towards the people who adhered to Georgia in the late dissensions over the boundary. If possible, said officers will forbear to institute suit and execute forfeitures and penalties incurred between December 10, 1803, and the date of this agreement, until the sense of the Legislature can be made known.[119]

The commissioners formally agreed that the supplementary articles and those of June 18, signed at Buncombe County Court House, "are to be considered as standing together" and forming a "final agreement" between the two States.[120] They informed the civil and military officials of Buncombe of these conventions in order that they might aid in giving amnesty provided in one agreement, and in the remission of forfeitures and penalties in accord with the other. The commissioners were confident that Buncombe citizens would receive the terms of settlement with satisfaction, but to re-inforce their own efforts to check the prevailing violence and bloodshed, they recommended that Governor Alexander should also issue a proclamation to the officials and inhabitants urging a strict observance of the agreements "until the sense of the Legislature shall be had thereon."[121]

On the day following the signing of the supplementary articles,

---

[119] *American State Papers-Miscellaneous,,* II, 75. The articles are there copied in full; they are here only summarized by the writer.

[120] *Steele Papers,* II, 524.

[121] *Steele Papers,* II, 524.

Caldwell, Meigs, and Hall, continuing their work at Douthat's Gap, took the last observations with the following results.[122]

Meigs	. . . .	35°	2' 57"	56'''
Caldwell	. . . . . .	35°	4' 54"	4'''
Hall	. . . .	35°	4' 55"	49'''

After going southward a number of miles below Georgia's old locations of the thirty-fifth parallel, therefore, the surveyors found that they were still approximately four miles north of the true line. The Georgians' inaccuracies were destined to prolong the time when an amicable settlement could be reached.

It is evident from the foregoing discussion, that early ignorance of geography and later incompetence of Georgia surveyors had combined to originate and encourage an unfortunate boundary controversy. Endeavoring to clarify the vague provisions of her original charter, Georgia had described her northern line by statute and then made it more nearly permanent by superseding the statute by incorporating its provisions in her constitution of 1798. South Carolina, it appears, had broken faith with Georgia during the process of changing ownership of the territory over which North Carolina and Georgia were later to quarrel. After South Carolina had appointed representatives with power to treat with Georgia in 1787, she was not justified in ignoring their work and ceding the territory to the Federal Government before they could complete their agreements.

After Congress had ceded the twelve-mile strip to Georgia in 1802 and the latter had organized the county of Walton, smouldering opposition became active and violent. The effect on the life of the two States was marked. Confusion characterized the local court system, administrative officials were "beat and abused" and became helpless to perform their duties, taxes could not be collected, citizens of the two States were "warring" among themselves. Imprisonment was common, and at one time during the "Walton War" two companies of militia had to be called out to maintain order. The regular functioning of the State government of Georgia was interfered with when various political factions in the disturbed region took advantage of the general confusion and

[122] *Ibid.*, II, 816-7; *American State Papers-Miscellaneous*, II, 76. These readings were taken on a very inclement day, and were admitted by all the astronomers to be very inaccurate.

sent their "Representatives" to the Legislature only to have them rejected.

The United States Congress was wise enough to stay out of the quarrel. The legislative branch of the Federal Government was the wrong agent to be asked to settle a violent dispute, particularly at a time when the States concerned were taking great pride in their sovereignty. One or the other could only have developed a strong prejudice against the general government by congressional attempts to adjust their differences. Apparently neither State desired to submit the controversy to the United States Supreme Court for adjudication.

A concession by each party opened the way to a settlement, though it was to be deferred a number of years. When Georgia stated in her memorial to Congress that the thirty-fifth parallel would be accepted if located with absolute accuracy, and when North Carolina agreed to drop her demand for a provision protecting land titles, the first crisis had passed. The agreements of 1807 were a logical consequence. The survey which followed convinced the Georgia commissioners of the gross errors in their State's impressions as to the location of the line, and caused the County of Walton temporarily to vanish. The fate of these agreements will next be considered.

CHAPTER II

THE CONTROVERSY RENEWED AND FINALLY CLOSED

It was the general opinion that the dispute with Georgia was closed after the signing of the agreements of June, 1807, and that there remained only the process of extending the line according to their provisions. The Georgia commissioners were decidedly under this impression. The relations between the commissioners of the two States had been very friendly. The Georgians were unexceptionable in their attitude and spirit during the proceedings. Steele reported that "we found the Gentlemen who acted on the part of the State of Georgia ready to meet us with the same just, elevated and conciliatory views."[1] They had conceded to North Carolina full ownership of the territory comprising Walton County and had agreed to urge their Legislature to abolish the county. It must be noted, however, that the Georgians declined to enter into any agreement with regard to land titles, as the North Carolinians had requested at the outset.[2]

North Carolina felt that the difference of opinion between the States had been "happily" adjusted in a "friendly and satisfactory manner." Governor Alexander expressed great satisfaction at the outcome of the negotiations, and the State was gratified with "the diplomatic and masterly manner," in which the negotiations were conducted by her commissioners.[3] A leading contemporary newspaper carried the following gratifying notice:[4] "It is with satisfaction we inform our readers that the dispute with Georgia for jurisdiction over a certain portion of territory is happily adjusted."

The commissioners for Georgia submitted a written report to Governor Irwin on July 25, 1807, containing the facts revealed

---

[1] *Steele Papers,* II, 525.
[2] See Article II of the agreement of June 18, 1807.
[3] Haywood to Steele, August 7, 1807. *Steele Papers,* II, 527.
[4] *The Minerva* (Raleigh), July 23, 1807.

and the signed agreements growing out of their discussion.[5] A similar report of the North Carolina commissioners, written by John Steele, was formally submitted to Governor Alexander.[6]

On December 17 of the same year, the Legislature of North Carolina enacted a law by which it was "fully ratified and confirmed."[7] Georgia, however, was plainly displeased with the proceedings of her commissioners. Governor Irwin announced to the Legislature in a tone of disappointment that, in accord with the observations of the astronomers of the two States, "Walton County will be found to be within the limits of North Carolina." Stating further that he had expected the Legislature to be concerned only with enacting further laws for the better organization of the county, he admitted that "a law of a far different nature is expected."[8] He requested the Legislature to consider the situation, and intimated that he expected prudent and appropriate action.

The Governor was not disappointed. His message was referred to the Committee on the State of the Republic, which reported as follows:

1. That "a difference and coincidence" in the various observations of the scientists, taken at the same time and place and with similar instruments, should have "raised in their minds rational doubts as to the accuracy of the instruments then used," or the truth of their observations.
2. That the Georgia commissioners were anxious to postpone the proceedings until new instruments could be secured and further readings be taken to test the former results.
3. That the committee were quite certain that North Carolina would not, if in her power, "stifle enquiry, when the object was the ascertainment of truth" and when a second trial might "calm inquietude."
4. Therefore, the committee recommended the adoption of a resolution favoring the appointment of three commissioners to be attended by two "artists" and the Surveyor-General, who were to use new instruments as well as the former ones in carefully making observations on the north side of the Blue Ridge. If the thirty-fifth parallel can be

[5] *American State Papers-Miscellaneous*, II, 73-6 This report was signed by Thomas Carnes and William Barnett.
[6] Executive Letter Book, XVI, 145; *Steele Papers*, II, 816-7.
[7] *Revised Statutes of the State of North Carolina* (1837), II, 90-2.
[8] Governor's annual message to Georgia Legislature. House and Senate Journals, November 3, 1807. This is the first topic discussed in the message, indicating the importance attached to the boundary controversy.

located there, the commissioners should have it plainly marked and report their proceedings to the governor by November 1, 1808.
5. The governor should be requested to notify the Governor of North Carolina of the doubts entertained by the Georgia Legislature as to the accuracy of the recent observations, and to request the appointment of new commissioners to join in a second effort to locate accurately the said parallel. Futhermore, "on the score of good neighborhood," he should request that North Carolina laws should not be enforced in Walton County, and that Georgia citizens there should not be disturbed in person or property by any officials of North Carolina.
6. That in case North Carolina should refuse to cooperate, the Georgia commissioners should proceed alone on their duties. Three thousand dollars was to be appropriated to meet the expense.

The resolutions, which in effect repudiated the work of the commissioners, were adopted.[9] A second resolution was even proposed in the House for appointing a committee to enquire into the official conduct of Surveyor-General Sturges regarding his report on the boundary, but the resolution was tabled.[10] The Legislature was plainly skeptical and dissatisfied with the work of their own capable astronomer, Dr. Meigs, in locating the line. The loss of an entire county at a period when a whole young nation was land hungry, was more than could be accepted without a new effort to verify the results. It must be said, however, that the Georgia Senate wavered on the issue of repudiating the work of the State's competent scientist. On the strength of his report the Senate passed a resolution suspending for the time being the election of officers for Walton County, but the Lower House tabled the resolution.[11]

The new commissioners appointed to act for Georgia were Nicholas Long, Leroy Pope, and James E. Houston. They were directed to ascertain again the thirty-fifth degree of north latitude and run and mark the line.[12] Two competent "artists" were to be

[9] Georgia House Journals, November 25, 1807; Senate Journals, November 30, 1807; Governor's Letter Book, 1802-1809, p. 288; Clayton, *Laws of Georgia*, p. 682 et seq.
[10] Georgia House Journals, November 7, 1807.
[11] House and Senate Journals, December 9, 1807.
[12] Georgia House and Senate Journals, December 1, 1807; Governor's Letter Book, 1802-1809, p. 263.

procured and they and the commissioners were each to receive $3.00 per day of actual service and a similar amount per twenty miles of necessary travel.[13]

In two written communications of March and June, 1808, to Governor Williams of North Carolina, one of which contained a copy of the resolutions of the Legislature, the Governor of Georgia urged the appointment of new commissioners to join in another survey. Governor Williams laid the matter before the Legislature where it was referred to a committee. The Legislature concurred in the later report of this committee,[14] which was to the effect that the Legislature "consider[ed] the subject of difference as solemnly adjusted."[15] Governor David Stone took the same firm stand in the following year. Replying to a previous request of Governor Irwin for the appointment of commissioners, he concluded as follows:

Indeed, it does not readily occur on what basis the adjustment is to rest if not upon that where it now stands.

The plighted faith of the two States to abide by the determination of commissioners, mutually chosen for the purpose of making the adjustment, and the adjustment of those commissioners actually made, I cannot, therefore, consistently with any sense of duty, make the appointments urged in your letter of December last.[16]

In the meantime, Governor Irwin again had earnestly urged North Carolina to cooperate in having the dividing line "permanently fixed," declaring that the "unhappy situation" of the inhabitants of Walton County "calls aloud for an adjustment" of the controversy.[17] Governor Stone only referred him to his previous letter as a reply.[18] It was plain that North Carolina's position was unalterable. She was in a strong position, having compromised on two vital questions; that is, on the question of

[13] Georgia House Journals, December 4, 1807; Senate Journals, December 8, 1807; Clayton, *op. cit.*, p. 684.

[14] N. C. Senate Journals, December 7, 1808; House Journals, December 8, 1808. These journals are also copied in *American State Papers-Miscellaneous*, II, 72-79.

[15] *American State Papers-Miscellaneous*, II, 72-78.

[16] Governor Stone to Governor Irwin, March 21, 1809. *American State Papers-Miscellaneous*, II, 76-7.

[17] Irwin to Stone, March 16, 1809. Governor's Letter Book, 1802-1809, pp. 283-284.

[18] Stone to Irwin, April 19, 1809. *American State Papers-Miscellaneous*, II, 77.

the confirmation of land titles, and the punishment of criminals in the disputed territory. On December 18, 1807, the Legislature had enacted a law providing that all crimes and misdemeanors, the punishment of which was by law capital, which had been committed between December 10, 1803, and June 27, 1807,[19] in the portion of Buncombe County formerly claimed by the State of Georgia and called Walton County, were "pardoned, released, and put into total oblivion."[20] The act was to take effect from the date of enactment of a law by the Legislature of Georgia "ratifying and confirming" the conventions of June 18 and June 27, 1807, between the commissioners of the two States.

The Legislature of Georgia made it known that they expected their new commissioners, with their new astronomical instruments, to proceed in the summer of 1809 either to verify or disprove the observations of the first scientists.[21] This was demanded despite a careful recheck by North Carolina.[22] Georgia held that, because the observations were contrary to all previous ones, because they were directly against the opinion of persons best informed on the subject, because they were not accepted by Georgia citizens residing in the territory, and because the observations varied sufficiently to strongly indicate errors,[23] she must have new observations made to satisfy her as to the real ownership of the disputed area.[24] Georgia was somewhat justified for demanding satisfaction on grounds of the last reason given, but the others—previous ob-

[19] The date of the establishing of Walton County and the agreement at Douthat's Gap, respectively.
[20] Laws of North Carolina (1821), chap. 718, section 1.
[21] Governor's Letter Book, 1802-1809, p. 288.
[22] Dr. Caldwell had carefully made observations with a new sextant early in 1809, which closely corresponded with the original readings. Steele to Governor Stone, April 30, 1809. *Steele Papers*, II, 591-2; Executive Letter Book, XVII, 68. Stone to Steele, May 24, 1809. *Ibid.*, XVII, 73. Governor Stone declared that North Carolina's position in the matter, and her fairness, were therefore sustained.
[23] The variation in Caldwell's and Meigs' observations of June, 1807, were:
    For June 22—1' 2" 49'''
    For June 24—1' 45" 39'''
    For June 26—1' 0" 47'''
Abstracts of astronomer's report, *Steele Papers*, II, 525.
[24] These reasons were stated later in resolutions of the Georgia Legislature. House Journals, December 13, 1809; Clayton, *op. cit.*, p. 690. Georgia's aim, in case her claim to ownership proved to be unfounded, was to go to Congress and press for remuneration for the loss of territory which the United States ceded to her in good faith in 1802.

servations, opinions of individuals, rejection by the inhabitants—were not of sufficient weight to stand against the observations made on the ground by a scientist of each State whose ability and integrity had never been questioned. Especially was this true when both Caldwell and Meigs were satisfied that, unquestionably, Georgia's previous impressions as to the location of the thirty-fifth parallel were erroneous.

As North Carolina could not be persuaded to participate in a new survey, the Georgia commissioners never attempted to carry out their instructions, but declined to make preparations to proceed.[25]

Governor Irwin informed the Legislature in 1809 that North Carolina continued her refusal to renew negotiations and again endeavor to ascertain the dividing line.[26] His message was tabled and later referred to a committee. A few days later, a resolution was presented providing for suspension of the Act of December 10, 1803, establishing Walton County until the thirty-fifth parallel was "properly ascertained, the line run and marked."[27] A week later a committee of three members was appointed to draw up a bill for carrying out the purpose of the resolution,[28] and after passing the second reading, further consideration of the bill was postponed until the following June.[29]

Governor Stone of North Carolina made only a brief reference to the dispute in his annual message of 1809, informing the Legislature of the new proof of the State's contentions regarding the location of the line as a result of Caldwell's recent careful observations. He expressed the hope that such proof would lead Georgia to an early ratification of the agreement of 1807, though admitting that the only communications received from her government were the requests for appointment of new commissioners to again join in locating and running the line.[30] The governor made no recommendations as to future policy, apparently desiring to await further action from Georgia.

Impatient at their failure to move North Carolina from her

[25] Governor's Annual message to Georgia Legislature. Georgia House and Senate Journals, November 7, 1809.
[26] Annual message to Georgia Legislature, November 7, 1809.
[27] Georgia House Journals, November 17, 1809.
[28] *Ibid.*, November 25, 1809.   [29] *Ibid.*, November 30, 1809.
[30] Governor's message to North Carolina Legislature, November 22, 1809. Executive Letter Book, XVII, 123 *et seq.*

NORTH CAROLINA BOUNDARY DISPUTES 197

position, the Legislature of Georgia again decided to turn to the United States Congress and the President with a new request to appoint a commissioner for locating the thirty-fifth parallel and running the line. A memorial was accordingly approved by the Senate and unanimously agreed to by the House.[31]

The memorial reviewed the history of the controversy through the proceedings of 1807, stating the reasons for refusing to ratify the results and adding that the government had pressed North Carolina "to a wearisome length" to join in a new effort to reach a satisfactory settlement, but had met only continued refusals. Hence, the Legislature saw but one mode of "calming the irritations that have arisen between the two States on the subject"; namely, an application to the Federal Government.

The Georgia Senators and Representatives were directed to urge favorable action on Congress, and the governor was requested to transmit the memorial and resolutions to all concerned. He promptly carried out the request. The memorial was communicated to the House of Representatives on April 26, 1810, by Representative Bibb of Georgia.[32]

The House took no action in the case but ordered the memorial or "representation" to lie on the table. The current session of Congress never resumed consideration of the question.

Soon after the opening of the third session of the Eleventh Congress, however, Representative Bibb called up the memorial and on his motion the House ordered that it be referred to a "select committee." Representative Bibb of Georgia, Macon of North Carolina, Calhoun of South Carolina, Stephenson of Virginia, and Ringgold of Maryland, were appointed as the committee to consider Georgia's request and report their findings to the House.[33]

Congress was slow to act, and Georgia had serious doubts that, even when action was taken, it would be favorable to the State. In November the governor announced that no decision had been made and that the time when such a decision would be made was uncertain, "as well as the nature of that decision";

[31] Georgia House Journals, December 13, 1809. A copy of these resolutions may be found in Clayton, *op. cit.*, p. 690, and in *American State Papers-Miscellaneous*, II, 72.

[32] *Annals of Congress*, 11 Congress, 2 session, pp. 2274-5; Georgia House and Senate Journals, November 6, 1810.

[33] *Ibid.*, 11 Congress, 3 session, p. 466.

hence, he suggested that other steps be taken.[34] Under such circumstances, and since previous efforts to determine the dividing line had proven so unsatisfactory, he recommended that an "artist" whose ability was unquestionable be secured; and in order to "preclude all idea of partiality," he should come from neither State concerned. Furthermore, he should go upon the ground and "ascertain with precision this much disputed point," which would better satisfy the State of Georgia by enabling her to support her pretentions before Congress with more effect, or "to relinquish the pursuit."

The governor urged the necessity of some immediate step toward a solution because of the "particular situation" of the people of Walton County. They had been organized into a county called Haywood, and were represented in the Legislature of North Carolina and performed all duties required of citizens by her laws.[35] At the same time, they were holding "partial elections" and sending representatives to the Georgia Legislature. "The dignity of the State demands that this controversy should be brought to a close," the governor declared; and he added that if the Legislature felt that another attempt to ascertain the thirty-fifth parallel would be useful or satisfactory, the State might have the services of an able scientist in the person of Andrew Ellicott.[36]

The governor's message was referred to the Committee on the State of the Republic.[37] In the following month their report was made, deploring the evil of a lack of harmony between sister States, and stating that it was honorable, dignified, and just for a State to offer such "openings of accomodation" as reason and justice might require in order to restore harmony and prevent future dissensions. The committee stated that they could not "divine" how long the dispute might be pending before Congress, nor how long the inhabitants might be deprived of citizenship,

[34] Governor Mitchell's annual message to the Georgia Legislature. House and Senate Journals, November 6, 1810.

[35] Haywood County had been established by act of the Legislature of North Carolina on December 23, 1808, and the county government began functioning March 4, 1809. *Laws of North Carolina, 1808,* chap. I; Arthur, *Western North Carolina,* pp. 166-167.

[36] Ellicott was from Lancaster, Pa., and a very capable man, having surveyed the disputed boundary lines of Pennsylvania, New York, the northern boundary of Virginia, as well as the southern boundary of the United States. Governor's Letter Book, February 26, 1811. However, Georgia became a victim of his selfishness, as will later appear.

[37] Georgia House Journals, 1810 (Printed), p. 18.

unless the foundation of the claims of each State was clearly established, thus affording the State which was in error a "decent and honorable opportunity of receding."[38] The adoption of a resolution was therefore recommended, providing that the governor be authorized to employ Ellicott to ascertain the thirty-fifth parallel, and in case North Carolina should decline to send a scientist to cooperate, that he instruct Ellicott to locate the line for the satisfaction of the State of Georgia. The governor should also notify the Governor of North Carolina of Georgia's "wishes and reasons" for an immediate and final adjustment of the controversy; that Georgia had employed Ellicott for the purpose, and that in case North Carolina should join in the new venture, the observations made should be "final and conclusive." The committee's report was read and agreed to.[39]

Ellicott was notified of the action of the Legislature by the governor and urged to accept responsibility for an accurate determination of the thirty-fifth parallel, setting a date and place of meeting, in case North Carolina should decide to send a commissioner to join in the survey. If not, he was assured, Georgia would expect him to proceed alone.[40]

Governor Mitchell transmitted to the North Carolina executive a copy of the resolutions of the previous December and informed him that he had taken steps to have Ellicott on the ground in the near future, and that he had accepted.[41] After promising to inform him of any date and place which Ellicott might designate, Governor Mitchell requested the Governor of North Carolina to give the matter "early attention." He expressed confidence that the State would join in this final survey to "put to rest" the lengthy and troublesome dispute.

North Carolina was not moved by this appeal. Confident that her claims were just, the governor again declined to appoint commissioners.[42] It proved to be the last time Georgia was to make

[38] Georgia House Journals, December 13, 1810.
[39] Ibid., December 13, 1810.
[40] Governor Mitchell to Ellicott, February 26, 1811. Governor's Letter Book, 1810-1815 (MSS.), p. 19.
[41] Mitchell to Governor of North Carolina, February 26, 1811. Governor's Letter Book, 1809-1814, p. 18.
[42] Ibid., April 30, 1811; Governor Mitchell's message to Georgia Legislature. House and Senate Journals, November 6, 1811. Mitchell stated in his message that he received a "positive refusal" to make an appointment. The North Carolina government appears to have become impatient with

such a request. Ellicott was directed to proceed alone and, after many delays, he entered upon his duties in the fall of 1811.

In the meantime, Congress had resumed consideration of the memorial of the Georgia Legislature and had courteously declined to interfere in the dispute. Governor Mitchell was informed through the Georgia Congressmen that the House of Representatives declined to act on the grounds that, as a legislative body, it was beyond their authority. The House advised Georgia to resort to "judicial interposition" for a decision to determine her rights.[43]

The citizens of Walton County themselves seem to have concluded by this time that their county did not legally and justly exist; that the work of the astronomers of the two States was, to say the least, very close to accurate. They had no representative at Milledgeville, the State capital, when the Legislature convened in regular session in November, 1811,[44] though a Senator from Walton, John Davis, attended and took his seat.[45] The absence of a Representative is significant, in view of the fact that the county was never again represented in either House at the opening of a legislative session.[46]

Ellicott made careful astronomical observations in the general region of the boundary and located the thirty-fifth parallel in a position which bore out the original conclusion of Meigs and Caldwell. His work was completed on December 26, 1811, and he submitted a report to the Governor of Georgia, which was accompanied by a poorly drawn chart of the line. His conduct during the period of his labors is important because of its probable influence on Georgia's attitude toward the survey. He took advantage of Georgia in the matter of remuneration for his efforts. Regardless of the governor's insistence, he would never commit himself as to the amount he would expect in payment. He would simply reply that he would expect the same amount he had received for running the boundaries of Pennsylvania, New York, Virginia, and other States. When asked what those rates were,

---

constantly repeated requests after it was felt that Georgia should have realized the finality of the State's refusal.

[43] Mitchell's annual message to Georgia Legislature, November 6, 1811. House and Senate Journals, 1811.

[44] House Journals, November 4, 1811.

[45] Senate Journals, November 4, 1811.

[46] House and Senate Journals, November 2, 1811, to November 2, 1818, *passim*. The writer has not found that the county was ever again represented.

NORTH CAROLINA BOUNDARY DISPUTES 201

he would evade and refuse to give the facts. On arriving in Georgia, he ignored the governor's request for a conference and communicated through messengers. When once in the region of the disputed boundary, he deliberately delayed his preliminary reports until the Georgia Legislature adjourned in order to forestall any legislative inquiry regarding his charges. When he finally reported, his charges were excessive and the succeeding Legislature hesitated long before approving them. He did not begin work until September, 1811, and completed his duties in December following; yet, in his letters, Governor Mitchell specifically mentions having paid him sums which total $3,700 and states that further remuneration allowed by the Legislature would also be paid. It is quite evident that his charges were extortionate. Moreover, he allowed his axe-men and other helpers to practice similar graft. Though Ellicott's report stated that the work was completed on December 26, 1811, the accounts of the subordinates called for daily wages to January 17, 1812. In a letter filled with stinging sarcasm, written after the reception of Ellicott's final report, Governor Mitchell stated that if the cost of publication of his journal was to be in proportion to the amount of his account, the government of Georgia "is perfectly indifferent as to its fate."[47] The government was greatly incensed over his conduct, and this costly experience undoubtedly played an important part in influencing the State to accept the line as located rather than face the expense of a new survey.

Ellicott's unusual ability as an astronomer and surveyor, however, produced results which were even more adverse to the claims of Georgia than those of the former scientists.[48] He ascertained the thirty-fifth parallel so closely that his work has since been accepted, and all standard maps of the region follow his line. A large stone on the eastern bank of the Chatooga River was made his marker and continued to be called "Ellicott's Rock" in the succeeding years.[49]

Governor Mitchell accepted the verdict resignedly and reported to the Legislature as follows: "By this report it appears

[47] On the quarrel with Ellicott, see Governor's Letter Book, August 29, 1811, to September 1, 1813, *passim;* House and Senate Journals, November 3, 1812.

[48] It must be remembered, however, that Caldwell, Meigs, and Hall never claimed to have reached southward to the thirty-fifth degree of latitude, but rather insisted that they were several miles north of that parallel.

[49] See, for example, Executive Letter Book, August 16, 1819.

that no part of the Territory heretofore claimed by this State as Walton County remains to Georgia."[50]

Though the Legislature realized that Ellicott's observations and conclusions also had terminated much to their dissatisfaction, they finally ratified the original articles of agreement of June 18 and 27, 1807.[51] The line was not run, however, at that time.[52] Failure to survey the line was probably caused by the pre-occupation of the two States with the War of 1812. The messages of the governors were largely taken up with questions of defense.[53] Naval craft were "skirting the coasts of . . . the Carolinas, and Georgia" from 1813 to the beginning of 1815.[54] The boundary question thus became submerged for a time. Furthermore, the usual interest in the boundary question naturally subsided after Georgia reluctantly accepted the conclusions of Andrew Ellicott.

Within a short period after the close of the War of 1812, when conditions and interests again became normal, efforts were begun looking toward a survey of the line as described in the agreements of 1807. It is probable that the necessity of a survey was called to the attention of the authorities by the westward movement then taking on such proportions and importance, and the consequent demand for definite and reliable land grants. Georgia assumed the initiative in securing a line when her Legislature took definite action in favor of a joint survey. Basing their action on the desire to promote harmony between the States, the Legislature passed a resolution on November 9, 1818, directing the governor to appoint commissioners, the number not to exceed three, who should "ascertain, run and plainly mark" the dividing line. The governor was requested to transmit a copy of the resolution to the Governor of North Carolina, requesting that it be

---

[50] Annual message to Georgia Legislature, November 3, 1812. Georgia House and Senate Journals, 1812.

[51] The authority for this statement is Dr. Caldwell, who stated seven years later that Georgia ratified the agreements of 1807 after Ellicott's adverse report. Caldwell to Governor Branch of North Carolina, August 16, 1819. Executive Letter Book, XXIII, 203. The State of Georgia "acquiesced in" Ellicott's observations, thus ending for a time the dispute as to the location of the thirty-fifth parallel. Prince, *Digest*, p. 54.

[52] Prince, *Digest*, p. 54.

[53] Georgia House and Senate Journals, 1812-1814, *passim*.

[54] Theodore Roosevelt, *The Naval War of 1812 or the History of the United States Navy During the Last War with Great Britain* (New York: G. P. Putnam's Sons, 1882), pp. 161, 400.

laid before the Legislature, and urging that he appoint commissioners to join in carrying out the purpose of the resolution.[55]

Governor William Rabun of Georgia immediately transmitted the resolution to Raleigh where the Legislature of North Carolina was in session. He stated that, if the purpose of the resolution were approved by North Carolina, the question of time and place of meeting of commissioners should be taken up immediately after he received notification of such approval.[56]

The Legislature of North Carolina lost no time in taking favorable action. A resolution was adopted authorizing the appointment of commissioners, a copy of which was forwarded to Governor Rabun in January following.[57]

The spirit of the correspondence was on a high plane and both States looked forward to a speedy settlement. Governor Rabun was "particularly gratified in believing that the object . . . will be accomplished to the satisfaction of both Legislatures."[58] He suggested a joint meeting of the commissioners to be held at Ellicott's Rock on Chatooga River, May 15, 1819. The date was inconvenient for the North Carolinians and the governor made a counter proposal of September 10 of the same year as the date. It was accepted by Georgia and preparations began accordingly.[59] Governor Rabun appointed as commissioners Benjamin Cleveland and Allen Daniel, and as surveyors James Camack and Timothy Tyrrel. Robert Love acted in the capacity of surveyor for the North Carolinians.[60]

The commissioners met at Ellicott's Rock on the appointed day and began the survey. The line was begun at that point,

[55] L. Q. C. Lamar, *Laws of Georgia, 1811-1819* (Augusta: T. I. Hannon, 1821), p. 1196. The full text of the resolutions may be found in this work.
[56] Governor Rabun to Governor of North Carolina, November 13, 1818. Governor's Letter Book, 1814-1821.
[57] Governor Branch to Governor Rabun, Janurary 15, 1819. Cited in Governor's Letter Book, February 3, 1819.
[58] Rabun to Governor of North Carolina, February 3, 1819. *Ibid.*, 1814-1821, p. 252.
[59] Governor Rabun to Governor Branch, April 15, 1819. *Ibid.*, 1814-1821, p. 258.
[60] Governor Rabun to Allen Daniel, August 5, 1819. Governor's Letter Book, 1814-1821. See also, Battle, "The Georgia-Tennessee Boundary Dispute"; *Laws of North Carolina* (1821), II, chap. 1005; Georgia Treasury Receipts 1817-1820 (MSS.), no. 16. The Georgia commissioners received $1004\frac{60\frac{1}{4}}{100}$ dollars as remuneration for their services.

which was the termination of the North Carolina-South Carolina survey of 1815, and extended "just thirty miles due west," supposedly along the thirty-fifth parallel. By September 25, they had reached a point eleven miles beyond the first crossing of the Blue Ridge, where they erected a stone on the parallel; at the end of sixteen miles a locust post was set up beyond the Cowee River, dated October 14, 1819; at the end of the twenty-one and three-fourths miles—after the second crossing of the Blue Ridge— a second stone was erected. At the end of the thirty-mile survey a stone monument was erected "on the north side of a mountain, the waters of which fall into Shooting creek, a branch of the Highwassee. . . ."[61]

The Legislature of North Carolina passed an act declaring the boundary line as thus surveyed to be "fully established, ratified and confirmed forever."[62] The Legislature of Georgia acquiesced in the survey for a time and declined to give relief to grantees in the disputed region.[63]

The further establishment of the line westward to its present termination was an *ex parte* extension so far as Georgia was concerned. When in 1821 North Carolina and Tennessee had run their mutual dividing line, the Legislature of North Carolina passed an act ratifying the work of the commissioners. The last section of the act provided that a line running 661 yards due southward from the termination of the line run by commissioners of the State in cooperation with commissioners from the State of Georgia in 1819, to the old survey known as Montgomery's line, thence westward along said line to the marker erected during the survey of 1821 and designating the corner of Georgia and Tennessee, should, after confirmation by the State of Georgia, "be and forever remain the dividing line between the two States of North Carolina and Georgia. . . ."[64]

Georgia did not ratify the line from the Hiawassee River to the Tennessee line before the War between the States.[65] On the other hand, she became doubtful about and dissatisfied with the survey of 1819 and, pursuant to a resolution of her Legislature of 1826, James Camack, the same scientist who had participated

[61] *Laws of North Carolina* (1821), chap. 1005.
[62] *Laws of North Carolina* (1821), chap. 1005.
[63] Arthur, *Western North Carolina*, p. 36.
[64] *Revised Statutes of North Carolina* (1837), p. 97. See map, p. 32.
[65] *Laws of Georgia*, 1810-1860, *passim*.

in the former survey, ran the section again and located the thirty-fifth parallel slightly farther northward, stating that he had used newer instruments than in 1818. With regard to accuracy, therefore, he gave preference to the survey of 1826. North Carolina, however, did not participate in this survey.

The line as established by North Carolina in 1821, though not approved by Georgia before the war, nevertheless constituted a legal line during that period, it would seem, because both States came to recognize it for a sufficient length of time for it to become the legal dividing line automatically.[66] Moreover, Georgia herself took definite action in 1861 and passed an act declaring the boundary between her territory and the States of North Carolina and Tennessee to be the thirty-fifth parallel of north latitude from its intersection with the Chatooga River westward to the place called Nickajack.[67] Nickajack was a small place marking the point at which the northern boundary of Georgia joined that of Alabama. The line thus described included the section established by North Carolina in 1821.

Thus the last State had acquiesced in the location of North Carolina's southern boundary line after a period of one hundred and fifty years of agitation, negotiation, and procedure. The line has since remained substantially in the location then established.[68] It will be well now to review briefly some of the outstanding points relative to the entire southern boundary line, and to state the general conclusions reached as a result of this study.

[66] This principle was recognized and established by the Supreme Court of the United States in a case in which Virginia was attempting to secure the alteration of a line between her territory and that of Tennessee, after such line had been recognized for a number of years. The court, in denying Virginia's contentions, laid down the following broad principle: "A boundary line between States which has been run out, located and marked upon the earth and afterwards recognized and acquiesced in by them for a long course of years; is conclusive even if it be ascertained that it varies somewhat from the courses given in the original grant." State of Virginia vs. State of Tennessee, 148 U. S., p. 503. Cited in Battle, "The Georgia-Tennessee Boundary Dispute."

[67] *Georgia Code of 1861*, section 19. The provision is quoted in Battle, *op. cit.*, p. 21. The clause was repeated in subsequent statutes concerning State boundaries. See *Acts of 1887*, p. 105. Quoted in *The Georgia Code, 1926* (Charlottesville: The Mitchie Co., 1926), Title I, chap. I, paragraph 18.

[68] In 1879, on account of some confusion in Macon County, North Carolina, and Rabun County, Georgia, the Legislature of North Carolina passed an act for re-marking the line between those counties, but Georgia did not reciprocate and no joint survey was made.

CONCLUSION

It is seen from this study that North Carolina's boundary disputes were characteristic of similar controversies between various colonies and States throughout much of their history. The outcome was of supreme importance to the future of the political units concerned. Such important questions as security of territory, the rights of States, peace and war, economic welfare, right of settlement, national politics, national expansion, international relations, and even the existence of the States and the Union were involved.

The dispute between the Carolinas was one of the most lengthy of all, and involved elements which were unique in their nature and character. Racial differences and physical, commercial, and social conditions played a great part in maintaining the divergent tendencies between the two sections. The importance of topographical influences can hardly be exaggerated in these disputes, both with South Carolina and Georgia. Carelessness on the part of the Crown and officials in describing colonial boundaries also made its contribution to the encouragement of disputes. South Carolina's attitude of superiority contributed to the desire of the northern section of the province for permanent separation. The collective influence of all these elements, with lack of normal contacts as a result of poor methods of communication, made separation inevitable.

Agitation in both sections of Carolina, and later in Georgia, became strong and effective. The Legislatures assumed the responsibility of bringing about a settlement. It appears, however, that every action taken by the Georgia Legislature, and all negotiations and agreements participated in by the State's commissioners before the War between the States were illegal and void. The constitution of 1798 had specifically described the boundary, and the State drew up no new constitution until 1861. Furthermore, no amendments relating to the boundary were adopted. Hence, as the strip of territory secured from the United States in 1802 was never constitutionally incorporated in the State, one is forced to the conclusion that nothing that was done throughout that period as a result of legislative action was valid in law. The legal principle that constitutional law supersedes statute law would support this position.

The first major benefit partially gained from agitation for a dividing line by the original colony of Carolina was to get rid of the deadening influence of the inefficient Proprietary government. The second was the permanent separation of two sections into distinct political units whose respective interests and ideals—always different—could be worked out in their own peculiar way, without interference or unreasonable sacrifices.

However, the effects of the disputes on the three States were largely detrimental to their growth and progress. Colonial finances were frequently disturbed in the case of the Carolinas as a result of constant bickerings between the colonies themselves and between the colonies and the Crown as to who should meet the expense of the surveys.

The settlement of the disputed territory was effectively retarded by the controversies. As land grants became hopelessly confused and titles became uncertain, prospective settlers hesitated to secure grants for lands in the region of the boundary. Many of them even refused to take out such grants. In the case of the Georgia dispute with North Carolina, even after the settlers had taken the risk and obtained grants, the two States quarreled for years over the question of securing titles to the grantees in case of transfer to a different State by the extension of the boundary line. Furthermore, settlers were often forced by other claimants to leave their lands. The inability of the governments to collect taxes under such circumstances was a natural consequence. The colonies and States lost much revenue on account of the lack of definite knowledge on the part of many inhabitants as to which government they were really obligated to pay taxes. They usually solved the question, if possible, by refusing to remit to either government.

The agricultural and commercial life of the colonies and States was affected either directly or indirectly. With demands for river courses as boundary lines, and for the incorporation of broad agricultural lands with their white inhabitants to serve as a precaution against uprisings of black laborers on the plantations, both commercial and agricultural interests were constantly manoeuvering for advantage. Boundary agreements, decisions, and instructions affected both fields vitally.

The permanent location of the capital of North Carolina was delayed for years because of the lack of a permanent southern boundary.

The boundary question had an important effect upon Indian relations, both colonial and imperial. This was in evidence in the Carolinas in their relations with the Catawbas and the Cherokees; and in the case of Georgia, with the latter tribe. In many cases, boundary adjustments meant the differences of peace and war. The question of alloting certain Indians to the respective provinces also influenced British policy for a time.

Militia service was also affected. However, this was true only locally. So far as expansion of the militia service as a result of war psychology was concerned, there was no State-wide effect on the service. But locally it was important. With one government undoubtedly encouraging the organization of militia companies in a county of another jurisdiction, confusion in the respective military organization was serious. In the course of the Georgia-North Carolina dispute, as has been shown, local militia companies had to be called into service for the protection of the citizens.

Confusion and violence characterized the boundary situation from its early appearance until the line was extended to the western extremity of North Carolina. Interference with court procedure in connection with both of the disputes, arrest of magistrates, abuse of other officials, imprisonment of citizens beyond their own State involving the right of personal liberty, loss of homes, and many other disturbing elements created a situation which was impossible to endure. Criminal elements took full advantage of the situation. Horse thieves, tax evaders, violaters of the Indian trade regulations, probably dodgers of military duty, and various other degenerate classes sought refuge in the disputed regions.

The normal functioning of the State governments was seriously impaired. In the case of the Carolinas, the legislative and executive branches were often at odds over the boundary issue, and South Carolina even lost a chief executive over the question. In Georgia, membership and attendance in the State Legislature were confused and interfered with, forcing postponement of Legislative activities on occasion.

A more important and fundamental result of the disputes, however, was the development of ill will between the colonies and States and between the colonies and the authorities. Messages, acts, resolutions, and communications from one legislative body to another, and correspondence between governors reveal the strained relations growing out of the controversies. This situation affected all of the relationships of the governments for a time. Moreover, communications with the British officials show the development of a spirit of resentment on the part of the colonial governments against the manner in which the disputes were handled. By 1773, this situation was very noticeable in North Carolina and the ill feeling against the Crown was at fever heat.

The disputes hindered cooperation between the governments during crises of war. This was true in the wars with the Indians and in the Seven Years War. It was probably true in some degree in the Revolution, though there is no direct proof of this view. Wars, in turn, affected the progress of settlement of the boundaries by forcing postponement of negotiations and surveys during preparations for defense and the prosecution of hostilities, and by causing British officials to decline to consider the question or to issue instructions relative thereto during periods of danger to the territories and interests of the Empire.

Each colony or State contended for its own advantage during the course of the controversies, with a very few exceptions. In the case of the Carolinas, North Carolina was in far better position from the standpoint of justice of claims during the colonial period. The injustice of the Granville Grant and the expansion southwestwardly in 1763, afforded her an unanswerable demand for an adjustment southward. From a practical standpoint, however, South Carolina was decidedly in the better position, for she had the support of the British authorities. The removal of Governor Glen was an exception to this rule. North Carolina was greatly relieved by this summary action on the part of the Board of Trade and must have felt extremely grateful. But the decisions and proposals of the Board and the Crown in practically every other case were more favorable to South Carolina's claims. After the birth of the independent States, however, when North Carolina was free from the costly partition of her territory by the Granville Grant, the advantage was more nearly balanced.

It is interesting to note in regard to the claims and arguments put forward by the Carolinas that economic interests were more emphasized as the period of the Revolution approached. South Carolina naturally sought to preserve her advantage, while North

Carolina was constantly working toward economic as well as political independence of the southern province.

After the Revolution, State pride played an important part in delaying settlements. For a generation after 1776 nothing of importance could be accomplished toward adjustments. For a sovereign State to make any material concession to another State was almost impossible in view of the temper of the people. After the turn of the century, however, when decades of fruitless bickerings had meant nothing toward an adjustment, the States began to come to the conclusion that the controversies could never be settled without mutual concessions. The results were the amicable agreements with Georgia in 1807 and with South Carolina in 1808, out of which came permanent settlements and the completion of the entire southern boundary of North Carolina.

In the process of extension, however, Federal and State relations were tested—indirectly by the Carolinas and directly by Georgia on two different occasions. It is to the credit of the United States Congress that it refused to become embroiled in a dispute which would only have become more difficult of friendly adjustment. The theory of State's rights was too jealously defended to have made a mutual adjustment possible.

Adjustments were more satisfactory and successful after the Revolution than during the colonial period. The cause of this is easily found. During the earlier period the influence of the Crown was decisive, if necessary in order to secure a survey, whether the location specified was satisfactory to both colonies or not; but after the colonies attained the dignity of States, they made no surveys until both States had approved the agreements of their commmissioners, thereby placing an inescapable moral obligation upon them to live up to the stipulations. This usually involved a much longer period of negotiations before a settlement could be reached, but there was no lack of cooperation once an agreement was made and ratified.

With all of the adverse conditions accompanying the disputes, occasionally there appeared redeeming elements. Among these was the type of men who sometimes were connected with them. With governors such as Tryon and Dobbs, and commissioners and scientists of the character and capacity of Blythe, Steele, Davie, Carnes, Caldwell, and Meigs, adjustments were bound to be made until the southern boundary of North Carolina had made a junction with that of the State of Tennessee. During the two centuries of disputes and mutual concessions, the colonies and States concerned received valuable training in the field of diplomacy. The wonder is that, with so many occasions for ill feeling over so long a period of time, there was not a great deal more violence and bloodshed. The fact that more serious disorders did not occur during the course of disputes is a tribute to the character of the people of the three States concerned.

BIBLIOGRAPHY

I. Primary Sources

A. Manuscript Sources

1. Official Correspondence

Georgia Governors' Letter Book, November 12, 1802, to October 20, 1821. Three bound volumes of original manuscripts. Poorly indexed. Contain thirty-three letters which are useful in this study. This collection of letters of the Georgia governors is in the Department of Archives and History, Atlanta.

North Carolina Executive Letter Books, 32 vols., 1777-1844. These letters of the governors, preserved by their private secretaries and in the archives of the North Carolina Historical Commission, bear on various subjects of importance to the State. Many relate to the boundary disputes with South Carolina and Georgia and are indispensable to any treatment of those controversies. They reveal the attitudes, spirit, and policies of the governors in the disputes.

Correspondence between Governors McLean and Richards of North Carolina and South Carolina, respectively, 1927-1928. These letters supplement the materials in the executive letter books listed above. They bear on the survey of 1928 and are indispensable. The original manuscripts and duplicates are in the governors' offices at Raleigh and Columbia.

Letter from D. J. Ravenel, Secretary of State of South Carolina, to Josiah Kilgore, of Columbia, dated January 29, 1814. This single letter in the office of the South Carolina Historical Commission with a loose collection of letters and papers, bears on the survey of 1813. Of little value in this study.

Syme Correspondence. George F. Syme. Senior Engineer of the North Carolina State Highway Commission, was boundary commissioner for North Carolina during the resurvey of 1928. His valuable correspondence is in the office of the State Highway Commission, Raleigh. All letters written by and to him in his relations with the governors and other officials concerned are preserved. Very valuable.

2. Journals, minutes, records, and miscellaneous manuscripts

Executive Journal of South Carolina, September 18, 1801 to 1810. Incomplete. Contains correspondence of North Carolina and South Carolina governors, legislative messages, proclamations, instructions, grants, reports, etc. Two letters are included which bear on boundaries. No executive journals were preserved by the South Carolina governors before 1801, and even their State papers were carelessly lost.

Elvord, James M., Astronomical Observations of South Carolina. This is a record of observations of latitude and longitude of various points in the State, including that of Ellicott's Rock in Chattooga River, and the entrance of Little River near the coast. Useful in this study.

Georgia Governors' Proclamations, 1782-1823. Bound manuscripts. Proclamations relative to various subjects of public importance. Poorly indexed.

Georgia Treasury Receipts, 1817-1820. Arranged chronologically and numbered consecutively. Useful on costs of the surveys.

Index to [S. C.] Land Grants, A to K, 1695 to 1776. In possession of the Secretary of State, Columbia. Contains in successive columns the name of grantee, county, and volume of land grant records containing the particular grant, day, month, and year of each grant. Valuable in treating the conflicts over grants near the line.

Journal of the Grand Council of South Carolina, August 25, 1671, to June 24, 1680. These are the original Journals, found at Charleston and transferred to the office of the Historical Commission at Columbia. They are loose leaves. The records are complete from August 25, 1671 to January 16, 1676. Some are missing after the latter date. Several entries are almost illegible. They are the earliest legislative records South Carolina has. Badly arranged and inadequately indexed. After the colony became royal the records of the Council were called "Journals of His Majesty's Council of South Carolina." The Journals contain phrases used by the proprietors which show an early consciousness of division of Carolina. Portions of the records down to 1775 are intact. After May 17, 1725, they are the original manuscripts.

Journals of the Commons House of Assembly of South Carolina, September 20, 1692, to August 30, 1775. Contain bills, reports, messages, papers, memorials, and other items. Very useful.

Journals of the House of Representatives of South Carolina, March 26, 1776, to 1886. They are not complete, except for the period 1801 to 1886. The Journals have been printed since 1831. Resolutions, bills, presentments, petitions, and recommendations are numerous. Valuable.

Journal of the Privy Council of South Carolina. The Privy Council was established by the Constitution of 1776 and was abolished by that of 1790. Its functions were merely advisory. The Journals contain advisory opinions on various public and private questions. The Historical Commission has the manuscripts covering the period February 11, 1783, to August 25, 1786.

Journals of the House of Commons of the State of Georgia, August 17, 1782, to 1826. These are by no means complete for this period. Parts of some volumes and loose sheets are mutilated and others almost illegible from damage. After 1787 they are in newer binding and are much more usable. The manuscript records are missing for a short portion of the period of the dispute with North Carolina; that is, from December 14, 1809, to November 2, 1812. However, the printed Journals for this period are intact. Other missing portions of the manuscripts are: June 11, 1790, to January 2, 1796; February 11, 1797, to November 1, 1800. The Journals consist of bills, letters, petitions, orders, writs of election, governors' messages, resolutions, ballots, memorials, reports, recommendations, proclamations, pardons, political discussions, and tax accounts. Essential to a treatment of the boundary question. In the Department of Archives, Atlanta.

Journals of the Senate of the State of Georgia, 1803 to 1826. Contain bills, petitions, resolutions, financial statements, accounts of elections, motions, proposals, and governors' messages. Indispensable for this study.

Journals of the Senate of South Carolina, 1776-1820. Contain bills, reports, acts, petitions, resolutions, memorials, messages, etc. Very valuable.

Journals of the Council of State of North Carolina, 1788-1792, 1796-1820, 1811-1882, 1837-1855, 1855-1889. In the archives of the Historical Commission, Raleigh. Of little value in this study.

Journals of the Provincial Congress and General Assembly of South Carolina, November 1, 1775, to March 26, 1776. Records the election of Representatives to the General Assembly from the "New Acquisition," territory lost by North Carolina in the survey of 1772, and as a result of which so much ill feeling was aroused.

Legislative Papers of North Carolina, 1776-1820. The entire collection covers the period from 1729 to 1900. Contains bills, acts, committee reports, petitions, memorials, governors' correspondence, etc. Indispensable to a study of the State's boundary disputes.

Minutes, Executive Department of Georgia, November 8, 1799 to February 28, 1821. Contains orders, appointments, records of bonds and taxes, pardons, commissions. Useful. In Department of Archives, Atlanta.

Papers of the Continental Congress, 1777. In possession of the Manuscripts Division, Library of Congress. These papers have not been seen by the writer. They were examined for materials on State boundaries by Dr. J. F. Jameson, Chief of the Division. Dr. Jameson states that they contain nothing that is not found in the *Journals of the Continental Congress.*

Papers of the Secretary of State of North Carolina, 1805-1815. Valuable for their reports of commissioners for adjusting the dispute with South Carolina.

Public Records of South Carolina, 1663-1782. 36 vols. Records copied from the British Public Record Office, by W. Noel Sainsbury of London. An index has been prepared for them to the year 1697 by Mr. A. S. Salley, Secretary of the South Carolina Historical Commission. They contain letters, reports, petitions, acts of Assembly, tariff rates, commissions to officials, lists of land grants. Of great value.

Proprietors' Grants (S. C.), vol. 39, no. 2. Land grant records in the office of the Secretary of State, Columbia. Contain a description of grants of land relative to size, location, limits, date, etc. Valuable.

Trott, Nicholas, The Laws of the Province of South Carolina. These provincial laws were compiled by Chief Justice Trott in 1719, the last year of the Proprietary government. They are aranged in two divisions as follows: "Part I, Perpetual Laws; Part II, Temporary Laws; The Two Charters to the Lords Proprietors." The second division contains a description of the boundaries of the province. The compilation also contains a law establishing separate assemblies for the northern and southern sections of Carolina.

B. Published Works

1. Legislative Materials

The following records of the Georgia and South Carolina Legislatures have been used to supply missing manuscript records, or to aid in the use of illegible or mutilated passages.

Journals of the House of Representatives of the State of Georgia, November 5, 1810 to May 5, 1821. 8 vols. Milledgeville, 1810-1821. The last volume is indexed, though inadequately and carelessly. It includes only the journal of the adjourned session of 1821.

Journal of the Senate of the State of Georgia, November 1, 1813 to December 18, 1816. Milledgeville, n. d.

Journal of the Grand Council of South Carolina, August 25, 1671 to June 24, 1680 and April 11, 1692 to September 26, 1692. 2 vols. A. S. Salley, Jr. (ed.). Columbia, 1907.

Journals of the Commons House of Assembly of South Carolina, September 20, 1692 to December 5, 1696. 3 vols. A. S. Salley, Jr. (ed.). Columbia, 1907-1912.

Journal of the General Assembly of South Carolina, March 26, 1776 to October 20, 1776. 2 vols. A. S. Salley, Jr. (ed.). Columbia, 1906 and 1909.

Journal of the House of Representatives of South Carolina, January 8, 1782-February 26, 1782. A. S. Salley, Jr., (ed.) Columbia, 1916.

These materials have supplied many missing and illegible passages. Other similar sources which have been found of value are the following:

Journal of the House of Representatives of the General Assembly of the State of North Carolina, 1879. Raleigh, 1879.

Journal of the Senate of the General Assembly of the State of North Carolina, 1879. Raleigh, 1879. Contains a bill to establish a portion of the Georgia-North Carolina line.

Journal of the House of Representatives of the General Assembly of the State of North Carolina, 1915. Raleigh, 1915. Contains a general act for settlement of any State boundary dispute.

Journal of the Senate of the General Assembly of the State of North Carolina, Session 1915. Raleigh, 1915. Contains the record of the general act of 1915 for settling boundary disputes.

Journal of the House of Representatives of the State of North Carolina, Session 1919. Raleigh, 1919. Records the adoption of an amendment to the act of 1915 extending the scope of the re-survey of a portion of the line near the seacoast.

Journal of the Senate of the General Assembly of the State of North Carolina, Session 1919. Raleigh, 1919.

2. Other journals, records, collections, and debates

Annals of Congress, 9 Congress, 1st and 2nd Sessions; and 11 Congress, 2 Session. Contains correspondence, petitions of the Georgia Legislature, Congressional action thereon, committee reports, etc., relative to the boundary controversy.

Colonial Records of Georgia, 25 vols. (1904-1914). A similar collection but not so valuable.

Debates in the Several State Conventions on the Adoption of the Federal Constitution as Recommended by the General Convention at Philadelphia in 1787. Edited by Jonathan Elliott (Washington, 1836). Volume IV has been used in this study.

House Miscellaneous Documents, 49 Congress, 2 Session, 1886-7, vol. 10. Contains valuable maps for treatment of successive Indian boundary lines and their relation to colonial and State boundaries. Early roads and trails to the west are also shown.

Journals of the Continental Congress, 1776-1781, vols. VI-XXI (Ford edition, Washington, 1906-1912). The record of boundary provisions in the Articles of Confederation is contained in these journals.

Journal of the Public and Secret Proceedings of the Convention of the People of Georgia, 1861. Milledgeville, 1861. Contains the record of the first constitutional definition of the State's boundaries after 1798.

State Records of North Carolina (vols. XI-XXVI, 1895-1905). edited by Walter Clark. Similar to the *Colonial Records.* Very valuable. They are followed by four serviceable index volumes, edited by Stephen B. Weeks, 1909-1914.

3. Executive Materials

American State Papers-Miscellaneous, 2 vols. Washington, 1834.

Commissions and Instructions from the Lords Proprietors of Carolina to Public Officials of South Carolina, 1685-1715. A. S. Salley, Jr. (ed.). Columbia, 1916. These commissions are valuable for phrases which indicate administrative division of Carolina.

Journal of the Commissioners of Indian Trade of South Carolina, September 1710-April 12, 1715. A. S. Salley, Jr. (ed.). Columbia, 1926. Useful regarding Indian relations with the Carolinas.

"Letter Book of Governor Samuel Elbert, From January 1785, to November, 1785." *Collections of the Georgia Historical Society*, V, Part II (1902). Elbert was governor of Georgia during the dispute with the Creek Indians over the boundary. These letters relate largely to military affairs. Some of them bear on the boundary controversy.

North Carolina Executive and Legislative Documents, 1831-1919. The volumes covering the period from 1840 to 1919 have been used in the present work. Valuable.

Records in the British Public Record Office Relating to South Carolina, 1663-1684, 1691-1697, 2 vols. A. S. Salley, Jr. (ed.). Atlanta, 1931. These are reproductions in facsimile from transcript records procured in London. Useful.

4. Collections, compilations, revisals of laws, and special legal works. All laws and many resolutions bearing on the boundary disputes may be found in the works which follow.

Acts and Joint Resolutions of the General Assembly of the State of South Carolina, n. p., n. p., 1928.

Clayton, Augustus S. (Comp.), *A compilation of the Laws of the State of Georgia, 1800-1810.* Augusta, 1812. Contains an appendix of approved resolutions, some of which relate to the dispute with North Carolina.

Code of the Laws of South Carolina, 1923, 4 vols. Charlottesville, 1932.

Code of North Carolina, prepared by William T. Dortch, John Manning, and John S. Henderson, 2 vols. New York, 1883.

Code of North Carolina, 1931, A. H. Michie and B. Stedman (eds.). Charlottesville, 1931.

Dawson, William C. (Comp.), *Compilation of the Laws of the State of Georgia, Passed by the General Assembly, since the year 1819 to the year 1829 inclusive.* Milledgeville, 1831. Contains all laws passed during the period indicated, topically arranged, with references to those repealed or amended. Included also are all approved resolutions of general, local, or private nature, indexed separately for laws and resolutions.

Georgia Code of 1861. Atlanta, 1861.

Georgia Code, 1926. Charlottesville, 1926. Contains various laws on the dispute with North Carolina.

Lamar, L. Q. C. (comp.), *A compilation of the Laws of the State of Georgia, Passed by the Legislature since the year 1810 to the year 1819, Inclusive.* Augusta, 1821. Laws are topically arranged, with valuable references to those amended or repealed. All approved resolutions of the period are included. Very useful.

Laws of North Carolina, 1802-1816. n. p., n. p., n. d. Contains all laws bearing on the boundary question during the period indicated.

Laws of North Carolina, 1806. n. p., n. p., n. d. Includes the law of 1806 relating to South Carolina and Georgia boundaries—one of the most important of the boundary laws.

Laws and Resolutions of the State of North Carolina, 1889. Raleigh: Josephus Daniels, 1889. Contains one general law on State boundaries.

McElreath, Walter, *A Treatise on the Constitution of Georgia.* Atlanta, 1912.

McGehee, L. P. (comp.), *Consolidated Statutes of North Carolina,* 2 vols. Raleigh, 1919.

Martin, Francois X. (ed.), *The Public Acts of the General Assembly of North Carolina, 1715-1803,* 2 vols. in 1. Newbern, 1804. Contains eight laws on North Carolina boundary questions. Vol. I; Acts from 1715 to 1790. Revised and published by James Iredell and again revised by Martin. Vol. II: Acts, 1790-1802. Revised and published by Martin for the first time.

Nash, Frederick, Iredell, James, and Battle, William H. (comp.), *Revised Statutes of the State of North Carolina,* 2 vols. Raleigh, 1837.

Pell, George P. (comp.), *Revisal of 1908 of North Carolina,* 2 vols. Charleston, 1908.

Potter, Henry, J. L. Taylor, and Bartlett Yancey (comps.), *Laws of the State of North Carolina,* 2 vols. Raleigh, 1821.

Public Laws and Resolutions of the State of North Carolina 1915. Raleigh, 1915.

Public Laws and Resolutions of the State of North Carolina, 1919. Raleigh, 1919.

Prince, Oliver H., *A Digest of the Laws of the State of Georgia.* Milledgeville, 1822.

Revised Statutes of the State of South Carolina. Columbia, 1873.

South Carolina Statutes at Large, 1682-1866. Columbia, 1836-1875. Vols. I-V edited by Thomas Cooper; vols. VI-X edited by Daniel J. McCord; vols. XI-XIII have no editor. Vols. I-V have been particularly useful.

Taylor, J. L. (ed.), *A Revisal of the Laws of the State of North Carolina, Passed From 1821 to 1825.* Raleigh, 1827.

Thorpe, Francis n. (ed.), *The Federal and State Constitutions, Colonial Charters, and other Organic Laws of the United States, and Colonies now or heretofore Forming the United States of America,* 7 vols. Washington, 1909.

Vattel, M. de, *The Law of Nations: or Principles of the Law of Nature; Applied to the conduct and affairs of Nations and Sovereigns.* New York, 1796. Contains a section warning of the dangers of unsettled boundary lines.

Watson, Robert and George, *A Digest of the Laws of the State of Georgia.* Philadelphia, 1810.

Wilson, W. S. (comp.), *Amendments to Revisal of 1905, 1907-1915.* Raleigh, 1915.

Womack, T. B., Gulley, N. Y., and Rodman, W. B. (comps.), *Revisal of 1905 of North Carolina.* Raleigh, 1905.

5. Letters, documents, memoirs, and travels

The following collection of letters, personal papers, travels etc. are of great value in determining the claims, facts, and settlements of the controversies.

Battle, Kemp P. (ed.), "Letters and Documents Relating to the Early History of the Lower Cape Fear." *James Sprunt Historical Publications,* No. 4, 1903.

―――, "Letters of Nathaniel Macon, John Steele, and William Barry Grove." *Sprunt Publications,* No. 3, 1902. Steele was a North Carolina boundary commissioner.

―――, "Letters of William R. Davie." *Sprunt Publications,* No. 7, 1907. Davie was governor of the State as well as a boundary commissioner. A few of his letters bear on the dispute over the dividing line.

Burnett, Edmund C. (ed.), *Letters of Members of the Continental Congress,* 5 vols. Washington: Carnegie Institution, 1921-31. Vol. II contains a few letters of North Carolina members which shed light on the State's votes on the boundary provisions in the Articles of Confederation. Useful.

Carroll, B. R. (ed.), *Historical Collections of South Carolina,* 2 vols. New York: Harper & Bros., 1836. Contains numerous pamphlets and documents bearing on the history of the State before 1776. Useful in this study.

Corbitt, D. L. (ed.), *Public Papers and Letters of Angus Wilton McLean, 1925-1929.* Raleigh, 1931. Relative to the boundary question, the collection contains only Governor McLean's proclamation of 1928 officially establishing the new survey of that year on the seacoast.

Digges, George A. (comp.), *Buncombe County North Carolina Grantor Deed Index,* 3 vols. Asheville: The Miller Press, 1926. Embraces all deeds filed for recording in Buncombe County prior to March 1, 1924. Gives date granted, size of grant, location, and date recorded. Very useful.

Fries, A. L. (ed.), *Records of the Moravians in North Carolina,* 4 vols. Raleigh, 1922-1930. An extremely valuable collection of sources on the early Moravian settlements. Sheds light on travel and trade in North Carolina and in South Carolina.

"Georgia-South Carolina Territorial Disputes." *Georgia Historical Quarterly,* XII (1928). This is a single, lengthy letter from William Few, a Georgian in New York, to the Speaker of the Georgia Assembly, dated October 19, 1786. It concerns the dispute with South Carolina over the twelve-mile strip of territory north of Georgia and adjacent to North Carolina. The letter is a vigorous defense of Georgia's claims.

Hamilton, J. G. deR., "William Richardson Davie: A memoir." *Sprunt Publications,* No. 7, 1907. Contains statements relative to Davie's public and private life which are useful in this study. The memoir is followed by a collection of Davie's letters.

Hillyer, George, "Boundary between Georgia and South Carolina." *Georgia Historical Quarterly,* I (1917). Hillyer was an arbiter in a dispute between Georgia and the Georgia Railway and Power Company over a tax assessment. The controversy "turns mainly on the proper location of the boundary."

Hoyt, W. H. (ed.), *The Papers of Archibald D. Murphy,* 2 vols. Publications of the North Carolina Historical Commission, 1914. This is a collection of letters and important papers bearing on public questions. In Murphy's report of 1819 on internal improvements is a brief sketch of North Carolina's boundary disputes and their settlement up to that time.

"Journal of a French Traveler in the Colonies, 1765." *American Historical Review,* XXVI, 1920-21. Valuable in the study of travel and communication in the colonial period.

McRee, G. J., *Life and Correspondence of James Iredell,* 2 vols. New York: D. Appleton & Co., 1858. These letters and papers of Judge Iredell, poorly edited, are useful in this study in treating communication in North Carolina before the Revolution.

MacDonald, William (ed.), *Documentary Source Book of American History,* 1606-1913. New York: The Macmillan Co., 1916. Contains the treaty of 1783 describing the southern boundary of the United States, which at that time was Georgia's southern boundary.

Meredith, Hugh, *An Account of the Cape Fear Country, 1731.* Edited by Earl G. Swem. Perth Amboy, N. J. 1922. Meredith was a partner in the printing business with Benjamin Franklin, 1727-1729. Having come to the Cape Fear, he explored the region and recorded his impressions in two lengthy letters. His descriptions of the topography of the region have been useful in the present work,

Smith, J. F. S., *A Tour in the United States of American; Containing an Account of the Present Situation of that Country,* 2 vols. London, 1784. The observations of this pre-revolutionary English visitor concerning economic life and methods of travel give light on conditions as they must have existed at a much earlier period when the boundary question was developing.

Wagstaff, H. M. (ed.), "The Harris Letters," *James Sprunt Historical Publications,* XIV (1916), No. 1 Harris, then a former professor in the University of North Carolina, was connected with the history of the boundary disputes in the matter of selecting astronomers to locate the line.

———, *The Papers of John Steele,* 2 vols. *Publications of the North Carolina Historical Commission,* 1924. Steele served as chief commissioner for the State during a portion of the controversies with both South Carolina and Georgia. This carefully edited collection of his letters is extremely valuable in treating Steele's part in bringing about amicable settlement.

6. Newspapers

Newspapers in general are not very important in the treatment of the boundary disputes. The Press was apparently not greatly concerned in the question. Editors and publishers were more interested in foreign news that in location of a boundary line with its technical and documentary details. If they mentioned the controversies at all it was usually a mere notice that commissioners had been appointed or were setting out to meet other commissioners for negotiation or to survey a line. A number of papers have been examined; those which have been of some use are listed below.

Augusta Chronicle. A weekly paper, with a number of extras and supplements issued during the War of 1812. The Georgia State Library, Atlanta, has the issues from May 31, 1811, to July 26, 1816. The issues for June 23, 1804, and April 12, 1806, are in the Department of Archives and History, Atlanta.

Augusta Herald. The Department of Archives and History has only a single issue—that of December, 1806.

The Minerva (Raleigh). Issues of the years 1806 and 1807 have been of value in this study.

The Monitor (Washington, Georgia). The Georgia State Library has twenty-two numbers covering a part of the period from June 15, 1805, to March 22, 1806. The issues are in fair condition and readable.

News and Observer (Raleigh). Issues of 1927 and 1928 are useful.

The South Carolina Gazette. The library of the University of South Carolina has the issues from January 4, 1735, to December 11, 1736. The South Carolina Historical Commission, Columbia, has the issues for September 17 and October 21,

1732. Professor Meriwether of the University of South Carolina examined the collection in the Charleston library and stated to the writer in a personal conference that it contains nothing of importance on boundary disputes. The issues cited above have been used in this study.

The Star (Raleigh). The University of North Carolina has various issues of the years 1810, 1811, 1812, and 1813, which have been examined for this work.

State Gazette of North Carolina (Edenton). Photostatic copies of various issues for the years 1788-1790, 1794-1795, 1797, 1799, have been examined. They are in possession of the library of the University of North Carolina. Of little use in the present study.

II. Secondary Works

A. Unpublished Works

Crittenden, C. C., Transportation and Commerce in North Carolina, 1763-1789. A doctoral dissertation, Yale University, 1930. Valuable in treating economic conditions which tended to cause a physical division of the Carolinas.

Deskins, S. C., The Boundary Dispute Between the Carolinas. An M.A. thesis of the University of North Carolina, 1926. 37 pages. Very limited in research.

McPherson, Elizabeth, Edward Mosely: A study in Colonial Politics. Moseley was a commissioner for North Carolina during the surveys of 1735 and 1737. This study, an M.A. thesis, University of North Carolina, 1925, contains brief references to his services as a boundary commissioner.

Meriwether, R. L., Expansion of South Carolina, 1730-1776. A doctoral dissertation to be submitted to the Department of History, Columbia University. Careful and thorough. Valuable in treating racial settlements in the boundary region.

B. Published Works

1. General, State, and local histories

   State and local histories are usually poor, particularly county histories. Local histories are often written by ministers or other untrained historical writers and, consequently, are unscientific. Little aid for this study has been found in them. The following have been examined, some of which include brief sketches of the boundary controversies.

   Arthur, John P., Western North Carolina: *A History, from 1730 to 1913*. Raleigh, 1914. This volume contains a brief chapter on boundary disputes. It must be used with caution because of inaccuracies.

NORTH CAROLINA BOUNDARY DISPUTES

Ashe, Samuel A., *History of North Carolina,* 2 vols. Vol. I, Greensboro, 1908; vol. II, Raleigh, 1925. Treating in a simple chronological manner, this is the best reference work on the State's history. It is accurate and dependable.

Connor, R. D. W., Boyd, W. K., and Hamilton, J. G. deR., *History of North Carolina,* 3 vols. Chicago and New York; Lewis Publishing Co., 1919. This is the most scholarly and readable history of the State, but disappointing to the student because of the very few reference citations. The first volume contains a brief account of the early boundary disputes.

Connor, R. D. W., *North Carolina: Rebuilding an Ancient Commonwealth, 1584-1925,* 4 vols. Chicago and New York: The American Historical Society, 1929. Volumes I and II treat the State's history from the beginning to 1925. The last two volumes contain sympathetic biographical sketches of prominent North Carolinians.

Gregg, Alexander, *History of the Old Cheraws, containing an account of the Aborigines of the Pedee.* Columbia, 1905. Sketches briefly the dispute with South Carolina.

Hawks, F. L., *History of North Carolina From 1663 to 1729.* Fayetteville, 1858. This volume carries the history of the colony through 1729, but does not treat the appearance of agitation for a division of Carolina.

Landrum, J. B. O., *History of Spartanburg County.* Atlanta, 1900. This history of a border county of South Carolina makes only the briefest statement concerning the boundary dispute between the Carolinas. Of little value.

McCrady, Edward, *The History of South Carolina under the Proprietary Government, 1670-1776.* New York: The Macmillan Co., 1879.

———, *The History of South Carolina under the Royal Government, 1719-1776.* New York: The Macmillan Co., 1899. These two volumes afford a good account of South Carolina during the colonial period. Useful in this study.

McMaster, J. B., *A History of the People of the United States from the Revolution to the Civil War,* 6 vols. New York: D. Appleton & Co., 1884-1895.

Martin, Francis X., *The History of North Carolina From the Earliest Period,* 2 vols. New Orleans, 1829. Useful description of natural barriers between northern and southern Carolina.

Moore, J. W., *History of North Carolina: from the earliest Discoveries to the present Time.* Raleigh, 1880. Must be used critically.

Smith, W. Roy, *South Carolina as a Royal Province, 1719-1776.* New York: The Macmillan Co., 1903. A valuable study, placing emphasis on the constitutional struggle in South Carolina.

Sondley, F. A., *Asheville and Buncombe County.* Asheville, 1922. Contains a brief sketch of the Georgia-North Carolina dispute.

Tompkins, D. A., *History of Mecklenburg County and the city of Charlotte From 1740 to 1903*, 2 vols. Charlotte, 1903. Describes briefly the confusion and violence in the county caused by the lack of a boundary line.

Waddell, Alfred M., *A History of New Hanover County and the Lower Cape Fear Region.* n. p., n. p., 1909. Contains a brief sketch of the dispute between the Carolinas.

Wheeler, J. H., *Historical Sketches of North Carolina from 1584 to 1851*, 2 vols. Philadelphia, Lippincott, 1851. Volume I consists of a brief general narrative with references to the boundary dispute with South Carolina. Vol. II treats briefly of the counties, giving biographical sketches. Very inaccurate in statement.

2. Biographical Works

Connor, R. D. W., *Cornelius Harnett*. Raleigh, 1909. Useful in the discussion of racial settlements in the Cape Fear region.

———, *Revolutionary Leaders of North Carolina*. Raleigh, 1916.

Davis, George, *A Study in Colonial History*. Wilmington, 1880. Discusses Edward Moseley briefly, including his services as a commissioner on the Virginia and South Carolina boundaries.

Henderson, Archibald, "John Steele," *North Carolina Booklet*, XVIII, nos. 3 and 4, January and April, 1919. Written in a popular and uncritical style. The author lavishes praise on an early kinsman.

Shinn, J. T. "Edward Moseley: A North Carolina Colonial Patriot and Statesman." *Southern Historical Association Publications*, III (1899), no. 1. A sympathetic treatment of one of North Carolina's commissioners.

South Carolina Historical and Genealogical Magazine, vols. I-XXXIII (1900 to date), published by the South Carolina Historical Society. Contains sketches of some of the South Carolina commissioners. Some issues also contain copies of official communications of South Carolina to the Board of Trade relative to the boundary question. Occasional quotations from contemporary publications are also included.

3. Monographs and Special Articles

Adams, H. B., "Maryland's Influence upon Land Cessions to the United States." *Johns Hopkins University Studies*, III, 1885.

Bassett, J. S., "Influence of Coast Line and Rivers on North Carolina." *American Historical Association Report*, I, 1908. An enlightening and useful monograph on the topographical features of eastern Carolina.

Battle, Charles E., "The Georgia-Tennessee Boundary Dispute." *19th Report Georgia Bar Association*, 1902. Contains some brief references to the Georgia-North Carolina controversy. Useful. Treated from a scholarly lawyer's viewpoint.

Clonts, F. W., "Travel and Transportation in Colonial North Carolina," *North Carolina Historical Review,* II, January, 1926. Treats only the Albemarle section. Valuable in the treatment of facilities of communication and their effects.

Coulter, E. M., "The Granville District." *Sprunt Publications,* vol. XIII, 1913, No 1. A careful study. Useful in showing the injustice to North Carolina of the Granville grant.

A series of articles on land travel and navigation in North Carolina from 1763 to 1789, written by Dr. C. C. Crittenden of the University of North Carolina, and appearing in the *North Carolina Historical Review,* Vols. VII and VIII (October, 1930, to October, 1931), shows the general conditions of travel and transportation which contributed so much to the development of a spiritual division between the inhabitants of northern and southern Carolina at an earlier period. The articles follow.

Crittenden, C. C., "Inland Navigation in North Carolina, 1763-1789."

———, "Means of Communication in North Carolina, 1763-1789."

———, "Overland Travel and Transportation in North Carolina, 1763 to 1789."

———, "The Seacoast in North Carolina History, 1763-1789."

———, "Ships and Shipping in North Carolina, 1763-1789."

Two bulletins of the United States Geological Survey contain brief sketches of boundary disputes between various States. Though not always accurate, they have been found valuable in this study. They are as follows:

Douglas, Edward M., "Boundaries, areas, geographic centers and altitudes of the United States and the several states and territories, with a brief record of the important changes in their territory." (*Bulletin,* No. 689, 1923).

Gannett, Henry, "Boundaries of the United States and of the several states and territories, with an outline of all important changes of territory." This is an earlier edition of the preceding work and was published in 1900 (*Bulletin* No. 171).

Farrand, Max, "The Indian Boundary Line." *American Historical Review,* X (1904-05), No. 4. A valuable monograph treating successive Indian boundary lines from 1763 to 1800.

Garrett, W. R., "History of the South Carolina Cession and the Northern Boundary of Tennessee." *Tennessee Historical Society Papers,* 1884. Brief but useful. Contains a valuable map showing vividly the strip of territory over which Georgia contended with North and South Carolina.

Goodloe, Daniel R., "The North Carolina and Georgia Boundary," *North Carolina Booklet,* III (1904), No. 12. A readable sketch of the controversy. The author quotes some valuable source materials.

Hinsdale, B. A., "The Establishment of the first Southern Boundary of the United States," *American Historical Association Re-*

port, 1893. Treats of the survey by Andrew Ellicott following the signing of the Pinckney Treaty of 1795. The recognition of this westward expansion encouraged demands by North Carolina for extension of South Carolina westward so as to make it possible for the former State to extend her line southward.

Phillips, P. L., "The Value of Maps in Boundary Disputes, especially in Connection with Venezuela and British Guiana," *American Historical Association Report,* I (1896). Contains valuable information and suggestions regarding the use of maps in the study of State boundaries. A great number of maps are discussed and evaluated.

Phillips, U. B., *History of Transportation in the Eastern Cotton Belt.* New York: Columbia University Press, 1908. A valuable study. Useful in treating transportation in the Carolinas in the early period.

4. Miscellaneous Works

Battle, Kemp P., *History of the University of North Carolina from its Beginning to the Death of President Swain, 1798-1868,* 2 vols. Raleigh, 1907, 1912. Useful in connection with the character and training of astronomers selected by North Carolina officials to locate the State's southern boundary line. A valuable history of the State University.

Connor, R. D. W., *Race Elements in the White Population of North Carolina.* North Carolina State Normal and Industrial College Historical Publications, 1920, No. 1. Valuable in treating the non-English elements in North Carolina's population.

Ford, Henry Jones, *The Scotch-Irish in America.* Princeton: University Press, 1915.

Hamilton, J. G. deR., *Reconstruction in North Carolina. Columbia University Studies,* LVIII (1914), No 141. The facts presented in this study on the conditions existing in the State during the period of military occupation account for the lull in the boundary controversies for fifteen years after the close of the War between the States.

Kerr, W. C., *Report of the Geological Survey of North Carolina.* Vol. I, Raleigh, 1875. Contains brief sketches of the State's boundary disputes. Not always accurate.

McConnell, J. J., *Catholicity in the Carolinas and Georgia.* New York, 1879. Useful regarding Irish elements in the Carolinas.

McLaughlin, A. C., *The Confederation and the Constitution, 1783-1789.* New York: Harper & Bros., 1905. A valuable study. Useful in a study of the western boundaries of the original States.

MacLean, J. P., *An Historical Account of the Settlements of Scotch Highlanders in America prior to the Peace of 1783.* Cleveland, 1900. Useful in treating racial settlements on the Cape Fear.

Nevins, Allan, *The American States During and after the Revolution, 1775-1789*. New York: The Macmillan Co., 1927. The relations of the States during this period are treated interestingly. The work contains a brief sketch of boundary controversies between the States.

Roosevelt, Theodore, *The Naval War of 1812 or the History of the United States Navy During the Last War with Great Britian*. New York: G. P. Putnam's Sons, 1882. Useful in showing the effect of war on the progress of boundary settlements.

Ruffin, Edmund, *Sketches of Lower North Carolina*. Raleigh, 1861. Descriptive of topographical features of the Cape Fear section. Useful in this study.

Scaife, Walter B., *America: Its Geographical History, 1492-1892*. Baltimore: Johns Hopkins University Press, 1892. Contains brief accounts of various State boundary disputes, including those of the Carolinas, Maryland and Virginia.

INDEX

Abercrombie, James, S. C. commissioner, 1735, 36n; writes Royal Council of physical conditions in Carolina, 5n; reports fruitless conferences, 38; declines to continue survey, 42; continues survey, 1737, 42-43.

Adams, John, President of U. S., sends Davie to France, 105.

Administrative division, influence of on physical division, 4.

Alabama, joins Georgia line, 205.

Alamance County, N. C., German settlements in, 12.

Albemarle, N. C., began as part of Virginia, 4; first Assembly held in, 23; included in Carolina, 1665, 23n; called "North Carolina" by Virginia Council, 1688, 24. *See* 24n.

Alexander, Nathaniel, Governor of N. C., urges legislative action on boundary question, 1806, 124; requests resumption of negotiations, 1807, 125; sends Moore to Columbia, 126; suggests Supreme Court trial as last resort, 126; requested to issue proclamation, 188; gratified with Georgia agreement, 191; receives report, 192.

Alexander, S. B., N. C. commissioner on independent survey, 1886, 148; reports necessity of joint survey, 1886, 149.

Alexander, Wallace, N. C. commissioner, 1799, 105; on legislative committee, 115.

Allegheny Mountains, in N. C., German settlers in region of, 12.

Allen, Eleazer, N. C. boundary commissioner, 1735, 36n.

Allen, Reuben, contests Nicholson's seat, 174; is denied seat, 175.

Allston, William, S. C. commissioner, failed to attend conference of 1808, 129; *see also* 134n; Governor of S. C., gratified at settlement, 1813, 140.

Altamaha River, partial boundary of Georgia, 161.

American Revolution, roads in N. C. before the, 17; delays boundary settlement, 89; influence of dispute on, 91.

Anderson, General, to defend S. C. claims before Supreme Court, 110n.

Anson County, N. C., Scotch Highlanders settle in, 10; animosity toward S. C. in, 11; Irish Protestants settle in, 12; Germans in, 12; McCulloh grant in, 45n; citizens of form militia, 46; citizens of abuse Dobbs, 46; denounces the king, 46; violence in, 48; conflicts over grants in, 47; irregular tax collections in, 50; commissioners in, 1762, 52.

Articles of confederation, boundary disputes to be settled by, 94; N. C. ratification of, 95.

Ashe, Samuel, Governor of N. C., 102; active on boundary question, 102; on legislative committee, 115n.

Asheville, N. C., observations in region of, 186.

Ashley and Cooper rivers, settlement on, 8; region favored by Proprietors, 8.

Atlantic Ocean, final boundary to begin at, 130; survey near, 1915, 150; re-survey begins at, 153.

Augusta, Ga., conference of with Indians, 1763, 52; South Carolina-Catawba boundary agreement confirmed, 52.

Avery, Waightstill, N. C. commissioner on Cherokee boundary, 93n, 96.

Barnett, William, Ga. commissioner, 1806, 182; signs report, 192.

Barnwell, John, informed Board of Trade of physical features of Carolina, 5; states to Board of Trade in 1720 that North and South Carolina are separate "in all respects," 25n; complains to Board of Trade over carelessness of Proprietors regarding boundary, 26.

Bath, N. C., negro slaves enter, 13.

Beaufort, N. C., negro slaves enter, 13.

Beaufort, S. C., commissioners meet at, 162; Treaty of, 162, 162n; Treaty of ratified, 163.

Berkley, Sir William, Governor of Va., instructed to appoint governors over Albemarle, 1663, 23; appoints William Drummond Governor of Albemarle, 23.

Bibb, Ga. congressman, requests federal intervention, 197.

Bill of Rights, of N. C., 1776, incorporated in constitution, 92-93; describes State boundaries, 92; boundary rights in protected, 100, 100n; contains a solution, 110; delays settlement, 121.

Bladen County, N. C., Scotch Highlanders settle in, 10.

Blair, Reverend John, comments on poor roads in N. C. in 1704, 17.

Blasingame, John, S. C. commissioner, 1813, 139n; again commissioner, 1815, 142n.

Block House, in survey of 1772, 134, 134n, 135; commissioners meet near, 136, 137.

Bloodworth, Timothy, on legislative committee, 114n.

Blue Ridge, junction of with "Green River Mountains," divisional point, 1815, 143; observations taken on, 186; 35th parallel not on, 187; commissioners cross, 1819, 204.

Blythe, Joseph, S. C. commissioner, 1807, 125; commits murder, 125, 126n; in conference at Columbia, 1808, 128-129; character of, 129; plans to resign, 1808, 134n; again commissioner, 1813, 139n; serves again, 1815, 142n.

Board of Trade, ignorant of geography of Carolina, 5; criticizes S. C. for her heavy tariff duties against N. C., 16; specifies Cape Fear as dividing line, 27; agrees with provisional governors on location of line, 31, 31n; orders governors to have line run, 31; favors S. C., 35; interviews Burrington on boundary, 37; consults Ex-governor Craven on boundary, 37; approves compromise agreement of 1735, 39; approves survey of 1735, 40-41; orders Broughton to send signed copy of survey, 41; receives draught of survey of 1735, 41; promises further action on boundary, 45; repeats old boundary instructions, 1739, 45-46; alters instructions on boundary, 60, 60n; instructs Dobbs to communicate with S. C. as to boundary location, 1754, 60; ignores Glen's proposal, 66; directs Lyttleton to submit boundary proposal, 66. See also Lyttleton; postpones action on boundary, 68; proposes to Crown a temporary line, 70-71; suggests survey of 1735, 71, 71n; drafts instructions to governors, 71; considers return to Cape Fear River line, 1765, 76; promises Montagu to arrange boundary agreement, 76-77; proposes a compromise line, 1771, 83; suggests final boundary, 84; instructs Montagu on boundary, 1771, 84; orders commissioners appointed, 1771, 84.

Boone, Thomas, Governor of S. C., informs Board of Trade of physical features of Carolina, 5; complains to Board of Trade of carelessness of Proprietors in references to boundary, 26; writes bitter letter to Dobbs, 1762, 48, 48n; threatens to accuse Dobbs before Board of Trade, 49; cooperates in Catawba survey, 52; leaves Catawba Lands question to arbiters, 69; reports many evictions of grantees, 70-71; promises to carry out instructions of 1763, 72; issues proclamation against violence, 73.

Boundary controversies, in Virginia and Pennsylvania, 2; in Vermont

INDEX 231

and Connecticut, 3; in Vermont and Massachusetts, 3; in Anson and Mecklenburg counties, 11.

Boundary House, commissioners meet near, 1764, 73; line re-marked to, 156.

Boundary tree, block of, 155n.

Boyd, William K., estimate of importance of boundary dispute, 2.

British and colonial authorities, bitter toward each other, 90.

Broad River, relation of to Catawba River, 78; Spartanburg County west of, 88; York County east of, 88.

Broughton, Thomas, Lieutenant-Governor, approves compromise agreement of commissioners, 1735, 39, 39n; ordered to send draught of survey, 41.

Brunswick, N. C., isolation of in 1774, 5; Dobbs in, 50.

Brunswick County, N. C., confusion in, 151; loss of territory in feared, 154-155.

Bull, William, Lieutenant-Governor of S. C., claims territorial agreement with Catawbas, 52; orders of concerning survey, 73n; proposes a line, 1764, 75, 75n; describes confusion over line, 75; reports chaos in courts, militia, tax collections, 77.

Buncombe County, N. C., citizens of raise boundary question, 120; Georgia citizen imprisoned in, 166; citizens of defy N. C. laws, 166; officials of adopt supplementary articles, 188; contains Walton County, 195.

Buncombe County Court House, settlers near, 135; commissioners meet at, 1807, 183; articles of amended, 187-188.

Burke, Thomas, absent for vote on boundary clause in Articles of Confederation, 94n.

Burke County, N. C., German settlements in, 12.

Burrington, George, appointed Governor of N. C., 1729, 30; ignores his official instructions as to land sales in Cape Fear region, 8; renews efforts for dividing line, 30-31; announces agreement with Governor Johnson on boundary line, 1729, 31, 31n; requested by Johnson to appoint boundary commissioners, 33, 33n; differs with Johnson over interpretation of boundary instructions, 33; opposes Cape Fear parallel line, 34; writes Newcastle urging Pee Dee River line, 34; warns South Carolinians against buying land north of Waccamaw River, 34; prevents unreasonable survey, 35; urges Pee Dee River line, 1735, 37, 37n; succeeded by Johnston, 35.

Burton, Robert, N. C. commissioner, 137; instructions to, 137n.

Business in S. C., affected by lack of boundary line, 28; demands Cape Fear as boundary, 28; affected by proposed line, 25, 63; in N. C. affected by tariffs, 70.

Butler, Pierce, S. C. commissioner, 99n; to defend S. C. claims before Supreme Court, 110; S. C. commissioner, 1787, 162n.

Cabarrus County, N. C., German settlements in, 12.

"Caesar's Head," observations near, 187.

Caldwell, Joseph, re-checks part of line, 1807, 111n; expected to aid in survey of 1807, 126; takes readings on line, 126; surveyor for N. C., 1813, 137; serves as scientist for N. C., 183, 186, 189; takes new readings, 1809, 195n; sustained by Ellicott, 200, 201n.

Calhoun, John C., S. C. Congressman, 197.

Camack, James, Ga. surveyor, 203; survey of, 1826, 204-205.

Camden, S. C., Montagu at, 86.

Cameron, Duncan, N. C. commissioner, 1812, 137; resigns as commissioner, 137.

Camp Creek, 96. *See* Cherokee boundary.

Campbell, George W., Tenn. Congressman, on special committee, 179n.

232 INDEX

Campbellton, N. C., incorporated as a market town, 1762, 16.

Cape Carteret, N. C., administrative division at, 24.

Cape Fear River, N. C., physical dividing line, 4; relation of to Waccamaw River, 6; river section a logical nucleus for a future State, 7; land sales forbidden within twenty miles of, 8; numerous official references to, 8n; growth of settlement on, 10; Scotch Highlanders settle on, 10. 10n; Swiss settlement on, 11; Welsh settlement on, 1730, 12, 12n; market town of Campbellton established on, 16; region of slowly developed because of poor means of communication, 20; claimed by South Carolina as boundary line, 26; S. C. land grants on, 26; N. C. grants land on 26; called the "Ancient Boundary," 27; S. C. fugitives escape to region of, 27; urged by Governor Johnson of S. C. as the boundary line, 28; north branch of suggested by South Carolina as part of boundary, 29; line parallel to approved by Board of Trade, 1729, 31, 31n; boundary line to be parallel to, 35; commissioners meet on, 1735, 36; first survey near, 1735, 38; fruitless conferences on, 38. *See also* 26n.

Carnes, Thomas P., Ga. commissioner, 1806, 182; signs report, 192.

Carolina, consciousness of division in, 3; governor appointed over southern section of, 1671, 4; governor appointed over northern section of, 1689, 4; governor appointed over all Carolina, 4; Deputy-Governor appointed over northern section of, 4; administrative independence in northern section of after 1711, 4; racial elements in, 9; effect of racial groups on physical division of, 12-13; negroes surpass whites in east, 13; means of communication poor in, 20; separate governments established in, 23; first agitation in for dividing line, 27;

change in form of government of, 29, 29n; Proprietors offer to sell, 30; official division of follows purchase by Crown, 30; efforts renewed, 1729, for division of, 30-31; boundary line of ordered run, 31; commissioners for, 1735, 36n; dividing line of begun, 40; line extended, 1737, 43; summary of boundary progress in, 52-59; stresses point of U. S. Supreme Court jurisdiction over disputes between States, 1788, 95.

Caswell, Richard, Governor of N. C., 99; describes poor communication in N. C., 20n; appoints commissioners on Cherokee line, 96; cooperates with Moultrie on boundary question, 99.

Catawba County, N. C., German settlements in, 12.

Catawba Indians, presence of in region of boundary, 12n; to be within South Carolina, 38; accused of destroying N. C. property, 51; Glen claims as "his Indians," 51; accused of insulting the Chief Justice, 51n; enlist in N. C. forces, 59; to be kept within N. C., 63; help control slaves, 82.

Catawba Lands, violence over control of, 50; Dobbs desires to divide part of, 50; protection of ordered, 72; survey to extend to, 1764, 73; Tryon County established west of, 78; to be part of line, 83; from part of survey of 1772, 87; indirectly demanded by N. C., 93; boundary intersection of altered, 1813, 138; independent survey around, 1886, 148-149.

Catawba River, in northern Carolina, 4; possible dividing line, 4; McCulloh's grant in region of, 11; German settlements on, 12; settlers in region of trade with S. C., 15; portion of to be line, 77; independent survey along, 1886, 148-149.

Catawba Town, proposed meeting place of commissioners, 1772, 86.

Charles II, King of England, charter of, 30; commissions Burrington and Johnson governors, 30.

INDEX 233

Charleston, S. C., capital of Carolina province, 7; immense distance from northern section, 7; courts in, 8; feeling of superiority of, 9; important commercial center, 9; commercial trend away from, 16; discriminates against N. C. products, 17; N. C. resentment toward, 17; bi-monthly postal express for established in 1765 on the Cape Fear River, 20; settlement of, 24; commissioners return to, 1772, 87.
Charlestonians, spirit of, 9.
Charlotte, N. C., proposed as meeting place for commissioners, 104, 121; 1806, 123.
Charter, first, of Carolina, 1663, 23; second, of Carolina, 1665, 4.
Chatooga River, divisional point in survey of 1813, 138; Ga. boundary point, 161; *see also* 163; "Ellicott's Rock" on, 201.
Cherokee border, boundary latitude near, 88; changes in, 96; proposed survey to, 116, 138, 142; boundary settled to, 140.
Cherokee boundary, importance of, 96; commissioners on, 96; agreement on, 96; Carolina line completed to, 1813, 150. *See also* Cherokee border.
Cherokee Indians, to be within S. C., 38; enlist in N. C. forces, 59; defense against, 81; land of, 93; boundary line of, 96.
Cherokee Mountains, N. C., involved in Montagu's proposal, 1768, 77.
Cherokee War, affects tax collections and boundary dispute, 50; delays South Carolina's boundary plans, 69-70.
Chester, S. C., proposed as meeting place for commissioners, 1804, 121.
Chickasaw Indians, S. C., trade with, 79.
"Chimney Top," 96. *See* Cherokee boundary.
Chiswell's mine, in Virginia, Cherokee line to, 96.
Choctaw Indians, S. C., trade with, 79.

Chowan Precinct, transportation in region of, 20.
Christian, Reverend Nicholas, describes early conditions of transportation, 5.
Civil War, effect of on boundary dispute, 145; Ga. line not ratified before, 204.
Clayton, Augustin S., Ga. assemblyman, plans representation, 175.
Cleveland, Benjamin, Ga. commissioner, 203.
Clouds Creek, 96. *See* Cherokee boundary.
Cogsdell, Joseph T., Swain complains to, 145.
Collins, J. H., N. C. surveyor on independent survey, 1886, 148.
Columbia, S. C., commissioners meet at, 1808, 128; agreement of altered, 1813, 138.
Columbus County, N. C., proposed survey near, 1919, 151; loss of territory in feared, 154-155; line re-marked to, 156.
Connecticut, Vermont's boundary dispute with, 3.
Connor, R. D. W., estimate of importance of boundary dispute, 1; estimates number of slaves in S. C., 14; on commercial unity, 16n.
Continental Congress, attitude of on boundary disputes, 3n.
Cook, James, S. C. surveyor, 1772, 84.
Council, of S. C. request Proprietors to have dividing line established, 1813, 27.
County, elections in, 7n; courts not allowed in S. C., 7.
Cowee River, line marker near, 1819, 204.
Craven, Charles, Governor of S. C., 37; consulted on boundary by Board of Trade, 1735, 37.
Crawford, of Ga., presents memorial, 176.
Creek Indians, S. C. trade with, 79.
Crockatt, James, S. Carolina's Agent in London, 65, 65n.
Crymble, partner in McCulloh's land grant, 1736, 11; bitterness over lands of, 49.

Cumberland County, N. C., Scotch Highlanders settle in, 10.
Daniel, Allen, Ga. commissioner, 203.
Davidson County, N. C., German settlements in, 12.
Davie, William Richardson, N. C. commissioner, 99; Governor of N. C., 103; urges S. C. to resume negotiations, 1799, 103; pleads for compromise, 103-104; both commissioner and governor, 104; resigns as commissioner, 105; threatens an appeal to Supreme Court, 105; resigns as governor, 105; commissioner to France, 105; to defend North Carolina's rights before Supreme Court, 105; plans case, 111; in error on survey, 111n; prepares to re-check old surveys, 1801, 112; fails to find documentary proof on survey of 1735, 112; finds no proof of appointment of commissioners on survey of 1764, 113-114n; collects boundary documents in S. C., 114; returns from S. C., 114; persuades N. C. to reverse boundary policy, 115, 115n; convinces legislative committee of necessity to support surveys, 116; re-appointed commissioner, 119; resigns as commissioner, 1805, 121-122; admits South Carolina's claim, 122.
Davis, John, Walton County senator, 1811, 200.
Dean, Silas, warning of as to danger to the "union of the colonies" over boundary disputes, 3.
De Graffenreid, Count, describes difficulties of travel in N. C., 20.
Delaware, Welsh settlers come to N. C. from, 12, 12n.
"Desausser, Mr." to defend S. C. claims before Supreme Court, 110n.
Dissenters, in N. C., 10; opposed to Anglican establishment in S. C., 10.
Dobbs, Arthur, Governor of N. C., protests against spirit and attitude of Governor Glen of S. C., 9; sponsors a land company in N. C., 11; grant of in Anson County, 45n; plans to survey lands, 46; complains to Board of Trade against S. C. land grants, 47; reports to Board of Trade that border counties "can't be settled," 47; urges S. C. to act, 47; reports magistrate violently captured, 47; writes bitter letter to Boone, 1762, 48; reports wide tax evasion to Board of Trade, 49; threatens to use force, 49; reports wide-spread violence, 49; reports "great confusion" over boundary line and taxes, 50; accuses S. C. of encouraging Catawba's violence, 50; attempts to enthrone puppet "king" over Catawbas, 51; complains of excessive lands allotted to Catawbas, 51; cooperates in survey of Catawba line, 52, 52n; suggests to Board of Trade extension of boundary along 35th parallel, 52n; desires to resume survey, 59; instructed by Board of Trade to communicate with S. C. as to "proper line," 1754, 60; promises to report to Board, 60; refuses to deal further with Glen, 60; proposes line, 60-63; causes Glen's removal, 61n; cites danger of inter-colonial conflict, 63-64; pleads for action on boundary, 66-67, 67n; requests Board of Trade to include Catawbas in N. C., 67; proposes adjustment of Ga. territory, 67; complains of South Carolina's delays, 67n; leaves Catawba Lands question to arbiters, 69; visits Charleston, 72, 72n.
Douthat's Gap, observations taken at, 186, 189.
Drayton, John, Governor of S. C., 105; continues boundary policy of predecessor, 106; defends survey of 1772, 108; implies resort to U. S. Supreme Court, 108, 108n; threatens N. C. with violence, 109n; invites Williams to institute suit in Supreme Court, 110; offers to appoint commissioners, 110; refuses to compromise, 1802, 116-

117; lays boundary question before Legislature, 1802, 118.

Drummond, William, Governor of Albemarle, 23.

Dry, William, N. C. commissioner, 1772, 85; visits Montagu, 1772, 86-87.

Duplin County, N. C., location of portion of McCulloh's and Dobbs' land grant, 11.

Earle, George W., S. C. commissioner, 1815, 142n.

Earle's Tavern, proposed meeting near, 125.

Ellicott, Andrew, Pennsylvania surveyor, employed by Ga., 198, 198n, 199; begins survey, 1811, 200; sustains Caldwell and Meigs, 200; unpleasant relations with Ga., 200-201.

"Ellicott's Rock," line marker, 1811, 201; commissioners meet at, 1819, 203.

Elvard, James M., makes astronomical observations for S. C., 1820, 143n.

England, officials in ignorant concerning Catawba River, 6; settlers from on Cape Fear in 1667, 10; secures N. C. trade, 17; authorities in support Johnston, 45; officials in suspect errors in survey, 73; action in on boundary, 83.

Eno River, S. C., McCulloh's grant in region of, 11.

Epps, John W., Va. congressman, on special committee, 179n.

Errors, in survey, 1737, 73; not detected, 1764, 73; cause disputes, 74, 80.

Fain, Ebenezer, presents credentials of election, 173; denied seat, 173.

"Falconer, Mr.," to defend S. C. claims before Supreme Court, 110n.

Farrar, Benjamin, Surveyor for S. C., 1772, 84.

Federal courts, and boundary disputes, 95.

Federal government, affected by boundary disputes, 20; cedes land to Ga., 168; S. C. cedes land to, 189; declines to mediate, 190; proposed appeal to, 197.

Federal tribunal. *See* Federal courts, and U. S. Supreme Court.

Fish Warden, of S. C., arrests N. C. fishermen, 1928, 152.

"Flagetius outrages," in Walton County, 172. *See also* Walton County.

Flournoy, Thomas, Ga. commissioner, 1806, 182; absent from survey, 1807, 185n.

Forsyth County, N. C., a center of Moravians, 12.

Fort Dobbs, built near Statesville, 82.

Fort Prince George, built by S. C., 81; danger of loss of, 81.

Franklin County, Ga., grand jury of urges settlement of Ga. boundary, 172-173; Walton County election held in, 173.

French and Indian War, non-English groups in N. C. in majority by time of, 13; effect of on surveys, 59.

French Broad River, demanded as western boundary, 97; settlers driven from, 97; settlers near threaten officials, 166.

Fury, Perege, S. C. Agent in London, 37; reports South Carolina's approval of survey of 1735, 41, 41n.

Garth, Charles, S. C. Agent in London, 69; requested to confer with Board of Trade, 69.

Geddes, John, Governor of S. C., orders astronomical readings along boundary, 1820, 143.

George I, King of England, death of, 1727, affects boundary question, 29-30n.

George II, King of England, commissions Burrington and Johnson governors of North and South Carolina, 1729, 30; status of dispute at end of reign of, 52 *et. seq.*

George III, King of England, receives boundary reports, 83; status of dispute in reign of, 89.

Georgia, founding of affects boundary demands, 29; territory of affected by Treaty of Paris, 98; dispute with N. C. begins, 1804, 120, 120n; settlement urgent, 1806, 124; dispute of complicates that of Carolinas, 139; boundaries of vague, 161; legislative act of 1783 regarding boundary, 161; constitution of omits boundary, 1777, 161; legislative act of describes boundary, 1783, 161; constitution of describes boundary, 1798, 161; dispute of with N. C. begins, 162; sued by S. C., 162; government of appoints N. C. boundary commissioners, 162, 162n; ratifies Treaty of Beaufort, 163; disappointed by S. C., 163; cedes western territory, 1802, 164; receives S. C. strip, 1802, 164; receives twelve-mile strip, 164; takes steps to mark boundary, 1803, 164; organizes county of Walton, 1803, 164; requests N. C. to join in survey, 165; Governor of urges legislative action, 166; enacts law to appoint commissioners, 166; objects to N. C. land title clause, 167-169; enacts law for appointing commissioners, 168; claims of divergent from own governor's 172; governor of suggests arbitration, 173; Assembly of denies seat to Nicholson and Allen, 175; alters boundary policy, 175-176; arguments of to Congress, 176-178; claims thirty-fifth parallel line, 178; authorizes appointment of Commissioners, 180; proposes appointment of commissioners, 181; threatens *ex parte* survey, 181; declines to compensate Walton citizens, 181; University of lends services of a professor, 183; commissioners of concede land titles provisionally, 184-185; commissioners of take independent observations, 186; commissioners of desire to discontinue survey, 187; commissioners of modify agreement, 1807, 187-188; coöperative attitude of, 191; protects land titles, 191; commissioners of make report, 191-192; repudiates own commissioners, 192-193; appoints new commissioners, 193; arguments of against agreement, 195, 195n; commissioners of decline to re-survey, 196; renews request to Congress, 197; employs Ellicott, 198, 198n, 199; unpleasant relations of with Ellicott, 200-201; ratifies agreement of 1807, 202, 202n; accepts survey of 1819, 204; fails to ratify survey, 1821, 204; *ex parte* survey of, 1826, 204-205; recognizes survey of 1821, 205, 205n.

German Reformed church, in N. C., 12.

Germans, settle in N. C., 12.

Glen, James, Governor of S. C., receives boundary instructions from Board of Trade, 46; reports wide evasion of taxes to Board of Trade, 49, cultivates Catawbas' friendship, 51; urges Catawba Indians to evict white people, 51, 51n; claims Catawbas as "his Indians," 51; is shocked at change of Board of Trade's policy, 61; refuses to accept change, 61; is removed from office, 61n; vigorously opposes Dobbs' proposed line, 64.

Goat Island, N. C., line marked to, 155.

Granville, Lord, line of, 50.

Granville County, N. C., Scotch-Irish and Germans settle in, 12.

Granville District. *See* Granville Grant.

Granville Grant, injustice of, 62, 66, 83; to be in S. C., 78.

Granville Tract, confiscated by N. C., 144.

Granville's line, S. C. claims all lands south of, 50.

Great Kanawha River, 96. *See* Cherokee boundary.

Green River, division point in survey of 1813, 138.

"Green River Mountains," adjacent to Blue Ridge; divisional point, 1815, 143.
Greenville, S. C., meeting place of commissioners, 1815, 142; Agreement of, 1815, 142; Agreement of ratified, 143-144.
Greenville, Agreement of, 142; agreement ratified, 143-144.
Guilford County, N. C., Germans settle in, 12.

Habersham, John, Ga. commissioner, 1787, 162n.
Haglar, "King" of Catawba Indians, favors S. C. claims, 51; Bull claims agreement with, 52.
Hagood, Johnson, Governor of S. C., requests N. C. governor to appoint commissioner, 1881, 146.
Halifax, N. C., convention of, describes State boundaries, 1776, 92.
Hall, James, N. C. commissioner, 99; scientist for N. C., 183, 189.
Halton, Robert, N. C. commissioner, 1735, 36n; continues survey, 1737, 43.
Hamer, John, collector for Anson County, reports threats against his life, 50, 50n.
Hamilton, Paul, Governor of S. C., delays appointment of commissioners, 121, 121n.
Harnett, Cornelius, asked to petition king for redress, 1771, 85; votes against boundary clause in Articles of Confederation, 94n.
Harnett County, N. C., Scotch Highlanders settle in, 10.
Harris, Charles H., of North Carolina, commissioner, 112, 112n; expected to re-check surveys, 1801, 114n.
Harvey, Thomas, Deputy-Governor of N. C., 24.
Hawkins, Benjamin, Governor of N. C., 136; notifies S. C. convention of Columbia must stand, 1812, 136; appoints commissioners, 1812, 137; expects settlement, 1813, 138; confident of final settlement, 141.

Haywood, John, commends Steele for boundary work, 1808, 125n.
Haywood County, N. C., erected in former Walton County, 1809, 198.
"Head-Northern-Stream-Savannah River," S. C. insists on joint meaning of, 162.
"Highwassee River," boundary line near, 204.
Hillsboro, N. C., convention of 1788, 95.
Hillsborough, Secretary of State, declines to report Bull's proposal to King, 76; urged by Bull to act on boundary, 77; rebukes N. C., 1772, 86.
Hillyer, George, quotes from Treaty of Beaufort, 163n.
Hoke County, N. C., Scotch Highlanders settle in, 10.
Holston River, 96. See Cherokee boundary.
Hooper, William, writes James Iredell about poor communication in N. C., 21n.
Horry County, S. C., confusion in, 151.
Houston, James E., Ga. commissioner, 193.
Howe, Robert, asked to petition king for redress, 1771, 85.
Huey, partner in McCulloh's land grant, 1736, 11; bitterness over lands of, 49.
Hunter, Colonel, to defend S. C. claims before Supreme Court, 110n.
Hyde, Edward, appointed Governor of N. C., 25.

Indian affairs. See Indian relations.
Indian relations, conflicts with whites, 56, 69; favorable effects of proposed survey on, 63; delay settlement, 68; affected by controversy, 88.
Indian titles, to be extinguished in Ga., 164.
Indian treaties, relation of to boundary dispute, 129, 133, 171.
Indians, as slaves in S. C., 14n;

provocations of hasten survey, 35; promises to not kept, 97.

Iredell County, German settlements in, 12.

Ireland, large immigration from to N. C. in eighteenth century, 11.

Irish, land at New Bern, 1753, 11; hatred of for Anglicans in S. C., 11; Protestant groups of, 12.

Irwin, Jared, Governor of Ga., hopeful of settlement, 182; receives report, 191; disappointment of, 192; requests new survey, 194; pleads for Walton County citizens, 194; notifies Legislature of N. C. refusal, 196.

Jarvis, T. J., Governor of N. C., requested by Hagood to appoint commissioners, 1881, 146. *See also* Hagood.

Jay, John, warns Livingstone on dangers of boundary disputes to the union, 3.

Jefferson, Thomas, Governor of Va., writes Governor of N. C. in 1780 about establishing an express system, 20.

Johnson, J. Monroe, S. C. commissioner, 1928, 153; confers with Syme, 154n.

Johnson, Robert, appointed Governor of S. C., 1729, 30; estimates number of negroes in S. C., 13n; writes Board of Trade of necessity of establishing boundary line to protect business men, 28; renews efforts for dividing line, 1729, 30-31; announces agreement with Governor Burrington on boundary line, 31, 31n; boundary suggestion of approved by Board of Trade, 1730, 31; requests Burrington to appoint boundary commissioners, 33; differs with Burrington over interpretation of boundary instructions, 33; protests adoption of Waccamaw River as boundary, 34; urges Board of Trade to continue original boundary instructions, 35, 35n; sets date for meeting commissioners, 36; writes to Agent in London insisting on Waccamaw line, 1735, 37; death of, May 3, 1735, 38, 38n; succeeded by Thomas Broughton, 38n.

Johnston, Gabriel, Governor of N. C., 10-13, 35; promotes settlement to Cape Fear region, 11; replies to Johnson of S. C. on boundary, 36; arranges compromise boundary line with commissioners, 1735, 37; arranges second compromise, 38; writes Governor Johnson of new agreement, 38; informs Board of Trade compromise was ratified, 40; urges speed in the survey, 40, 40n; pushes the survey, 42; informs Board of Trade of North Carolina's refusal to pay, 43; opposes changes of boundary, 44; arguments of against altering line, 44-45; urges further boundary extension, 1738, 45; instructed to raise troops, 46; secures compromise line, 53, 132.

Johnston County, Scotch-Irish and Germans in, 12.

Jones, Allen, objects to use of militia beyond N. C., 91.

Justice, Amos, readings taken at home of, 186.

Keowee River, disputed boundary, 162. *See also* 163.

Kerr, W. C., errors of concerning boundary, 44, 73n.

Kilgore, James, S. C. commissioner, 1809, 136n.

King George's War, causes delay in surveys, 58, 59.

Lancaster, S. C., proposed meeting place of commissioners, 1805, 121.

Lancaster Court House, S. C., commissioners meet at, 123.

Land grants, abuses in, 47, 48n.

Land titles, protected, 119, 121.

Lanier, Robert, N. C. commissioner on Cherokee line, 96.

Lincoln County, German settlements in, 12.

Little Peedee, survey near, 43.

Little River, in Brunswick County, N. C., 93; survey begins near, 1735, 40; re-survey begins, 1928, 155; designated in N. C. constitution, 93.

Livingston, Robert, John Jay writes to, 3.

Lloyd, John, S. C. Agent in London, instructed to work for settlement of boundary question, 1721, 28.

Lochabor, treaty of, 1770, 26. *See* Cherokee boundary.

London, merchant in aids S. C. request for Cape Fear as boundary line, 28; Drayton secures documents from, 115; Steele desires documents from, 125.

Long, Nicholas, Ga. commissioner, 193.

Long Island of Holston, 96. *See* Cherokee boundary.

Lords of Trade. *See* Board of Trade.

Lords Proprietors. *See* Proprietors, Lords.

Love, Robert, N. C. surveyor, 203.

Love, Thomas, N. C. commissioner, 1814, 141.

Ludwell, Philip, Governor of Carolina, 7, 24; provisionally instructed as to county elections, 1691, 7; to have assemblymen elected for counties of Albemarle, Colleton, Berkeley, and Craven, 24n.

Lumber River, proposed survey near, 1919, 151; swamps along, 155; re-check near, 1928, 155.

Lutherans, German settlers in N. C., 12.

Lyttleton, William H., Governor of S. C., succeeds Glen, 66; to submit boundary proposal, 66; appoints boundary committee, 67; sends proposal to Dobbs, 68n; postpones Catawba question, 69.

McCulloh, Henry, London merchant, sponsors land company in N. C., 11; grant of in Anson County, 45n; Agent in London, 84; opposes Board of Trade's line, 1771, 84.

McCulloh's lands, survey of planned by Dobbs, 46.

McDowell, Charles, General, N. C. commissioner on Cherokee boundary, 93n; authorized to drive settlers from French Broad region, 97.

McDowell, Joseph, Jr., N. C. commissioner, 99.

McIntosh, Lachlan, Ga. commissioner, 1787, 162n.

Mackay, Arthur, S. C. commissioner, 73n; appointment of questioned, 113.

"McKinney's on Toxaway river," meeting place of commissioners, 1813, 137, 140.

McLean, A. W., Governor of N. C., informs Richards of urgency of re-survey, 1928, 151; appoints Syme, commissioner, 153; confers with Nelson and Phillips, 153; proposes temporary re-survey, 153; confers with commissioners, 154; proclamation of, 1928, 156n; offers reward, 156.

McNamies Creek, 96. *See* Cherokee boundary.

Macon, Nathaniel, Speaker of the House, 178; writes Monroe in London about documents, 1807, 125n; receives compromise suggestion, 178; congressional committeeman, 197.

Macon County, N. C., confusion in, 205n.

Martin, Josiah, Governor of N. C., 1770, 84; receives instructions for survey, 1771, 84; opposes Board of Trade's proposal, 1771, 84n; requests funds for survey, 1771, 85; appoints commissioners, 1772, 85; complains to Hillsborough of Montagu's delay, 86; acts on Cherokee boundary, 97; urges Legislature to act on boundary, 1784, 97; fails to get action on boundary, 98; announces western land cession, 164.

Mecklenburg County, German settlements in, 12; loses territory, 1772,

88n; S. C. survey along, 147; conditions in grow worse, 148.
Meigs, Josiah, of Ga., takes readings, 1813, 137; serves as scientist for Ga., 183, 186, 189; work of questioned, 193; finds Ga. in error, 196; sustained by Ellicott, 200, 201n.
Meredith, Hugh, statement of regarding topography of Carolina, 4n.
Middleton, Henry, S. C. commissioner, 1813, 139n.
Middleton, William H., Governor of S. C., 59.
Militia, organized in Anson County, 57.
Milledge, John, Governor of Ga., declines to act on boundary, 168; proposes to appoint commissioners, 169; sends petition to Congress, 178; suggests arbitration, 180; U. S. senator, 182.
Milledgeville, Ga. capital, Walton County not represented at, 1811, 200.
Miller, William, Governor of N. C., executes agreement of 1813, 141; reports survey to Legislature, 1815, 143.
Mississippi River, demanded as western boundary, 97; S. C. claims territory to, 162.
Mississippi Territory, ceded by Ga., 164.
Mitchell, David B., Governor of Ga., recommends neutral "artist," 198; employs Ellicott, 198, 198n, 199; urges N. C. to act, 199; informed Congress will not intervene, 200; compensates Ellicott, 201.
Monroe, James, Minister to England, procures boundary documents, 1807, 125.
Montagu, Charles G., Governor of S. C., 75; proposes line, 77; urges Tryon to join in proposed line, 77; refers boundary question to Council, 78; receives Board of Trade's instructions, 1771, 84; appoints commissioners, 84; "on a tour of amusement," 1772, 86.
Montgomery's line, portion of N. C.-S. C. line, 1821, 204.
Moore, Alfred, N. C. commissioner, 99; re-appointed commissioner, 102n; resigns as commissioner, 1799, 105; goes to Columbia, 1807, 126; resigns temporarily in anger at governor, 127, 128n.
Moore, James, S. C. commissioner, 73n; appointment of questioned, 113.
Moore, John, N. C. commissioner, 1803, 119.
Moore, Maurice, asked to petition king for redress, 1771, 85.
Moore, Roger, N. C. commissioner, 1735, 36n.
Moore, Thomas, S. C. congressman, on special committee, 179n.
Moore County, N. C., Scotch Highlanders settle in, 10.
Moravians, German settlers in N. C., 12. See Forsyth County.
Morris, Gouverneur, John Jay warns, 3.
Moseley, Edward, N. C. commissioner, 1735, 36n; continues survey, 1737, 42-43.
Moultrie, William, S. C. commissioner, 1772, 84, 85; Governor of S. C., 99; urges Caswell to act, 1786, 99; insists N. C. ratified survey of 1772, 100; sends boundary documents to Spaight, 101; boundary knowledge to be "perpetuated" by S. C., 110n; sends documents, 102.

Nelson, J. S., N. C. Commissioner of Fisheries; confers with McLean, 153.
Neuse River, Scotch-Irish settle in region of, 12; Swiss settlement on, 20.
Nevins, Allan, estimate of importance of boundary dispute, 2, 3.
"New Acquisition," gained by S. C., 1772, 88; later counties of Spartanburg and York, 88.

New Bern, N. C., Irish immigrants arrive in, 11, 20; Dobbs in, 60.

New Hanover precinct, established on the Cape Fear, 1729, 8.

Nicholson, Francis, appointed provisional royal governor of S. C., 25n, 29n.

Nicholson, John, Walton County representative, 173, 177n; deprived of seat, 173-174; see also 174n; Allen contests Assembly seat of, 174; pays taxes in N. C., 174.

Nickajack, corner of Ga. and Ala. line, 205.

Nollichucky River, 96. See Cherokee boundary.

North Carolina, natural unit north of Pee Dee River, 7, 7n; S. C. settlers enter, 10, 10n; McCulloh's land grant in, 11; variety of products in, 13; increase of slaves in, 13, 13n; democratic development in, 13, 14; unfavorable effect of geography on commerce in, 14; flow of rivers of, 15; Council petitions Crown to locate boundary at Pee Dee River, 15; retaliates against S. C. with high tariffs on liquors, 16; forbids grazing of S. C. cattle in N. C., 16; Leglislature of attempts to hold domestic trade on own bounds, 16; builds roads to encourage trade, 16; turns her trade from S. C. to other fields, 17; builds road from Mecklenburg County to Wilmington, 18; little travel in, 19; regular postal service in, 20; complete separation of from S. C. begins, 25; see also 25n; makes land grants on southern bank of Cape Fear, 26; permanent change in government of, 29; George Burrington appointed governor of, 30; governor of announces mutual agreement on boundary line, 1729, 31; boundary line of approved by Board of Trade, 1729, 31; Council of advises Burrington to postpone appointment of commissioners, 33, 33n; governor of appoints boundary commissioners, 36, 36n; commissioners of asked to compromise on boundary instructions, 40; commissioners run line, 1735, 40; urges speed in the survey, 40-41; proceeds independently, 41; resumes boundary negotiations, 1737, 42; Assembly of refuses to pay cost of survey, 43; Council of agrees to pay, 43, 43n; boundary of extended to private citizens, 44; Assemblymen accuse S. C. of secretly organizing militia in Anson County, 46; complains against S. C. land grants, 1753, 47; evicts S. C. grantees, 48; Council of exonerates Dobbs of S. C.'s charges, 49; Council of accuses S. C. of encouraging abuse of Dobbs, 49; grants land far south of 35th parallel, 1763, 49; protests S. C. survey of Catawbas' boundary, 52, 52n; summary of boundary progress in, 52-59; prepares for war, 59; declines to appoint surveyors, 65; consents to S. C. survey, 65; builds fort to protect Catawba Indians, 67; renews efforts for definite boundary, 1761, 68; requests royal action at close of War, 70; renews Pee Dee River proposal, 70; proposes alternate line of 34° 38', 70; evicts grantees, 70-71; governor of appoints commissioners, 72-73; commissioners of extend survey westward, 1764, 73, 73n; settlers of desire Pee Dee River line, 74, 74n; protests against Montagu's proposal, 77-78n; runs temporary line, 1767, 78, 78n; establishes Tryon County, 78; defends her position, 80; opposes Board of Trade's proposal, 1771, 84; resentful toward British officials, 1771, 85; Assembly of table Martin's request for funds, 1771, 85; asks Martin to petition the king, 85; commissioners for, 85; refusal of funds "ill received by the King," 1773, 86; boundary survey of begins, 1772, 87, 87n; gains territory, 1772, 88; refuses to recognize survey of 1772, 88; embittered against Britian and S. C., 1773, 88; boundary disputes of, 1775, summarized, 89-91; State of defines boundaries, 1776, 92; ignores part of previous surveys, 1776, 93, 93n; Legislature of makes agreement of 1735 binding, 93n; considers Cherokee land question with Virginia, 93; attitude of toward Articles of Confederation affected by boundary question, 94, 94n; votes to make Congress final arbiter on boundary disputes, 95; proposes to submit dispute to U. S. Supreme Court, 96; authorizes presents for Cherokees, 97; renews boundary negotiations, 1784, 97; Legislature fails to act, 98; appoints commissioners, 1792, 99; fails to get S. C.'s cooperation, 101; appoints other commissioners, 1797, 102, 102n; threatens to appeal to Supreme Court, 105; confuses provisions of charter, 106-107; alters position on previous surveys, 1800, 107; decides to appeal to Supreme Court, 1800, 109-110; protests against whole survey, 113; to blame for delay in procedure; reverses her boundary policy, 115; abandons appeal to Supreme Court, 1802, 116; refuses to permit appointment of commissioners, 118; enacts law appointing commissioners, 118-119n; begins boundary dispute with Ga., 1804, 120, 120n; amends boundary law to include Ga., 120; commissioners of make progress, 1805, 123; drops defense of Bill of Rights clause, 1806, 124; requests resumption of negotiations, 1806-1807, 125; reaches agreement with Ga., 1807, 126; agrees to compromise with S. C., 1808, 129-131; loses territory to S. C., 132; refuses to cede land titles, 132; ratifies Columbia Agreement, 1808, 132; repudiates Stone's policy, 136; commissioners of meet, 1813, 137; ratifies Provisional Agreement, 1813, 138; appoints commissioners, 1814, 141; commissioners of run survey, 1815, 141; gains territory, 143; commissioners of report survey to Miller, 1815, 143, 143n; instructs governor to notify S. C. of ratification of survey of 1815, 143-144; provides by law for re-marking portion of line, 1880, 145; enacts law to adjust boundary of any "contiguous States," 1881, 146-147; provides for arbitration, 147; enacts law, 1888, similar to that of 1881, 147n; gives governor initiative in boundary disputes, 1909, 147; governor of requests S. C. survey, 148; makes independent survey, 1886, around Catawba Lands, 148-149; empowers governor to make joint survey, 1915, 150; provides for survey to Lumber River, 1919, 150-151; governor of requested to re-survey line, 151; fishermen of arrested by S. C., 151-152; governor of initiates re-survey, 1928, 152; commissioners of meet on Little River, 1928, 155; joint re-survey of 1928, 156; official proclamations of, 156n; adopts general policy on boundary, 157; dispute of with Ga. begins, 162; government of appoints Ga. boundary commissioners, 1787, 162, 162n; cedes western lands, 1789, 164; territory of adjacent to Ga., 1802, 164; requested by Ga. to join in survey, 165; amends boundary act, 1804, 167; amends Act of 1804, 182; University of supplies scientist, 183; commissioners of defend land titles, 183-184; commissioners modify agreement, 1807, 187-188; confident of final settlement, 191; commissioners of make report, 192; Legislature of confirms Ga. agreement, 192; declines a new survey, 1808, 194; pardons Walton County citizens, 195; again declines to appoint commissioners, 1811, 199; Legislature of authorizes appointment of commissioners, 203; ratifies survey of

INDEX 243

1819, 204; *ex parte* extension of line to Tennessee, 1821, 204; connects southern line with Tennessee, 204; southern boundary of completed, 205.

Northeast River, in N. C., location of Irish settlement, 11.

Oglethorpe, James, N. C. sends aid to, 58.

Ohio River, 96. *See* Cherokee boundary.

Old Fort, in N. C., built, 1756, 82.

Orange County, N. C., Irish Protestants and Germans settle in, 12.

Overhill Cherokees, 97. *See* Cherokee boundary.

Pacolet River, north fork of a division point, 138; line marker near, 143.

"Painted Rock," on Chatooga River, corner of three States, 1815, 143.

Pamlico River, poor transportation in region of, 17.

Parliament, act of 1728 authorizes purchase of Carolina by the Crown, 30.

Patton, John, N. C. commissioner, 1814, 141.

Pawley, George, recommended by S. C. "Commons House" for commissioner, 42n; appointed commissioner, 1763, 73n; appointment of questioned, 113.

Pee Dee River, influence of on physical division, 4; Welch settlement in valley of, 12, 12n; settlers in region of trade with S. C., 15; survey of 1737 near, 43.

Penn, John, N. C. delegate to Congress, 94; votes against boundary clause in Articles of Confederation, 94n.

"Pennamite Wars," in Pa., over boundary dispute, 3, 3n.

Pennsylvania, boundary dispute of with Va., 2; with Conn., 3; Scotch-Irish come from to N. C., 11; Welsh settlers come to N. C. from, 12, 12n.

Phillips, Wade, N. C. Director of Conservation and Development, confers with McLean, 153.

Pickens, Andrew, S. C. commissioner, 99n; to defend S. C. claims before Supreme Court, 110n; S. C. commissioner, 1787, 162n.

Pinckney, C. C., S. C. commissioner, 99n; to defend S. C. claims before Supreme Court, 110n; S. C. commissioner, 1787, 162n.

Pinckney, Charles, Governor of S. C., 103; proposes meeting of commissioners, 1807, 126; expresses desire to compromise, 126; sets date of commissioners' meeting, 127.

Pitt, William, instructs Dobbs to prepare N. C. for defense, 59.

Polk, Thomas, N. C. surveyor, 1772, 85, 85n; is refused remuneration, 1773, 88.

Pollock, Thomas, 27.

Pope, Leroy, Ga. commissioner, 193.

Pownal, Thomas, Secretary of Board of Trade, 72; attempts to improve relations between Carolinas, 72.

Price, Jonathan, N. C. commissioner, 1796, 102n; discouraging report of to Williams, 107; fails to appear with surveyor's instruments, 114.

"Prince of Wales," half-breed Catawba Indian, favors N. C. boundary claims, 51; Dobbs attempts to enthrone, 51.

Proprietary Period, First Assembly, 1665, 23; Charters of 1663, 1665, 23.

Proprietors, Lords, forbid land sales within twenty miles of Cape Fear, 8; are conscious of a natural division of Carolina, 8, 8n; favor southern Carolina, 8; charter of 1665 to authorizes division of Carolina into colonies, 23; set up administrative divisions of Carolina, 23, 24; appoint Ludwell governor of northern Carolina, 24; appoint Edward Tynte governor of all Carolina, 24; urge King to resume practice of appointing a deputy-governor of N. C., 25n; admit their inability to protect S.

C. from enemies, 25; refer to Cape Fear River as boundary line, 26; refuse request of 1713 to have dividing line run, 27; secretary to Board of Trade promises to present S. C.'s request for dividing line to, 1713, 27; offer to sell interests in Carolina, 30; authorized by act of Parliament to sell interests in Carolina, 30; rights of deeded to Crown, 1729, 30.

Rabun, William, Governor of Ga., purposes further survey, 1818, 203; appoints commissioners, 1819, 203.
Rabun County, Ga., confusion in, 205n.
Raleigh, N. C., commissioners' conference in with McLean, 154; resolutions sent to, 203.
Randolph, Edward, Collector of Customs, recommends that N. C. be annexed to Va., 25n.
Randolph County, N. C., German settlements in, 12.
Reedy Creek, Anson County, settled by tax evaders, 46.
Reedy River, beginning of Tryon's line, 96.
Regulators, movement of causes delay, 89.
Revolution, American, delays surveys, 89.
Richards, John G., Governor of S. C., informed of urgency of resurvey, 1928, 151; replies favorably to McLean, 151; appoints commissioner, 1928, 152-153; appoints Johnson commissioner, 1928, 153; accepts McLean's proposal for temporary re-survey, 154, 154n; supports N. C.'s position, 154.
Richardson, James B., Governor of S. C., 118; instructed to seek amicable settlement, 118; delays coöperation, 1803, 119.
Richmond County, N. C., Scotch Highlanders settle in, 10.
Ringgold, Samuel, Maryland congressman, 197.
Robeson County, N. C., Scotch Highlanders settle in, 10; proposed survey near, 1919, 151; line remarked to, 156.
Rocky River, Scotch-Irish settle in region of, 12; desired for boundary line, 74-75.
Rowan, Mathew, Acting-governor of N. C., 1753, 11; of Scotch-Irish descent, 11; N. C. commissioner, 1735, 36n; continues survey, 1737, 42-43.
Rowan County, N. C., Irish Protestants and Germans settle in, 12.
Ruffin, Edmund, describes isolation of eastern Carolina, 5n.
Rutherford, Griffith, General, conquers western N. C., 184, 184n.
Rutherford, John, N. C. commissioner, 1772, 85.
Rutherford, Thomas, N. C. surveyor, 1772, 85.
Rutherford County, commissioners meet in, 141.
Rutledge, Edward, Governor of S. C., uncoöperative on survey, 106.

St. Augustine, N. C. aids Oglethorpe against, 58.
Salisbury Road, line extended to, 73; recommended as part of boundary, 77; Board of Trade recommends for boundary, 83; beginning of survey of 1772, 87; suggested as starting point of survey, 130; accepted by N. C. as starting point of survey, 132; rejected as boundary, 1813, 138-139; importance of alteration of line at, 140.
Saluda Gap, commissioner joins survey at, 142.
Saluda Mountains, in N. C.-S. C. boundary region, 135.
Saluda River, north fork of a division point, 138; line monument erected near, 143.
Sampson County, N. C., Scotch Highlanders settle in, 10; location of portion of McCulloh's and Dobbs' land grant, 11.
Santee Canal, built by S. C., 16.
Santee River, in southern Carolina,

INDEX

4; possible dividing line, 14; original boundary line, 34.

Saunders, W. L., states that Cape Fear River never was the dividing line, 27.

Savannah River, Dobbs suggests extension of S. C. to, 56, 63, 67; objections of S. C. to extending line to, 81; partial boundary of Ga., 161; head of disputed, 162. *See also* 162-163.

Scales, A. M., Governor of N. C., urged to re-mark line, 148; urges joint survey, 1888, 149-150.

Scotch Highlanders, settle on Cape Fear, 10, 10n.

Scotch-Irish, settle in Piedmont, N. C., 11; driven from Ireland by Test Act of 1714, 11; are opposed to Anglicans of S. C., 11; settlements on Catawba, Yadkin, Cape Fear and Neuse rivers, 12.

Scotland County, N. C., Scotch Highlanders settle in, 10, 10n.

Seven Years' War, effect of on boundary disputes, 59; territorial gains by, 89.

Sevier, John, N. C. commissioner on Cherokee boundary, 93n.

Sharpe, William, N. C. commissioner on Cherokee boundary, 96.

Shooting Creek, branch of Hiawassee River, 204.

Simpson, clerk of S. C. Council, accused by Dobbs, 48.

Skene, Alexander, S. C. commissioner, writes Royal Council of physical conditions in S. C., 36n; reports fruitless conferences, 38, 38n; refuses to continue survey, 42; continues survey, 1737, 42-43.

Slaves, in S. C., escape to Cape Fear region, 27; affect the boundary question, 28; S. C. fears revolt of, 81.

Smith, Thomas, Governor of Carolina, 1693, 7n; provisionally instructed as to county elections, 7n.

South Carolina, racial groups in N. C. opposed to remaining under, 13; large estates and staple product in, 13; petitions king to ascertain boundary line, 29; slavery in, 14, 14n; industrial development in, 14; enacts tariff laws against N. C. trade, 15; builds Santee Canal, 1790, 16; first road building by in 1682, 18, 18n; travel in by horseback and carriage, 19, 19n; little visiting in N. C., 19; urges king to make her a royal colony, 25; ignores Proprietors' authority, 25n; applies to England for troops for protection, 25; revolts against Proprietary government, 26; considers question of boundary line, 28; *see also* 26n; claims Cape Fear River as boundary, 26; grants land on southern bank of Cape Fear, 26; officials insist Cape Fear River is dividing line, 28; governor of requests Proprietors to have dividing line established, 1713, 27; Proprietors refuse request of 1713 to have dividing line run, 27; fugitives from escape to Cape Fear region, 27; Assembly of accuses N. C. of encouraging slaves to escape, 27; business in affected by lack of boundary line, 28, 28n; merchants of demand royal government, 1719 and 1727, 28; requests royal order declaring Cape Fear a part of S. C., 28; instructs her agents in London to work for settlement of boundary question, 28; suggests north branch of Cape Fear River as portion of boundary line, 29; requests that N. C. be put under her jurisdiction, 29; prospect of founding of Ga. affects boundary claims of, 29; petitions king in vain, 1725, for adjustment of boundary, 29; permanent change in government of, 29; Robert Johnson appointed governor of, 1729, 30; endeavors to run boundary, 31; Assembly of admits Burrington's contentions, 34; Assembly of insists on Cape Fear parallel line, 36; requires citizens along Waccamaw River to pay taxes, 36; governor of appoints commissioners to run boundary line, 1735, 36; appointments in cause government friction, 36; to include Catawaba and Cherokee Indians, 38; denies legality of survey of 1735, 39; Council of approves compromise agreement of 1735, 39; commissioners run line, 1735, 40, 40n; tries to delay survey, 40-41; accepts work of commissioners, 41, 41n; dissension of with her commissioners, 41-42; commissioners of decline to continue survey, 42; council of urges reply to Johnston, 42; delays over expense, 42; officials of wrangle, 42; resumes boundary negotiations, 1737, 42; urges alteration of surveys, 44; makes second attempt to alter line, 44; governor and council of accuse Dobbs of "creating disturbances," 48-49; claims all lands south of Granville's line, 50, 50n; commissioners of attempt to run Catawba Indian line, 52; summary of boundary progress in, 52-59; engaged in war, 1755-1760, 59; protests to Board of Trade, 1749, over surveys of 1735 and 1737, 59; asks boundary extension to calm Indians, 59-60; urges extension, 61; Council of proposes survey of Pee Dee, Waccamaw and Cape Fear rivers, 64; urges that N. C. appoint surveyors to join in survey, 64; Council of sends letter to James Crockatt, 65; *see also,* James Crockatt; proposes "re-observance" of Cape Fear River line, 65-66; appoints Committee of inquiry of former proceedings, 66; causes delay, 67; asks Board of Trade to secure royal orders for establishing boundary, 69; demands that Crown defray expense of survey, 72; governor of issues proclamation against violence, 73; governor of states survey is made, 1764, 74; urges return to Cape Fear River line, 1764, 76; governor of proposes line, 77; replies to Tryon's objections, 78, 79; Council of objects to Tryon's proposal, 80; defends Catawba River proposal, 81; buys slaves, 81; builds fort, 83; sends report to Hillsborough, 1770, 83; modifies Catawba River proposal, 83; to bear expense of survey of 1772, 85; commissioners for, 1772, 85; gains by survey of 1772, 87, 88n; State constitution of fails to describe boundaries, 1776, 92; grants representation to "New Acquisition," 92, 92n; appoints commissioners, 99, 99n; objects to Bill of Rights clause, 100; declines to cooperate on boundary, 1797, 103; despairs of a settlement, 1800, 107; demands change in N. C. constitution, 108; to resort to Supreme Court, 1800, 109, 109n; prepares to defend boundary claims in Supreme Court, 110, 110n; refuses to cooperate with Davie, 114; enacts law for appointment of commissioners, 1803, 121; refuses to compromise, 127; attempts to use Indian Treaties, 129; urges simple extension of survey of 1772, 1808, 133; declines to ratify Agreement of Columbia, 133; secures alteration of Columbia agreement, 134-135; ratifies Convention of Columbia, 137; commissioners of meet, 1813, 137; ratifies Provisional Agreement of 1813, 138; gains territory, 1813, 139; erects district of Lancaster, 1813, 139; makes erroneous claims, 139; empowers governor to appoint commissioners, 141; commissioners of run survey, 1815, 141; ratifies Agreement of Greenville, 1815, 144; vaguely describes boundaries, 1873, 145; requires re-survey of portion of line, 1880, 145-146; makes independent survey, 147; declines to join in survey, 149-150; adopts N. C.'s policy, 150; arrests N. C. fishermen, 151-152; joint re-survey of, 1928, 156; citizen of removes monument, 1928, 156; claims territory to Mississippi River, 162; institutes suit against

Ga., 162; cedes western lands, 1787, 163; cedes twelve-mile strip to Ga., 164.
"South Seas," western extremity of boundary line, 38; designated in agreement of 1735, 107.
Spaight, Richard Dobbs, Governor of N. C., denies N. C. ratified survey of 1772, 100-101; requests information on boundary, 101; succeeded by Ashe, 102; on legislative committee, 115n.
Spalding, Thomas, Ga. congressman, on special committee 179n.
Spartanburg County, S. C., organized, 1785, 88.
Spencer, S. C. surveyor, makes *ex parte* survey, 1881, 148-149.
Spivey, S. C. senator, proposed law for re-survey, 1928, 152-153.
Spottswood, Alexander, Governor of Va., writes Board of Trade concerning poor roads in Albemarle section in 1711, 18.
Stanford, Richard, N. C. congressman on special committee, 179n.
Stanly County, German settlements in, 12.
Statesville, N. C., Fort Dobbs built near, 1755, 82.
Steele, John, N. C. commissioner, 1805, 122; spokesman for commissioners, 123; defends Bill of Rights clause, 123; insistent in conference, 123; requests Monroe to secure documents from England, 1807, 125; proposes meeting of commissioners, 125; persuades Moore to continue as commissioner, 128, 128n; plans to grant concessions, 128; defeats S. C.'s arguments, 129; accuses S. C. of stalling, 135-136; opposes alterations without specific legislative action, 136n; again serves as commissioner, 1812, 137; suggests compromise ground, 178; Milledge commends N. C. to, 182; commends Georgians, 191; submits report, 192.
Stephenson, James, Va. congressman, 197.

Stokes, Montford, N. C. commissioner, 1812, 137; again serves, 1814, 141.
Stone, David, Governor of N. C., 133n; opposes S. C.'s plans, 1808, 134; questions power of commissioners, 136; plans to protect N. C. from territorial loss, 136; declines new survey, 194; refers to Ga.'s proposed re-survey, 196.
Sturges, Surveyor-General of Ga., takes readings, 186; work of questioned, 193.
Suffolk, Va., post road established to Wilmington, 20.
Sugar Creek, Anson County, settled by tax evaders, 46.
Sumter, Thomas, Jr., S. C. commissioner, 1808, 128-129; appointed to an embassy, 1808, 134n; resignation of, 136n.
Survey, of 1735, 36, 40; of private citizens, 44; of 1764, 73; Tryon's survey, 1767, 96; of 1772, 87, 87n; of Ellicott, 1811, 200; of 1813, 138; of 1815, 142-143; of 1819, 203-204; *ex parte* survey, 1821, 204; of Camack, 1826, 204-205; of Spencer's 1881, 148-149; independent survey, 1886, 148; of 1928, 155.
Surveyor's table, 149.
Swain, David L., Governor of N. C., error of concerning boundary, 44; complains of boundary injustices of early surveys, 1835, 145.
Swiss, settle on Northeast River, 11.
Syme, George F., Senior engineer, N. C. Highway Commission, 88; estimates territory, 88n; appointed commissioner, 1928, 153, 153n; confers with Johnson, 154n; refuses to alter line, 154; describes topography, 155, 155n; makes report, 156n; reports amicable settlement, 156.

Taylor, C. Edward, N. C. citizen, urges re-survey, 151.
Taxes, confusion over, 49, 50, 55; Dobbs suggests adjustment for 56.

INDEX

Tellico, Treaty of, extinguishes Indian titles, 1798, 179.

Tennessee, basis of N. C. claim to, 116; boundary policy regarding, 146; boundary of joins N. C., 204; Ga. declares 35th parallel her boundary with, 205.

Thompson, William, S. C. commissioner, 1772, 84, 85.

Three Springs, near Saluda River, 142.

Tivoli, S. C., home of William R. Davie, 122.

Topography of Carolina, influence of on separation, 4.

Trade, ill feeling between the Carolinas over, 15.

Transportation, poor means of isolates N. C., 17; banking and credit in Charleston affected by, 17.

Treaty of Hard Labor, with Cherokees, 96.

Treaty of Paris, effect of on boundary discussions, 98.

Tryon, William, Lieutenant-Governor of N. C., 72, 72n; complains of poor means of communication in N. C., 20; appoints commissioners, 1763, 73; instructed to propose "proper final Boundary," 74, 74n; proposes a line, 1766, 74; defends S. C., 75; renews own proposal, 1767, 1768, 75; protests against return to Cape Fear River line, 76; urges Hillsborough to act on boundary, 77; reports chaos in boundary region, 77; runs temporary line, 1767, 78, 78n; opposes Montagu's proposal, 78, 78n; approves survey of 1764, 113.

Tryon County, established, 78; sheriff of opposed, 1771, 85; loses territory, 1772, 88n.

Tryon Mountain, end of survey of 1767, 96.

Tugaloo River, Georgia boundary point, 161; disputed boundary, 162; *see also* 163; observations taken near, 186.

Turner, James, Governor of N. C., 1802; urges early settlement of dispute, 118; *see also* 118n; appoints commissioners, 1803, 119; asks S. C. to appoint commissioners, 121; appoints Steele commissioner, 1805, 122; opposes views of own commissioners, 124; U. S. senator, 125; aids Steele to get documents from London, 125, 125n; notified of establishment of Walton County, 165; urges Georgia to act, 166; defends N. C. land titles, 167-168; designates commissioners for Ga. survey, 169; replies to Ga. on land titles, 170.

Tuscarora Indians, influence survey, 35; to be reprimanded, 36; land grants to, 51.

Twelve Mile Creek, near Catawba Lands, point in proposed line, 1764, 75; independent survey near, 1886, 148-149.

Tynte, Edward, appointed governor of all Carolina, 24, 24n.

Tyrrel, Timothy, Ga. surveyor, 203.

Unaka Mountains, and N. C. cession, 100, 100n.

Union County, German settlements in, 12.

U. S. Congress, accepts S. C. cession, 1787, 163; refers Ga. petition to committee, 178; declines to act, 180; declines to intervene, 197, 200; committee of considers Ga.'s request, 197; recommends Supreme Court action, 200.

U. S. Constitution, provides for settlement of inter-State disputes, 108.

U. S. Supreme Court, power of over inter-State disputes, 95; N. C. proposes appeal to, 96, 105, 109; S. C. requests resort to, 110, 114; Davie to represent N. C. before, 111; N. C. decides against appeal to, 116.

Vattel, M. de, quoted on importance of boundary disputes in general, 2.

INDEX

Vermont, boundary dispute of with Conn., 3.

Virginia, boundary dispute of with Pa., 2; governor of appoints a governor over Albemarle, 1664, 4; considers Cherokee boundary question, 93, 96; N. C. boundary policy regarding, 146.

Waccamaw River, in southern Carolina, ignorance of British authorities regarding, 6, 6n; provisionally to be boundary, 31; part of first proposed line, 1730, 33; Johnson opposes line along, 35; S. C. demands taxes in region of, 55; to be surveyed, 64; survey near, 1915, 150; swamps along, 155.

Walters, William, S. C. commissioner, 1735, 36n; continues survey, 1737, 42-43.

Walton County, Ga., organized 1803, 120, 120n, 164; confusion in, 165-166; settlers in, 171n; citizens of petition Ga. governor, 172; represented in Legislature, 173; represented in Senate, 1810, 174; see also 175; proposed re-survey of, 180; citizens of lose compensation, 181; amnesty for citizens of, 186; temporarily vanishes, 190; finally abolished, 191-193, 196; conceded to N. C., 201-202.

"Walton War." See Walton County.

War between the States. See Civil War.

War of 1812, status of dispute at close of, 139; delays boundary surveys, 202.

War of Jenkin's Ear, causes delay in boundary extensions, 46; co-operation in, 58.

Wateree River, in southern Carolina, 4; possible dividing line, 4.

Waxhaw region, settlers occupy lands in, 47; Caldwell takes readings in, 126.

Wellborn, James, N. C. commissioner, 1803, 119; again serves, 1812, 137; resigns, 1812, 137.

Welsh emigrants, from Pa. and Delaware, settle in Cape Fear region, 1730, 12.

Welsh Tract, in New Hanover County, named after original settlers, 12, 12n.

West Indies, secures N. C. trade, 17; Carolinians fight in, 58.

"Widow Earle's," Rutherford County, N. C., meeting place of commissioners, 1815, 141.

Williams, Benjamin, Governor of N. C., 105; invites Drayton to send commissioners, 1800, 105-106; complains of S. C.'s indifference, 106; postpones meeting of commissioners, 109n; to resort to Supreme Court, 109, 109n; stresses importance of Supreme Court case, 111; moves to settle controversy, 112; invites S. C. to send commissioners, 1801, 112; asks Davie's advice on future policy, 1802, 117; becomes impatient with Drayton, 117-118; second administration of, 126, 126n; persuades Moore to continue as commissioner, 128, 128n; insists on Bill of Rights clause, 1808, 128; presents Ga.'s request, 194.

Williams, D. R., Governor of S. C., empowered to appoint commissioners, 1815, 141n.

Williamson, Hugh, refers to effect of treaty of Paris, 98.

Williamson, Richard, Walton County representative, 173.

Wilmington, N. C., post road established to Suffolk, Va., 1757, 20.

Winslow, Arthur, N. C. surveyor on independent survey, 1886, 148.

Winston, Joseph, N. C. commissioner on Cherokee boundary, 96.

Winyaw Bay, Pee Dee River flows into, 4; N. C. desires line to, 15-16, 59, 63; Dobbs urges adoption of line to, 68; N. C. settlers urge line to, 74.

Woolens Act, 1699, effect of on Scotch-Irish emigration to N. C., 11.

Wyley, Samuel, S. C. commissioner, 73n; appointment of questioned, 113.

Yadkin River, course of, 4; logical dividing line, 4; McCulloh's grant in region of, 11; Scotch-Irish settle in region of, 12; German settlements on, 12; desired for boundary line, 74-75.

Yazoo claims, and Ga., 171.

Yeamans, Sir John, appointed governor of southern Carolina, 23n, 24.

Yemassee Indians, danger of leads S. C. to urge king to make her a royal colony, 25.

Yonge, Francis, S. C. Agent in London, instructed to work for settlement of boundary question, 1721, 28; receives petition on boundary from S. C., 1725, 29, 29n.

York County, S. C., organized, 1785, 88; western end of proposed resurvey of 1880, 146.

Yorkville, S. C., meeting place of commissioners, 127.

THE JAMES SPRUNT STUDIES IN HISTORY AND POLITICAL SCIENCE

No. 1. PERSONNEL OF THE CONVENTION OF 1861. By John Gilchrist McCormick. } (Out of print.)
LEGISLATION OF THE CONVENTION OF 1861. By Kemp P. Battle.
No. 2. THE CONGRESSIONAL CAREER OF NATHANIEL MACON. By Edwin Mood Wilson. (Out of print.)
No. 3. THE LETTERS OF NATHANIEL MACON, JOHN STEELE, AND WILLIAM BARRY GROVE, WITH NOTES. By Kemp P. Battle.
No. 4. LETTERS AND DOCUMENTS RELATING TO THE EARLY HISTORY OF THE LOWER CAPE FEAR, WITH INTRODUCTION AND NOTES. By Kemp P. Battle.
No. 5. MINUTES OF THE KEHUKEY ASSOCIATION, WITH INTRODUCTION AND NOTES. By Kemp P. Battle.
No. 6. DIARY OF A GEOLOGICAL TOUR BY ELISHA MITCHELL IN 1827 AND 1828, WITH INTRODUCTION AND NOTES. By Kemp P. Battle.
No. 7. WILLIAM RICHARDSON DAVIE: A MEMOIR. By J. G. de Roulhac Hamilton.
LETTERS OF WILLIAM RICHARDSON DAVIE, WITH NOTES. By Kemp P. Battle.
No. 8. THE PROVINCIAL COUNCIL AND COMMITTEES OF SAFETY IN NORTH CAROLINA. By Bessie Lewis Whitaker.
VOL. 9, No. 1. THE SOCIETY FOR THE PROPAGATION OF THE GOSPEL IN THE PROVINCE OF NORTH CAROLINA. By D. D. Oliver.
CORRESPONDENCE OF JOHN RUST EATON. Edited by J. G. de Roulhac Hamilton.
VOL. 9, No. 2. FEDERALISM IN NORTH CAROLINA. By Henry M. Wagstaff.
LETTERS OF WILLIAM BARRY GROVE. Edited by Henry M. Wagstaff.
VOL. 10, No. 1. BENJAMIN SHERWOOD HEDRICK. By J. G. de Roulhac Hamilton.
VOL. 10, No. 2. BARTLETT YANCEY. By George A. Anderson.
THE POLITICAL AND PROFESSIONAL CAREER OF BARTLETT YANCEY. By J. G. de Roulhac Hamilton.
LETTERS TO BARTLETT YANCEY.
VOL. 11, No. 1. COUNTY GOVERNMENT IN COLONIAL NORTH CAROLINA. By W. C. Guess.
VOL. 11, No. 2. THE NORTH CAROLINA CONSTITUTION OF 1776, AND ITS MAKERS. By Frank Nash.
THE GERMAN SETTLERS OF LINCOLN COUNTY AND WESTERN NORTH CAROLINA. By Joseph R. Nixon.
VOL. 12, No. 1. THE GOVERNOR, COUNCIL, AND ASSEMBLY IN ROYAL NORTH CAROLINA. By C. S. Cooke.
LAND TENURE IN PROPRIETARY NORTH CAROLINA. By L. N. Morgan.
VOL. 12, No. 2. THE NORTH CAROLINA INDIANS. By James Hall Rand.
VOL. 13, No. 1. THE GRANVILLE DISTRICT. By E. Merton Coulter.
THE NORTH CAROLINA COLONIAL BAR. By E. H. Alderman.
VOL. 13, No. 2. THE HARRINGTON LETTERS. Edited by H. M. Wagstaff.
VOL. 14, No. 1. THE HARRIS LETTERS. Edited by H. M. Wagstaff.
VOL. 14, No. 2. SOME COLONIAL HISTORY OF BEAUFORT COUNTY. By F. H. Cooper.
VOL. 15, Nos. 1 and 2. PARTY POLITICS IN NORTH CAROLINA, 1835-1860. By J. G. de Roulhac Hamilton
VOL. 16, No. 1. A COLONIAL HISTORY OF ROWAN COUNTY, NORTH CAROLINA. By S. J. Ervin. (Out of print.)
VOL. 16, No. 2. THE DIARY OF BARTLETT YANCEY MALONE. Edited by Wm. Whatley Pierson, Jr.
THE PROVINCIAL AGENTS OF NORTH CAROLINA. By Samuel James Ervin, Jr.
VOL. 17, No. 1. THE FREE NEGRO IN NORTH CAROLINA. By R. H. Taylor.
SOME COLONIAL HISTORY OF CRAVEN COUNTY, NORTH CAROLINA. By Francis H. Cooper.
VOL. 17, No. 2. JOURNAL OF A TOUR OF NORTH CAROLINA BY WILLIAM ATTMORE, 1787. Edited by Lida Tunstall Rodman.
VOL. 18, Nos. 1 and 2. SLAVEHOLDING IN NORTH CAROLINA: AN ECONOMIC VIEW. By Rosser Howard Taylor.
VOL. 19, No. 1. PRESENT STATUS OF MODERN EUROPEAN HISTORY IN THE UNITED STATES. By Chester Penn Higby.
VOL. 19, No. 2. STUDIES IN HISPANIC-AMERICAN HISTORY. Edited by W. W. Pierson, Jr.
VOL. 20, No. 1. NORTH CAROLINA NEWSPAPERS BEFORE 1790. By Charles Christopher Crittenden.
VOL. 20, No. 2. THE JAMES A. GRAHAM PAPERS, 1861-1884. Edited by H. M. Wagstaff.
VOL. 21, Nos. 1 and 2. THE DEMOCRATIC PARTY IN ANTE-BELLUM NORTH CAROLINA, 1835-1861. By Clarence Clifford Norton.
VOL. 22, Nos. 1 and 2. MINUTES OF THE NORTH CAROLINA MANUMISSION SOCIETY, 1816-1834. Edited by H. M. Wagstaff.
VOL. 23, No. 1. THE PRESIDENTIAL ELECTION OF 1824 IN NORTH CAROLINA. By Albert Ray Newsome.
VOL. 23, No. 2. THE SECESSION MOVEMENT IN NORTH CAROLINA. By Joseph Carlyle Sitterson.
VOL. 24, No. 1. JEFFERSONIAN DEMOCRACY IN SOUTH CAROLINA. By John Harold Wolfe.
VOL. 24, No. 2. GUIDE TO THE MANUSCRIPTS IN THE SOUTHERN HISTORICAL COLLECTION OF THE UNIVERSITY OF NORTH CAROLINA.
VOL. 25, No. 1. NORTH CAROLINA BOUNDARY DISPUTES INVOLVING HER SOUTHERN LINE

www.ingramcontent.com/pod-product-compliance
Lightning Source LLC
Chambersburg PA
CBHW021359290426
44108CB00010B/306